2.75

SELECTIONS FROM
MEDIEVAL PHILOSOPHERS

I
AUGUSTINE TO ALBERT THE GREAT

SELECTIONS FROM MEDIEVAL PHILOSOPHERS

I
AUGUSTINE TO ALBERT THE GREAT

EDITED AND TRANSLATED, WITH
INTRODUCTORY NOTES BY

RICHARD McKEON

CHARLES SCRIBNER'S SONS
NEW YORK

CONTENTS

vii

GENERAL INTRODUCTION

The reestimation of medieval culture began, about eighty years ago, to make difficult the continued currency of the old strictures against medieval philosophy. Judgments of philosophers in the ordinary tradition had, up to that time, continued almost unchanged from the form in which they first appeared in the writings of sixteenth and seventeenth century philosophers who represented themselves in revolt against a scholasticism, vain, authority-ridden, tenuous, repetitious, logic-chopping, inadequate to the revolutions of modern thought. Only slowly have these opinions been altered until in more recent years increasingly impressive contributions in scholarly research have made possible the return of medieval speculations to a place of dignity in the history of thought. The noises of these changes have by now spread rather generally in literary and philosophical discussions, but the layman, the student who has no access to writings in latin and greek, and the casual essayist of the day who is tempted to generalities concerning centuries and cultures, are still limited to the vaguest of secondary and tertiary impressions. Little of the material examined in the reestimation has been translated into the modern languages, and the translations in english are perhaps fewer than in most languages. Between Augustine and the seventeenth century, twelve hundred years which are crammed with the writings of voluminous workers who initiated some of the most significant, though almost forgotten, developments of philosophic thought, there is almost nothing in english save some partial and not always satisfactory translations of Anselm and Aquinas. So striking is the paucity that, although the present selections, translated from fifteen philosophers of the middle ages, were made with an eye only to the importance of the pages selected, subsequent inquiry disclosed that none of the passages had ever been translated into english before.[1] Indeed several of the selections are translated from works that have been published for the first time, even in latin, during the past twenty years.

Yet doubtless the writers of the period and their thought can come to be known generally only by translation. The following translations are to be justified only as a device to open medieval philosophy to a larger audience, for the selection of a few pages among a little more than a dozen out of hundreds of prolific writers could not serve to present an adequate outline of all the tendencies of medieval thought. No single volume would be adequate, even if the present state of scholarship made it possible, to the diversity of philosophical problems which were discussed between Augustine and Ockham; in the following selections, therefore, one problem has been chosen as central, and its evolution through the centuries has been followed in the hope that the orientation of philosophy from that central problem may in each case be indicated. The problem of knowledge has been inquired into, with different emphases and different consequences, throughout not only the medieval period but through the whole age of western philosophy. The significant characteristics of the philosophy, no less than the further prob-

---

[1] Since the preparation of the manuscript an english translation of the *Opus Majus* of Roger Bacon has appeared: *The Opus Majus of Roger Bacon*, translated by R. B. Burke (Philadelphia: University of Pennsylvania Press, 1928), 2 vols.

lems to which attention was turned, has been determined
in large part by the answer which has been given in
each case to the problem of how we know. The platonist and the augustinian looked for warrant of knowledge to the eternal things presented directly to the
human mind in the light of divine illumination. The
discovery of truth indicated the necessity of Truth; and
the contingent beings, the partial truths and incomplete
goods which man discovers are inexplicable to them
save on the background of the necessary, the unique,
the simple, the eternal. The demonstration of the existence of God and the exploration of the eternal structure of divine ideas constitutes the philosophic enterprise
most in keeping with this attitude. Any truth is the
manifestation of the presence of an eternal principle or
a divine illumination to us, and there were therefore
few things in the metaphysics of the universe which
reason and intellect were not equipped to penetrate;
even the trinity, the incarnation and the mysteries of
faith could be demonstrated. Significantly, too, the interest in mathematics and the beginnings of science at
Chartres and Oxford were connected with augustinism,
for mathematics shows forth the eternal structure of
things, and the knowledge of things conceived in their
changeless natures must further the knowledge of God.
But if the platonist turned to God and eternal ideas in
answer to the question how we know, the aristotelian
sought the answer in terms and ideas, and in their com-
binations and separations, which are accomplished by
the human intellect. The eternal truth, divine illumination, the truth of things, which constitutes their being,
remain the same, for there is divine as well as human
knowledge, but the problem of human knowledge as such
centers in the truth of discourse. The orientation therefore is toward the problems of logic rather than to the

discovery of divinity. Significantly, too, though the basis of certainty is still in first principles known *per se* by the human mind, the origin of knowledge in experience is emphasized more and more, and mind loses its power to demonstrate with certainty whatever it knows; the proofs of the existence of God, the necessity of the trinity, incarnation, the creation of the world lose their cogency; of these some can be proved *a posteriori* from the data of experience, others are impossible of demonstration, since the mind can as easily prove their contrary on the data it possesses. It was the aristotelian logic and the platonist philosophy, not science, which first turned the philosophers of the thirteenth and fourteenth centuries to the data of experience.

For all the doctrinal diversity that the evolution of the discussion of knowledge displays, there is none the less a considerable homogeneity among the opposed positions. The mark of this is, for example, in the fashion in which the early selections, those of Augustine, Boethius and Anselm, continue to be influential in the later discussions, even to the extent of frequent explicit quotations in the twelfth and thirteen centuries. In one sense augustinism continues to be dominant throughout the sequence of philosophers, and the addition of problems does no violence to the outline of the philosophy. In another sense, the doctrinal alteration is tremendous. Thus the ontological argument, which is developed by Anselm, is present almost explicitly stated in Augustine, and continues in the chief adherents of the augustinian philosophy, notwithstanding its frequent refutation at the hands of philosophers like Thomas Aquinas or the "coloring" of it by philosophers like Duns Scotus that it may be *a posteriori* rather than *a priori*. And as the data of the demonstrations of philosophic doctrines are derived in this augustinian approach from the character of the mind, so the fact of selfconsciousness, the fact that if I think, if even I doubt, I am and I live and I think, can be made the sufficient beginning of the demonstration of God and the elucidation of the character of the universe. The data of selfconsciousness becomes, nevertheless, far from central to the thought of an aristotelian; but for all the mounting concern of aristotelianism with the certainty of first principles and with the materials of experience, it is a significant commentary on philosophic refutation and philosophic evolution that Descartes could initiate the modern period in philosophy with the discovery of a basis for certainty in the fact of selfconsciousness and with the statement of an *a priori* demonstration of the existence of God.

Parallel to such shifts of interest and problems is the evolution of philosophic method in the development of what has come to be called the scholastic method. The development is illustrated in the sequence of the selections which follow. Three of the first selections (Augustine, Eriugena, Anselm) are in the form of dialogues. One (Boethius) is a commentary on the *Isagoge* of Porphyry (which in turn is a commentary on the *Organon* of Aristotle); there is another (Abailard) which is a gloss on the section of Boethius's commentary which had previously been presented. One (Lombard) is a selection of sentences from the Scripture and church fathers relevant to problems proposed; two (Bonaventura, Duns Scotus) are selections from courses presented at universities in commentary on the *Sentences* of Peter Lombard, which had come to form the center of theological education. Two (Grosseteste, Albert the Great) are opuscula devoted to the detailed study of particular problems. One (the pseudo-Grosseteste) is a summa; one (Bacon) is the opus of a projected new instauration of science. Two (Aquinas, Matthew of Aquaspartas) are *quaestiones disputatae,* products of the medieval pedagogical system in which problems were presented in sequence about fortnightly for debate by the students and finally for resolution and discussion by the master. And one (William of Ockham) is a selection from *quaestiones quodlibetales,* debates on a grander scale conducted before the gathered university twice a year, at Christmas and Easter.

The method of the later works, used with variations and more or less formally, combined the virtues of the dialogue and the commentary. The dialogue is the obvious form of dialectical presentation: the principles no less than the deductions from them are arrived at by the discussions and agreements of interlocutors. The commentary and gloss are no less powerful instruments of philosophic development: the text of an important philosophic work is submitted to careful scrutiny and its implications are developed, supplemented, criticized. The method of the scholastics was to present a question, quote whatever had been said by authorities on either side, then resolve the question. The method took on a set form in some philosophers, Alexander of Hales, Bonaventura, Thomas Aquinas being among the number, and every question was resolved in some precise sequence of authority and refutation and resolution. In others the method is used but without formality (the selections from the pseudo-Grosseteste and Albert the Great, below, are examples), and the uninitiated reader must be warned lest in reading he take the first statement of solution as the author's opinion to find that it is refuted toward the end of the chapter and another doctrine substituted for it. The method indicates the relative place of authority and reason in the solution of philosophical problems. A philosopher must be careful to have examined the solutions to problems which the wise men of the past have found before presuming to a resolution of his own. But the common criticism that scholastic problems were solved by reference only to authority is without foundation: a good scholastic was one who could find authority for either side of a question and who was convinced further that truth could be discovered best by examining the interplay of such possible contradictory statements. Authority was only the reason of past thinkers solidified in brief statement, and if reason could not be found for it, the opinion could not be held. Authority, as one of the scholastics remarked, has a nose of wax: it may be turned in any direction whatsoever unless it is fortified by reason. There were questions, to be sure, concerning how first principles were known, in which platonist and aristotelian disagreed; moreover it was conceived that the end of human life exceeded the time and place of this age and planet, that to pursue his end man must have supernatural revelation of the means to it; there were therefore metaphysical differences to be considered, and there were theological problems which, depending on the metaphysical foundations, sometimes fell without the domain of reason, sometimes dominated it. But whatever the metaphysics or the theology of a writer, his appeal to authority was literally an appeal to what authors had in the past said on the subject: to be free from authority was to be unaware of the history of the problem discussed. And indeed all the fresh starts in the history of philosophy, even the fortunate ones, have proved distressingly innocent of philosophical sophistication. The constant appeal to authority in a medieval work does not shackle the imagination and enslave the reason; rather it permits the author, as Bernard of Chartres suggested, to mount the shoulders of the ancients that he may see further than he could with his own unaided vision and at his own stature.

The sequence of the selections which follow is chronological; where the authors are contemporaries, the sequence is by date of birth of the authors. It is not always easy to date the composition of the works themselves, but probably with two exceptions (the work of Roger Bacon and probably the *Summa of Philosophy* were composed after the works of Bonaventura and Thomas Aquinas which they precede here) the sequence is according to the chronology of the works. The merits of the purely chronological order will be obvious if one considers the groupings into schools which have become traditional in the study of medieval philosophy. It happens fortunately that the selection from Albert the Great is separated from the selection from Thomas Aquinas by Roger Bacon and Bonaventura, and Albert in turn appears between Grosseteste and Bacon. It may be possible by that arrangement to read Albert as other than only the preparation for Thomas, and the Oxford school may be seen more easily in relation to augustinism and the philosophic problems of the age. Finally the problems themselves and the relevance of discussions to genuine philosophical difficulties, many of which persist recognizable today though in a different guise, can be indicated best by the circlings and oppositions of solutions.

The rendering of latin philosophy into english, faces the difficulties and impossibilities which early latin writers bewailed in the translation of greek philosophy into latin: there is no philosophic vocabulary in english suitable to express distinctions which are made easily in greek and in late latin. In addition, the point of view expressed in medieval philosophy is one misunderstood and largely forgotten in modern discussions, and therefore arguments which are obvious when stated briefly in the latin and on the background of greek philosophy, are difficult when rendered literally, and uncogent to an audience little read in aristotelian philosophy. In many cases it is difficult to know whether it would be wiser to translate a term by its english cognate, which has been loaded with foreign connotations, or to engage in a lengthy paraphrase to make the meaning clear. It has seemed to the present translator that the course of paraphrases was too crowded with dangers to be practicable. For example, *subject* for medievals is that which underlies accidents and properties, and therefore the subjective aspect of things is that which corresponds in the nature of things to the objective aspect in the mind; modern usage is precisely the reverse, and one has a choice therefore of substituting subject for object and vice versa, running the risk of introducing all the irrelevant implications of later discussions, or else of using the cognate english forms in the hope that the strangeness of the statements will warn the reader that the distinction is the opposite to that of later psychology. Words like intention, individuation, specification, adequation express distinctions to which no english words are adequate, and there is little choice but to use them, with warnings concerning their meaning when it is not clear from the context. Other words are common enough in meanings other than those conveyed in the medieval: imagination, for example, is the storehouse in which are recorded past sense-perceptions; it knows by means of phantasms, and its usual contrast is with the intellect (to which it supplies materials) in that it is concerned with particulars, while the intellect is concerned with abstractions or ideas or theophanies. Or again, reason is an impossible substitute for *ratio*, for *ratio* means not only a faculty of the mind, but also a relation in things or a rationale of related elements, a substantial ground (*raison d'être; ratio essendi*), a principle of knowledge, a seminal cause (*ratio seminalis*); to translate *ratio* successively by half a dozen terms is to lose the centralizing force which the single word possesses and by which it is indicated that in a fundamental sense the various *rationes* are the same. The english word reason has therefore been employed as broadly as possible in the following translations and where the sense demands another word too insistently, the latin has been inserted in brackets. Finally etymological arguments, which are introduced frequently and unobtrusely, are lost unless the original is given in brackets; that course therefore has been adopted here, for the cogency of the sequence of ideas depends often on the connection the eye detects between words as unrelated in translation as would be the english for *notio* and *nomen.* Wherever possible cognates and related words have been used or even invented; but for purposes of clarity the selections would be read with constant references to the gloss of words which is appended to the second volume. A number of emendations have been made in several of the texts where the reading was obviously corrupt, but it has seemed unnecessary to make special note of them in this work.

The exigencies of the plan of these selections, no less than the limitations of space, has necessitated the omission of a great many philosophers of the first importance and has determined the choice of portions of the writings of even the philosophers selected and the exclusion of other portions. To go into the list of the regrettable omissions would be to write the outline of the history of medieval philosophy; the plan which has been followed must be justified in that it achieves a maximum number of diversified ends: a relatively coherent development of one of the central problems of philosophy, the indication of the variety of philosophic positions in medieval thought, a sampling of the major traditions and of the outstanding philosophers, an example of each of the important forms of philosophic composition. The limitation indicated in the dates of the first and the last philosophers in these selections is more easily rectified than the paucity of materials that could be presented. Ancient philosophy and modern philosophy are widely and currently known; it would be too bad if medieval philosophy were read as a strange unconnected island between, particularly since connections can be made at the one end by the study of hellenistic, medieval greek and roman developments from greek thought and at the other by the study of the transition from the fourteenth to the seventeenth century; possibly two more volumes of selections might profitably be prepared, one in introduction to medieval latin philosophy, another in transition to the modern period. The problem of truth has its obvious roots not only in Plato and in Aristotle, but in writers posterior to them, and it has continuations which would elucidate doctrines of Galileo, Frances Bacon, Descartes and Leibniz. The major affinities of thought, however, will be obvious if the project of these selections as introduction to medieval philosophy is successful. To accomplish the project attempted in this book has been to forego whatever temptation there was to prepare another book, even in the face of the certain risk of criticism that this book is not that other: the collection of the more famous gems and sayings from the works of medieval philosophers would perhaps be more nearly what the present age would naturally seek in the middle ages, but it would have been less useful as introduction to medieval thought; there is the certainty, however, that this compilation is more nearly the outline of a problem in medieval philosophy in the spirit which a medieval *compilator* would have understood.

RICHARD McKEON.

SELECTIONS FROM
MEDIEVAL PHILOSOPHERS

I
AUGUSTINE TO ALBERT THE GREAT

ST. AUGUSTINE (354-430)

The philosophy of Augustine, whatever its origins—
for it would not be difficult to find traces of most of
his arguments and beliefs in more ancient statements
—was to determine the problems, and in part even the
conclusions, of a thousand years of philosophers. In
his work there emerges, for the first time, from the attempt to express an understanding of the tenets of
faith, a system of christian philosophy, and whereas it
is conceivable that an understanding of the faith might
have taken any of a variety of directions in the early
centuries of Christianity, by the time of Augustine most
of the major outlines have been fixed. The testimony
of frequent citation of Augustine in the works of his
medieval successors is indication of the part he played
in the determination of doctrines.

That a faith should find its intellectual statement in
a platonizing tendency seems in the retrospect of western religious history, with its broad repetitions in mo-
hammedan, jewish, and christian developments, inevitable and proper. The most persistent problem of
Augustine yields nicely to a modified platonism. The
resolution recurs in many forms, though the question is
never posed in the abstract. If one is to find, it is
necessary to have searched; God intended the soul to
have fallen into the error of pride before it should find
grace and salvation; therefore the life even of the saint
shall be interrupted in spiritual luxury and spiritual
fornication. Yet when grace is granted, intelligence
shall find only those things which have been revealed in

the illumination of God or by faith. Truth, as a philosophic consequence, must be a thing which is received, recognized by intimations of it to be present to the mind, but arrived at, for all that, only after moral and logical preparations.

The orientation of Augustine's philosophy is, for the excellent reason of this preoccupation, toward eternal things: the soul must be turned to God who is the source of illumination and who must be known if anything is to be intelligible. God is considered first in philosophy, since he is before all things and all ideas. Whereas pagans fell into error in the ordering of their knowledge because they assigned to each science and subject of inquiry an independent domain, the christian can recognize the affinity of the sciences to each other, for he is aware that they would be unintelligible save in view of their source. God is known in everything as he created all things. There is, therefore, little need for a proof of the existence of God, since any one who understands himself or things recognizes God in them. Yet the discovery of God is constant and central in the works of Augustine; only the detail of the way to that discovery can be, and usually is, abbreviated. Whenever it need be specified, the existence of God can be shown in any of a number of indications: in the movements of the world whose arrangements, order, and beauty are signs of him; in the existence of finite, contingent things, since their existence needs an infinite, necessary artificer; but most important, in the nature and structure of human thought. All three types of proof, however, serve the purpose only of revealing a truth that any man can find in himself. God is present and to be recognized in the workings of the world and the soul. Proof of him is a way of intimating the

presence of a structure in the universe and of displaying
to the mind a truth from which it has fallen.

The need, consequently, for a demonstration of God's
existence is a comparatively rare one, since knowledge
of God is at the bottom of all knowledge. But there
is always the fool, brought by the Psalms into philosophy, who says in his heart there is no God; and
since he exemplifies at least the possibility of fundamental ignorance, Augustine must pause frequently to
insist that the case is extreme and rare; to protest that
even the fool says this only in his heart; and to show
that even in his case demonstration can do much to
resolve the ignorance. Such demonstration, nevertheless, is always introduced preliminary to some doctrine
which could not be understood without the divine principles on which all knowledge is grounded: the passage
presented in the following selection is from the middle
book of the three devoted to the Free Will, and it can
be supplemented and explained best by passages in the
treatises on Music, on the Master, and on the Trinity.
Significantly the demonstration of the existence of God
is used to adumbrate or definitely to state a theory of
knowledge; it would serve the same necessary function
as foundation to physics or ethics.

By creatures we can raise ourselves to a knowledge
of God, and reason can convince us of his existence *as
clearly as the sun displays itself before our eyes.*[1] Intelligence always has need of the light of God, its sun,
for truth. Yet, the mysterious divine influence without
which our soul cannot attain intellectual truth does not
consist in the revelation of God to us *objective,* but in
the production in us *effective* of an image, as it were, of
those truths which determine our knowledge. Knowledge is not innate in us as it is in angels, but requires

[1] *Soliloquies,* I, 6.

a process which scholastics assigned to the activity of
the active intellect producing *species impressæ*. All
the figures in which Augustine writes of it are designed
to bring out this effective role of the divine light: knowledge is a transcription; it is the impression of an image;
it is a seal ring which marks its signet in the mind;
it is a sun, a master speaking within, an angel illuminat-
ing man. Emphatically, however, this light *sui generis*
is not God, but produced by God; it is the light by
which the mind sees, much as the senses see by the
external light.

By the divine light the soul perceives the unchangeable things of truth. That knowledge differs wholly
from knowledge by sensation, for sensation has to do
with particular, multiple, changing objects, whereas
thought moves among indivisible, eternal things. Moreover, no knowledge properly so called is derived from
sensation, for no movement of the body could exercise
a causal action on the soul; the lower can not be cause
of the higher. The alterations of the body therefore are
not the causes of the soul's perception, but the soul
draws from itself an image of the body; its action, as
is particularly clear in the case of the dolorous senti-
ments, is usually its response to a need of the body.
It is not the body which acts on the soul, but the soul
which acts on the body. This can be illustrated from
the interrelations of body and soul in teaching, where
words may seem to be the causes and the means of
conveying ideas, for, if one consider, there is a complete independence, not a parallelism, of words and
ideas. Conversation consists of two crossed monologues,
and even when there is no misunderstanding, it is not
the word which furnishes the idea, but rather the memory of things already known. Either one is ignorant
of the thing represented by the symbol, in which case

it means nothing; or else its meaning is known, then it teaches nothing. To learn means to understand and to be able to react to an external experience; but the pupil does not undergo or receive an idea: an idea is aroused in him which had been dormant. No one ever learns, precisely because a thought is never made of a body; the soul always draws its truth out of itself even when it seems to discover it. The truth of each person is his own proper truth. No other can be substituted for it. Nothing penetrates from without into the soul, but individuals who are hermetically sealed against each other, have a sort of agreement among themselves through the possession of the truth.[2] The presence of God to thought invisibly is the truth itself.

The fact of thought, therefore, is indication of the existence of God. One can not see without light, and though the light is not seen, there is no doubt, while one sees, that there is light. So too if one knows, God must exist whether one know God or not. But even while I doubt, Augustine insists, I know that I am, and in that knowledge are involved the further certainties that I live and that I understand. The reiterated insistence on this self-knowledge of the soul, which is the beginning of the knowledge of God, anticipates the cartesian proof in all the solidity of its thought, and possibly misses only the severity of its method. That God is present in all knowledge is particularly relevant to the knowledge of the soul, since of all knowledge that of the existence of thought is the most certain; and it can in turn be made the basis of other certainties. Therefore Augustine's gift of exquisite self-analysis and introspection, by which he is enabled to describe with precision the most delicate phenomena of intimate life, is turned wholly to the intimation of God. The axis

[2] Cf. below *on the Free Will,* Bk. II, ch. 9, no. 27, p. 43.

of life and philosophy must be God, since any study is in part the study of God; the analysis of the mind becomes a religious science inspired by the desire to know the ways of God in our soul and the ways of our soul toward God. Throughout his philosophy the world is of less interest to Augustine than the actions of God in the world and particularly in us. He says, in fact, in the *Soliloquies* that he wishes to know only God and soul, and it is clear there as elsewhere that he says *Noverim me* only after he has prayed *Noverim te*.

It is not surprising, in view of this, that philosophy should take its rationale from the nature of God. Following the Trinity, the divisions of philosophy are three. Even in ignorance of the Trinity, pagan philosophers had found that triple division into physics, logic, and ethics; God, however, is the cause of all being, all truth, all good—the *causa subsistendi, ratio intelligendi, et ordo vivendi*. In the order of things and in the ways of morals the workings of God are evident as they have been seen to be in discovery of truth. All things were created by God in the beginning as in a contexture of elements, and they are to develop and appear only when suitable circumstances occur (*acceptis opportunitatibus prodeunt*). Everything which will later become this or that particular thing is contained invisibly in the seminal reasons implanted at creation; the world blooms out of its primitive elements as a tree develops from its seed. And, to complete the trinity, as the movement of bodies is the growth of the seminal reasons formed by God, as knowledge of truth is knowledge in the light of God, so the pursuit of the good is a state of will which stands in need of the grace of God. The supreme good is as necessary to virtue as the supreme truth to wisdom. The ethical problem is the problem of what the soul seeks in seeking God and how it comes to seek that.

The happy life, obviously on these grounds, is nothing other than the enjoyment of the truth, that is, the enjoyment of God who is truth and the illumination. The soul seeks not only a knowledge which is true—if it were not true it would not satisfy the soul—but it must be so true that it sets an end to all research. The soul seeks, by way of incomplete doctrines, truth, that after movement it may have repose. The cause of all the movement of the soul is a truth which is present to our memory but superior to it. It is present without being part because we are variable and truth is immutable. The movement therefore of thought from things to God is possible only through the presence of a confused idea of God in the soul. The problems of morality are problems of guidance in the practical use of the faculty of knowing, and follow therefore from the nature of thought. As there is the distinction between wisdom and knowledge, between what the mind may learn of eternal things and what it may learn of temporal things, so there are the two cities, the city of God and the terrestrial city, for the will of men may become entangled in corporeal changing things as well as inspired to the search for God. Salvation must come with the love of God; he can be loved only if the mind is turned to him; but if he is known he can not but be loved; all knowledge must lead to God and therefore to the love of God. The intellect in wisdom and the soul in virtue travel the same road to salvation.

That there is a philosophy in Augustine, therefore, is the result of an error and an accident; if Adam had not fallen, man would have been like the angels in his knowledge and love. Philosophy is love and the search for wisdom; love is the desire for that which is perceived to be good. All revolves about the love of God, but love depends on knowledge, because one loves only that which one knows. It is important to faith that there be at least a limited certitude for the understanding. This indeed is faith—not a vague sentiment of the soul adhering to a doctrine without rational motivation, nor a mysticism without sure proofs, nor yet an intellectualist certainty imposed necessarily by the evidence of irresistible proofs—but an intellectual adherence to truths which are guaranteed in testimony worthy of credence and illustrated, once believed, in all the facts of the universe. All faith is placed in God; in the true philosophy the mind grasps him as truth, after him the soul, after the soul the body, after the body other bodies. Philosophy must, if this is so, consist in an inversion of perspective toward things. The mind must be prepared for it as for an initiation; the work of philosophy is first a work of conversion. It is to accomplish this preliminary task that Augustine most usually undertakes his excursions into spiritual biography. The knowledge of the world is so related to the knowledge of God that the mind passes immediately from the world to God. There is, consequently, no purely speculative curiosity in Augustine. The statement of his philosophy involves the selection from an infinity of possible truths of some few, useful to introduce tranquillity into the soul. The joy of knowing is sensed in truths, not that more truths may be added to the sum of knowledge, but rather that in truths may be achieved the happiness for which truth is sought. It is enough for philosophy to have discovered a profound tie between religion and intelligence and to have justified religion dialectically.

ST. AUGUSTINE

ON THE FREE WILL [1]

Book II

In which, a difficulty having arisen from the circumstance that freedom, by which sin is committed, was given by God, the following three questions are inquired into: by what reason it is manifest that God is; whether all goods are from God; whether the free will is to be considered among the number of goods.

CHAPTER I.

Why freedom, by which sin is committed, was given by God.

1. *Evodius.* Now explain to me, if you can, why God gave man free judgment of will, for obviously, if man had not received free will, he would not be able to sin.

Augustine. Is it certain and known to you then that God gave man this which you do not think should have been given?

E. So far as the preceding book is concerned I seem to have understood both that we have free judgment of will and that we sin only by it.

[1] SANCTI AURELII AUGUSTINI, HIPPONENSIS EPISCOPI, *De Libero Arbitrio, Lib. II,* in *Opera Omnia,* J. P. MIGNE, *Patrologia Latina,* vol. 32, col. 1239-1266.

A. I too recall that that has already been made clear to us. But I have just asked whether you know that God gave us this which we clearly have and by which clearly we sin.

E. I think no other than God. For we are from him; and whether we sin or act rightly, we merit punishment or reward from him.

A. I want to know also whether you know this clearly or whether you are moved, not unwillingly, to believe it by authority even though you do not know it.

E. I answer that in what concerns this thing I first believed by authority. But what is more true than that every good is from God and that every just act is good, and that the punishment of sinners and the reward of those who act rightly are just? From this it comes about both that sinners are afflicted by God with misery and that those who act rightly are visited with felicity.

2. *A.* To that I have no objection, but I raise this other question: how do you know that we are from him? For this you have not yet explained, but you have explained that we merit from him either punishment or reward.

E. That, too, I see is clear no otherwise than because we know already that God judges sins. Certainly, all justice is from him. For as it is not characteristic of any goodness to show its benefits in what is alien to it, so it is not of justice to judge in what is alien to it. Wherefore, it is clear that we pertain to him, not only because he is most benign in showing his benefits in us but also most just in judging. Finally, from what I have stated and from what you have conceded, every good, including man, can be understood to be from

God. For man himself in so far as he is man is something good, because he can, when he so wishes, live rightly.

3. *A.* Clearly if these things are so, the question which you proposed has been solved. For if man is something good and can not act rightly except when he wishes, he ought to have a free will without which he could not act rightly. For it is not to be believed that, because sin is committed by it too, God gave free will for sin. Therefore, since without it man can not live rightly, there is cause enough why it should have been given. It can, moreover, be understood to have been given for this and on this account, because if anyone shall have used it for sinning, it is condemned in him by God. But this would be done unjustly if free will had been given, not only that one might live rightly, but also that one might sin. For how could he be punished justly who had used his will for that purpose for which it has been given? But then, when God punishes the sinner, what else does he seem to you to say except, Why have you not used your free will for the purpose for which I gave it to you, that is, for doing rightly? Further, if man lacked free judgment of will, how would that be good, for which justice itself is commended when it condemns sins and honors deeds rightly done? For that which was not done by the will would be neither sinfully nor rightly done. And according to this if man did not have free will, both punishment and reward would be unjust. However, there must have been justice in both punishment and reward, since it is one of the goods which are from God. Therefore, God must have given man free will.

CHAPTER II

Objection: how is the free will pliant to evil if it has been given for good?

4. *E.* I concede now that God gave it. But I ask you, does it not seem to you that, if it has been given for acting rightly, it should not be susceptible of being turned to sinning? As in the case of justice itself, which was given to man that he might live well: for can anyone live evilly by his justice? So too, no one would be able by will to sin, if the will had been given for acting rightly.

A. God will grant, I hope, that I shall be able to answer you, or rather that you reply to yourself by the same truth, teaching within, which is the supreme mistress of all. But I want you to tell me briefly, if you hold as certain and known that of which I have asked you, that God has given us free will, whether or not it be necessary to say that that should not have been given which we acknowledge God to have given. For if it is uncertain whether or not he gave it, we inquire rightly whether it was well given, that it may be discovered also, when we shall have found it was well given, that he gave it by whom all goods have been given to man; if however we should find that it was not well given, we may understand that he did not give it, whom to blame is sinful. But if it is certain that he himself gave it we must acknowledge that, in whatsoever manner it has been given, it should neither not be given nor be given otherwise than it was given. For he gave it whose deed can not rightly be reprehended in any stipulation.

5. *E.* Although I hold these things with unshaken faith, still, since I do not yet hold them in knowledge; let us inquire as if all things were uncertain. For I see, since it is uncertain whether free will was given for doing rightly (since we can also sin by it) that it becomes uncertain too whether it should have been given. For if it is uncertain that it was given for doing rightly, it is also uncertain that it should have been given, and by that it will also be uncertain whether God gave it; because if it is uncertain that it should have been given, it is uncertain that it has been given by him, of whom it is sinful to believe that he has given anything which should not have been given.

A. At all events you are certain that God is.

E. That too I hold unshakable, not by contemplation, but by belief.

A. If, then, any of those fools of whom it is written, *The fool hath said in his heart, There is no God,*[2] should say that to you, and should not wish to believe with you what you believe, but wished to know whether you believed the truth; would you leave the man, or would you judge that he was to be persuaded in some way of what you hold unshakeable, particularly if he wished, not to oppose it obstinately, but seriously to learn it?

E. That which you stated last warns me sufficiently what I should answer him. For, of course, even if he were extremely stupid, he would grant me that one must not argue deceitfully and obstinately about anything whatever, and particularly not about so great a thing. After he had conceded that, it would first be important to me that I should believe he inquired this in good faith and did not conceal within himself any obstinacy and deceit in what pertains to this question. Then I should demonstrate (which I think would be extremely easy

2 *Psalm* 53:1; or in the Vulgate, *Psalm* 52:1.

for any one), how much more reasonable it would be (since he was willing to believe another who was not acquainted with them in respect to hidden matters of his own mind, which he himself knew) to believe also from the Books of so many men who left testimony in letters that they lived with the Son of God, that God is; for they have written that they saw deeds which could never have been done if there were no God; and he would be very stupid, if he, who for himself wanted me to believe these things, should reprove me for believing them. Moreover, since he would not be able to reprove me rightly, he would in no wise find a reason why he too should not imitate me.

A. If, then, you think it sufficient in the question of the existence of God for us to have judged that so many men could not have believed thoughtlessly, why, I ask you, do you not think similarly that the authority of those same men is to be credited in those matters too, which, uncertain and obviously unknown, we have undertaken to examine, and so spare us the labor of further investigation of them?

E. But we wish to know and to understand that which we believe.

6. *A.* You remember correctly what we undeniably asserted at the beginning of our previous discussion.[3] For if to believe were not one thing and to understand another and if we did not have to believe first whatever great and divine truths we wished to understand, the prophet would have said in vain, *If ye will not believe, ye shall not understand.*[4] Our Lord himself also urged

[3] Book I, chapter 2.
[4] *Isaiah* 7: 9, sec. LXX. In the Vulgate version *intelligetis* becomes *permanebitis;* the passage, consequently is now rendered, *If ye will not believe, surely ye shall not be established.*

by both his words and his deeds that they whom he
called to salvation should first believe.   But later when
he spoke of the very gift which was to be given those
who believe he did not say, And this is life eternal,
that they should believe; but he said, *And this is life
eternal that they should know thee the only true God
and him whom thou didst send, Jesus Christ.*[5]   Then
again he says to believers, *Seek and ye shall find;* [6] for
neither can that be said to have been found which is
believed while unknown, nor is any one made suitable
to find God unless he shall first believe what later he
is to know.   Wherefore, obedient to the precepts of
God, let us seek earnestly.   For what we seek when
he urges us, we shall find by his pointing the way, so
far as these things can be found in this life and by
such as we: for it is to be believed that they can be
distinguished and known very evidently and very perfectly by better men even while they inhabit this earth,
and certainly by all good and pious men after this life;
and it is to be hoped that it will be so with us.   Once
earthly and human things have been despised, these
things are in every manner to be desired and loved.

CHAPTER III.

*That it may become manifest that God is, it is inquired
what is most excellent in man.*

7. Let us, however, if that pleases you, take up the
question in this order: first, how it is manifest that God

The early writings of Augustine antecede, of course, the Vulgate translation, and for a time Augustine seems to have opposed the project of translation, although in his later works
the version of St. Jerome not infrequently appears in his
biblical citations.

[5] *John* 17:3.   [6] *Matthew* 7:7.

is; then, whether all things whatsoever, in so far as they are good, are from him; finally, whether free will is to be numbered among the goods. When these have been resolved it will appear sufficiently, I think, whether free will was rightly given to man. So, to begin with what is most manifest, I ask you first whether you yourself are. Or perhaps you have fears lest you be led astray in that question, although surely if you were not, you could not in the least be led astray?

E. Go on instead to the other questions.

A. Then, since it is clear to you that you are, and since it would not otherwise be clear to you unless you lived, this also is clear, that you live; do you understand these two to be extremely true?

E. I understand that immediately.

A. Therefore this third proposition too is clear, namely, that you understand.

E. Clearly.

A. Which of the three seems to you to excel?

E. Understanding.

A. Why does that seem so to you?

E. Because since there are these three, to be, to live, and to understand; and a stone is, and an animal lives, but nevertheless I do not think a stone lives nor an animal understands; but on the other hand it is most certain that he who understands both is and lives; so, I do not hesitate to judge that more excellent to which all three are present than that from which two or one are absent. For that which lives, surely also is, but it does not follow that it also understands: such I judge is the life of an animal. But, on the other hand it surely does not follow from the fact that something is, that it also lives and understands: for I may say that a corpse is, but no one would say that it lives. Moreover, that which does not live, much less understands.

A. We hold, then, that of these three two are absent from the corpse, one from the animal, and none from man.

E. That is true.

A. We hold further that that is most excellent in the three which man has together with the other two, namely, to understand; and having that it follows also that he is and lives.

E. Surely.

8. *A.* Tell me now, whether you know that you have those ordinary senses of the body, seeing, and hearing, and smelling, and tasting, and touching.

E. I do.

A. What do you think pertains to the sense of seeing? That is, what do you think we perceive in seeing?

E. All corporeal things.

A. Do we also perceive the hard and the soft by sight?

E. No.

A. Therefore, what pertains properly to the eyes, which we perceive through them?

E. Color.

A. What to the ears?

E. Sound.

A. What to smell?

E. Odor.

A. What to taste?

E. Flavor.

A. What to touch?

E. Soft or hard, smooth or rough, and many such qualities.

A. Then, do we not perceive the forms of bodies, large, small, square, round, and whatever other qualities there are of this sort, by both touching and seeing, and therefore can they not be attributed to neither sight nor touch properly, but to both?

E. I understand.

A. Do you understand then also, that single senses have certain properties concerning which they report, and that some of the senses have certain properties in common?

E. I understand this too.

A. Are we able then to distinguish by any one of the senses what pertains to each, and what all or certain of the senses have in common among them?

E. That can be distinguished in no way except by a certain interior sense.

A. Is that perhaps reason itself, which the beasts lack? For I believe, by reason we understand these things and know that they are so related.

E. Rather I think we understand by reason that there is a certain interior sense, to which all things are referred from those very well known five. For the beast sees by one process, by another he avoids or desires that which he perceives in seeing: for the one sense is in his eyes, but the other is within him, in the soul itself, by which animals either desire and seize if pleased, or turn from and reject if displeased, not only those things which are seen, but also those which are heard, and those which are grasped by other senses of the body. This sense, however, can not be called sight, nor hearing, nor smell, nor taste, nor touch, but something else which presides over all of them in common. This, as I have said, we may comprehend with reason, but we can not call it itself reason, since it is clear that it is present in beasts.

9. *A.* I recognize this, whatever it is, and I do not hesitate to call it the interior sense. But that which

is referred to us by the senses of the body, unless it also pass beyond this interior sense, can not come to knowledge. For whatever we know, we comprehend by reason. We know, however, to say nothing of many other facts, that colors can not be perceived by hearing nor voices by sight. And although we know this, we know it neither by eyes, nor ears, nor again by that interior sense which beasts do not lack. For it is not to be believed that they know that light is not perceived by the ears, nor the voice by the eyes, since we distinguish such things only by rational reflection and thought.

E. I can not say that I have observed that. In fact, what follows if they judge too by the interior sense, which you concede they do not lack, that colors can not be perceived by hearing, nor voices by sight?

A. Do you think also that they can distinguish these four one from the other—the color which is perceived, and the sense which is in the eye, and that interior sense in the soul, and the reason by which these are defined and enumerated one after the other?

E. Not at all.

A. Then, would reason be able to distinguish these four, one from the other, and determine them in definitions, if there were not referred to it, color through the sense of the eyes, and also that sense itself through the interior sense which presides over it, and the same interior sense through itself, if there is not still another intermediary interposed?

E. I do not see how it could be otherwise.

A. Do you see then that color is perceived by the sense of the eyes, but that the sense itself is not perceived by the same sense? For you do not see the seeing itself with the same sense by which you see color.

E. Not at all.

A. Try also to make this distinction: for I think that
you do not deny that it is one thing to be color and
another to see color, and that again it is still another
thing to have the sense, when color is not present, by
which it could be seen if it were present.

E. I see that too, and I concede that they differ from
each other.

A. Do you see any of these three, besides color, with
the eyes?

E. None.

A. Tell me then whence it is that you see the other
two, for you would not be able to distinguish them if
you had not seen them.

E. I know nothing further; I know that they are,
nothing more.

A. You do not know then whether it is reason, or that
life, which we call the interior sense, excelling the
senses of the body, or something else?

E. I do not know.

A. This however you know: that it can not be defined
except by reason, nor can reason define it except with
reference to those things which are offered to it for
examination.

E. That is certain.

A. Whatever else there is, then, by which all that we
know can be perceived, it is in the service of reason,
to which it brings and reports whatever it touches, so
that the things which are perceived can be distinguished
by their ends and can be comprehended not only by
being perceived but also by being known.

E. That is so.

A. Reason itself distinguishes its servant-senses and
that which they bring to it from each other, and further
recognizes what separates them from itself, and proves
itself to be more powerful than they. Does it then

comprehend itself by some other thing than itself, that
is, by reason? Or would you know that you have reason
otherwise than by perceiving it by reason?

E. Very true.

A. Since, therefore, when we perceive color, we do
not in like manner perceive, by the sense itself, ourselves perceiving; nor when we hear a sound, do we also
hear our own hearing; nor when we smell a rose, does
our very smelling also emit some odor to us; nor when
we taste something, does taste itself savor in our mouth;
nor when we touch something, are we able also to touch
the sense of touch itself; it is clear that these five senses
can be perceived by no one of the senses, although all
corporeal things are perceived by them.

E. That is clear.

CHAPTER IV.

*The interior sense perceives itself perceiving: whether it
also distinguishes itself apart.*

10. *A.* I think it is clear also that not only does
that interior sense perceive those things which it has
received from the five senses of the body, but also that
the senses themselves are perceived by it. For no otherwise would a beast move itself either in desiring something or in fleeing it, except by perceiving itself perceive, not in order to know, for this is the property of
reason, but only in order to move, which surely it perceives by no one of those five senses. But if this point
is still obscure it will be clarified if you consider, for
example, what is clear enough in any one of the senses,
as in sight. For, to open the eye and to move it that
it may look at that which it wishes to see, would in no
way be possible, if, when the eye was closed or not
so moved, the interior sense did not perceive that it did

not see the thing. If, however, it perceives that it does not see when it does not see, it is necessary too that it perceive that it sees when it does see; because it indicates that it perceives both, since it does not move the eye when it sees by that appetite by which it moves the eye when it does not see. But it is not so clear whether this life, which perceives itself perceiving corporeal things, also perceives itself, except that any one who inquires within himself finds that every living thing flees death; since death is the contrary of life, it is necessary that life, which flees its contrary, perceive itself too. But if it is still not clear, let it be passed over, that we may go on only by certain and clear instances to that which we wish. For the following points are clear, that corporeal things are perceived by the bodily sense; but sense itself can not be perceived by this same sense; yet both are perceived by the interior sense—corporeal things (by way of a sense of the body) and the sense of the body itself; finally, that by reason all these and reason itself are made known, and are held together in knowledge: does it not seem so to you?

E. It seems clearly so.

'A. Proceed then; tell me now how the question arises which has kept us so long on this path in our efforts to solve it.

Chapter V.

The interior sense excels the external senses of which it is the moderator and judge.

11. *E.* As I remember, the first of those three questions which we posed a little while ago to establish an order for this discussion is now being considered, that

is, how, even though it is to be believed most tenaciously
and most firmly, it can be made clear that God is.

A. You recall that correctly, but I want you to bear
this diligently in mind too, that when I asked you
whether you knew that you were, not only this but
two other facts which you knew appeared to us.

E. I remember that too.

A. Now then consider to which of those three you
would say pertains all that the bodily sense perceives;
that is, in which class of things does it seem to you
must be placed whatever our sense touches whether by
means of the eyes or by any other instrument of the
body; is it to be placed in the class which only is, or
in that which also lives, or in that which also understands?

E. In that which only is.

A. Then, in which class of these three do you judge
the sense itself to fall?

E. In that which lives.

A. Which of these two then do you judge to be the
better? The sense itself or that which the sense perceives?

E. The sense surely.

A. Why?

E. Because that which also lives is better than that
which only is.

12. *A.* Will you hesitate, then, to place above this
sense by which we perceive body (and which you have
just said is to be placed above the body itself) that
interior sense which in what precedes we have looked
for beneath reason and even as common in us with the
beasts?

E. I should certainly not hesitate.

A. I want you to tell me too why you do not hesitate.

For you can not say that this interior sense must now be put in that one of those three classes which also understands, but only in that which both is and lives, although it lacks understanding: for this sense is also present in beasts in which there is no understanding. Since these things are so, I ask you why you place the interior sense above the sense by which we perceive corporeal things, since they are both in the class which lives. Moreover, you have placed sense, which perceives bodies, above bodies, because they are in that class which only is, whereas sense is in the class which also lives: and since the interior sense is found in that class too, tell me why you think it is better. For if you should say, because it perceives this sense, I do not believe that you will find a rule by which we can establish that all perceiving is better than that which is perceived by it, lest perchance we be compelled by that to say also that all understanding is better than that which is understood by it. That in fact is false, because man understands wisdom and is not better than wisdom itself. Wherefore consider by what cause it appeared to you that the interior sense is to be preferred to this sense by which we perceive bodies.

E. Because I know it to be a kind of moderator and judge of the other. For if something should be lacking to it in the exercise of its function, it demands it as due from its servant, as was brought out a little while ago in the discussion. For the sense of the eye does not see itself see or not see, and because it does not see, it can not judge what is lacking to it or what is sufficient; but the interior sense does this, and by it the soul of the beast is admonished to open the closed eye and to supply that which it perceives to be lacking. But no one doubts that that which judges is better than that which is judged.

A. Do you see then that in a certain way this sense of the body also judges of bodies? For pleasure and pain pertain to sense when it comes in contact smoothly or roughly with a body. For just as the interior sense judges what is missing or what is sufficient to the sense of the eyes, so the sense of the eyes itself judges what is missing or what is sufficient in colors. Likewise, just as the interior sense judges whether our hearing is too little or sufficiently intent, so hearing itself judges in voices, which of them flows smoothly or which resounds harshly. We need not proceed further with the other senses of the body, for I believe you are now aware of what I mean, that obviously the interior sense judges of these senses of the body when it examines their integrity and when it demands what is needed, just as the senses of the body judge of bodies, accepting a smooth touch in them and rejecting the contrary.

E. I see clearly, and I grant that it is very true.

CHAPTER VI.

Reason excels other functions in man; if there is anything which excels it, it is God.

13. *A.* Consider now whether reason judges also of this interior sense. For now I do not ask whether you think that reason is better than it, because I have no doubt that you do; although again I do not think that it need even be asked whether reason judges of this sense. For how would one thing be better than another among the things which are below reason, that is, in bodies and in the senses of the body and in that interior sense, and how would reason itself be more excellent than the others, which indeed it is, unless it

proclaimed this itself? Which certainly it could in no way do unless it judged of them.

E. That is clear.

A. Then, since the nature which not only is, but also lives, but does not understand (such as the soul of beasts) stands above the nature which only is and does not live nor understand (such as an inanimate body); and again since above that there stands the nature which at the same time is and lives and understands (such as the rational mind in man) would you not think that in us, more particularly in those things by which our nature is fulfilled that we may be men, something could be found more excellent than what we placed in the third place in these three? For it is clear that we have a body, and a certain life by which the body itself is animated and quickened, which two we also recognize in beasts, and a third something which the nature of beasts does not have, the head or eye of our soul, as it were, or any other name by which reason and understanding may be designated more appropriately. Wherefore consider, I pray you, whether you can find in the nature of man something more sublime than reason.

E. I see absolutely nothing better.

14. *A.* Well, then, if we could find something which you not only do not doubt to be, but also to be more excellent than our reason itself, will you hesitate to call that, whatever it is, God?

E. I should not necessarily say, if I could find something better than that which is best in my nature, that it is God. For it does not please me to name God that to which my reason is inferior, but rather that to which nothing is superior.

A. Plainly so: for he has himself given to this reason of yours the power to feel so piously and truly of him.

But I ask you again, if you did not find that there was anything above our reason except what is eternal and immutable, would you hesitate to call that God? For you know that bodies are mutable, and it is clear that the very life by which the body is animated does not lack mutability in various states; and reason itself is surely shown to be mutable, since it sometimes attempts to arrive at truth and sometimes does not attempt to, and sometimes arrives and sometimes does not. It may be granted that if reason with the aid of no instrument of the body, not by touch, nor by taste, nor by smell, nor by ears, nor by eyes, nor by any other sense inferior to it, but by itself, discerns something eternal and immutable and at the same time discerns itself inferior to it, that must be its God.

E. I will readily grant that that is God than which nothing is known to be superior.

A. You hold a good doctrine: for it will be enough for me to show that there is something of that sort, which either you will grant to be God, or if there is something above, you will concede that that itself is God. Wherefore whether there be something above or not, it will be manifest that God is, since I shall have shown, with his aid, that which I promised, that there is something above reason.

E. Then demonstrate what you promised.

CHAPTER VII.

In what manner the same thing may be perceived by many, as a whole, or not as a whole, and at the same time by different persons.

15. *A.* I shall do that, but first I ask whether my bodily sense is the same as yours, or whether definitely

mine is only mine, and yours is only yours; because if it were not so, I would not be able to see anything with my eyes which you did not see.

E. I concede readily that although they are of the same genus, nevertheless, we have each of us senses of seeing, or hearing, or any one of the others. For a man can not only see but can also hear what another man does not hear, and one man can perceive by any of the other senses what another does not perceive. Wherefore it is clear both that your sense is only yours, and mine is only mine.

A. Will you make this same answer concerning that interior sense too? Or will you say something else?

E. Absolutely nothing else. For surely that sense of mine perceives my sense and yours perceives yours: for that very reason I am asked very frequently by a person who sees something, whether I too see it, because I perceive myself seeing or not seeing but he who asks does not.

A. And then, does not each one of us have his own reason? Inasmuch as it can happen that I understand something when you do not understand it; and you can not know whether I understand it; but I know.

E. It is clear, too, that we have, each of us, individual rational minds.

16. *A.* Will you be able to say too that we have the individual suns, which we see, or moons, or morning-stars, or other things of that sort, even though each one sees them with his own and proper sense?

E. I should certainly not say that.

A. Many of us, then, are able to see a single thing at the same time, although we have, each single one of us, our individual senses, by all of which we perceive that one thing which we see at the same time, so that although my sense is one and yours another, it may nevertheless happen that what we see is not one mine and another yours; but one only may be present for both of us, and may be seen by both at the same time.

E. That is very clear.

A. We can also hear some single voice at the same time, so that although my hearing is one and yours another, there is not, for all that, one voice mine and another voice yours which we hear at the same time, nor is one part of it caught by my hearing and another by yours, but whatsoever has sounded will be there to be heard at one time, one and whole, by both of us.

E. That too is clear.

17. *A.* Now you may also consider what we say in relation to the other senses of the body, that, with respect to what pertains to this thing, they are not constituted wholly as the two senses of eyes and ears, nor are they constituted wholly differently. For because you and I can fill our lungs from the same air and perceive the state of the air by odor; and again because we can both taste of the same honey or of any other food or drink, and perceive its state by flavor, even though it is one and our senses are individual, yours to you and mine to me, so that although we both perceive one odor and one flavor, nevertheless you do not perceive it with my sense, nor I with yours, nor with any one sense which could be common to both of us, but truly my sense is mine and yours is yours, even though a single odor or flavor is perceived by both: in this respect, therefore, these senses are found to have something like the above two in sight and hearing; but they are unlike in this (in so far as it pertains to what we are now treating) that although we both draw

one air into our nostrils or both take one food to taste it, nevertheless I do not draw in that part of the air which you do, nor do I take the same part of the food as you, but I take one and you another: and therefore of all the air I take a part, when I breathe, such as is sufficient for me, and you too take, of all of it, another part such as is sufficient for you: and although the food be consumed one and all by both of us, still it can not be consumed all by me and all by you, in the manner in which I hear a whole word and you the whole word at the same time, and as I see a certain species as much as you too see it at the same time; but it is necessary that one part of the food or drink pass into me and another part into you; do you understand these things clearly enough?

E. By all means; I grant them to be very apparent and most certain.

18. *A.* Do you think the sense of touch is to be compared with the senses of the eyes and ears in this matter which is now being discussed; because not only can we both perceive one body by touching it, but also you will be able to touch the same part as I have touched, so that we can both perceive by touch not only the same body but also the same part of the body? For in touching it is not as in eating of a given food, when we can not both of us, I and you, take all of it; but that which I have touched you will be able to touch, one and all, so that both of us touch it, not in single parts, but each of us the whole.

E. I confess that this sense of touch is in this respect very much like the two higher senses; but I see that they are unlike in this respect, that we can both see and hear at the same time, that is, at one time some single whole, but we can not both touch any whole at one time,

but only single parts, and we can touch the same part
only at separate times, for I can not touch any part
which you are inspecting by touch unless you remove
your touch.

19. *A.* You have replied very carefully, but you
must see this too, that since of all the things which
we perceive there are some which both of us perceive
and others which we may perceive individually, we perceive surely our senses themselves, as individuals, each
his own, so that I do not perceive your sense nor you
mine, because we can not both perceive, but only singly,
anything of those things which are perceived by us
through the senses of the body, that is, of corporeal
things, except what is so made ours that we are able
to transform and change it into ourselves, as is the case
with food and drink, of which you will be able to perceive no part that I have perceived; for even in the
case of nurses who give children masticated food, nevertheless that which the taste has taken therefrom and
has changed to the viscera of the chewer, can in no
way be recalled that it may be made again into food
of the child.   For when the throat tastes something
with pleasure, it claims for itself an irrevocable part,
however small, and this must be done because such is
the nature of the body: for if it were not so, no savor
would remain in the mouth after those masticated bits
had been passed on or spit out.   This can rightly be
said also of the parts of the air which we draw into
the nostrils; for although you may draw in some of
the air which I have expelled, nevertheless you can not
draw in that which has gone from the air into my
nutriment, because that can not be returned.   Physicians
say that we take nutriment through the nostrils too;
which nutriment I alone can perceive by breathing, and

I can not return it by breathing it out again for you to draw into your nostrils and perceive too. For there are other sensibles which although we perceive them, still we do not in perceiving change them into our body and corrupt them; we both can perceive them, whether at one time or successively at different times, inasmuch as either the whole or the part which I perceive, may be perceived by you too; of such sort are light or sound or bodies which we touch but nevertheless do not alter.

E. I understand.

A. It is clear then that those things which we do not alter and which we nevertheless perceive with the senses of the body, do not pertain to the nature of our senses and rather on that account are common to us, because they are not changed and altered into something proper, and as it were, private to us.

E. I agree readily.

A. Therefore, that must be understood to be proper, and as it were, private, which belongs to each one of us alone and which each alone perceives in himself, because it pertains properly to his nature; but that must be understood to be common, and as it were, public, which is perceived by all who are sentient, with no corruption or alteration of itself.

E. It is so.

CHAPTER VIII.

The reason or nature of numbers is perceived by no sense of the body; by whomsoever it is perceived in understanding, it is one and immutable.

20. *A.* Attend now, and tell me whether something may be found which all who reason see in common,

each with his own reason and mind, since that which is seen is present to all and is not altered for the use of those to whom it is present, as food or drink, but remains uncorrupted and whole whether they see it or do not see it: or would you perhaps think that there is nothing of this sort?

E. On the contrary, I see that there are many such things, of which it suffices to mention one; that the reason and truth of number is present to all who reason, so that every computer individually tries to apprehend it with his reason and understanding; and one can do it rather easily, another with more difficulty, still another can not do it at all: although notwithstanding it offers itself equally to all who can grasp it; nor when perceived by any one is it changed and altered for the nutriment, as it were, of its perceiver; nor does it cease when some one is deceived in it, but he is so much the more in error the less he sees it, while it remains true and whole.

21. *A.* Clearly true; but I notice that you found what you said quickly as if you were not unused to these things; nevertheless, if some one were to say to you that these numbers are not impressed on our mind by some nature of theirs, but by those things which we come upon by the bodily sense, as it were, certain images of visible things; what would you reply? or do you also think thus?

E. I should certainly not have thought thus: for if I have perceived numbers by the sense of the body, I have not thereby been able by the sense of the body to perceive also the nature of the separation and combination of numbers. For by this light of the mind I refute him who would report a false sum when he computes whether in adding or subtracting. And I do not know how long anything I touch by a bodily sense will persist, as for instance, this sky and this land, and whatever other bodies I perceive in them; but seven and three are ten, and not only now, but always; nor have seven and three in any way at any time not been ten, nor will seven and three at any time not be ten. I have said, therefore, that this incorruptible truth of number is common to me and any one at all who reasons.

22. *A.* I do not oppose you when you reply so very truly and with such certainty. But you will see also that numbers themselves are not easily drawn out by the sense of the body, if you will have considered that any number whatsoever is given its value according to the number of times it contains one; for example, if it contains one twice it is called two; if three times, three, and if it contains one ten times, then it is called ten: and the number of times that any number whatsoever contains one, that is its name, and it is called that much. Certainly whoever ponders one very truly, finds forthwith that it can not be perceived by the senses of the body. ,For whatever is touched upon by such a sense, is proved immediately to be not one but many: for it is body, and therefore has innumerable parts. But not to trace out any extremely minute and still more finely divided particles, however small that tiny body be, it surely has a right part and a left part; one higher and another lower; or one further and another nearer; or some at the ends and another in the middle; for it is necessary that these be present in the tiny mode of body however tiny we may say it is; and because of this we do not concede that any body is truly and purely one, in which, notwithstanding, so many could be enumerated except for the discrete consideration of that one. For when I seek one in body, and when I have no doubt

that I shall not find it, I know certainly what I seek
there, and what I shall and what I shall not find there,
and what can not be found there or rather can not be
there at all. When therefore I know that body is not
one, I know what one is: for if I did not know one I
should not be able to enumerate the many in body.
But wherever it may have been that I know one, I surely
do not know it through the sense of the body, because
through the sense of the body I know only body, which
we are persuaded is not truly and purely one. Moreover, if we have not perceived one by the sense of the
body, we have perceived no number by that sense, at
least so far as those numbers are concerned which we
distinguish by the understanding. For there is none
of them which is not given its value according to the
number of times it contains one, and the perception of
one is not encompassed by the sense of the body. For
the half of any small body whatsoever makes up a
whole of two halves, and it itself contains its half.
Therefore these two parts are in the body in such
fashion that they are not simply two themselves. But
since the number which is called two is called two because it contains twice that which is simply one, the
half of it, that is, that which is itself simply one, can not
further have a half or a third part or any part whatsoever, since it is simple and truly one.

23. Furthermore whereas when we follow the order
of numbers we see two after one, which number, compared to one, is found to be double; the double of two
is not joined next in series, but four which is the double
of two follows after the interposition of three. And this
relation is carried out through all the other numbers
by a most certain and immutable law, that the first
number after one, that is, after the first of all num-

bers, itself excepted, is double one, and in fact two follows one. The second number after the second moreover, that is, after two, itself excepted, is double two: indeed, after two there is first three, second four, which is double the second. The third number after the third, that is, three, itself excepted, is the double of three: indeed, after the third, that is, after three, there is first four, second five, third six, which is twice the third. And so, too, after the fourth, the fourth number, itself excepted, is double four: for after the fourth, that is after four, there is first five, second six, third seven, fourth eight, which is double the fourth. And so you will find through all the others what has been found in the sequence of the first numbers, that is, in one and two, that the double of any number is as many units after it as the original number is after one. Whence do we perceive this, then, which we perceive to be immobile, firm and uncorrupted through all numbers? For no one has perceived all the numbers by any sense of the body; for they are innumerable: whence then do we know that this is so through all; or by what phantasy or by what apparition is so certain a truth of number to be contemplated so faithfully through countless numbers except by an interior light which the corporeal senses do not know?

24. From these and many similar instances it must be granted by all inquirers to whom God has given natural perception and whom obstinacy has not overcast in obscurity, that the reason and truth of numbers is not perceived by the senses of the body, and that it persists unalterable and pure, and that it is common to be seen by all who use reason. Wherefore although many other things can be found, which are present in common and as it were publicly to those who reason,

and are seen by them by way of the mind and by way of the reason of each and every one who perceives, and these things remain inviolate and immutable, nevertheless I have taken it not unwillingly, that this reason and truth of numbers should occur most insistently to you when you wanted to answer what I asked: for not for nothing is number joined to wisdom in the Sacred Books where it was said: *I turned about and I inclined my heart that I might know and consider and inquire the wisdom and the number.*[7]

CHAPTER IX.

What wisdom is, without which no one is happy; whether it is one in all wise men.

25. Nevertheless, I ask you, what do you think must be judged of wisdom itself? Do you think that each individual man has his own individual wisdom? Or do you think that one wisdom is present in common for all, of which the more one is made participant the wiser he is?

E. I do not yet know what you call wisdom, inasmuch as I see that what is done and said wisely appears variously to men: for those who fight seem to themselves to act wisely, and those who, despising military matters, supervise the care and labor of cultivating the field, praise rather this and attribute it to wisdom; and those who are astute in thinking out ways of acquiring money, seem to themselves to be wise; and those who neglect or cast off all these and all things

---

[7] *Eccles.* 7:26. The Vulgate has *sapientiam et rationem* instead of *sapientiam et numerum. Ratio* is usually rendered the *reason of things* in the translation of this text; *Eccles.* 7:25, in english translation.

that are temporal of this sort, and turn their whole
care to the investigation of truth that they may know
themselves and God, they judge this to be the great
reward of wisdom; and they who do not wish to give
themselves to this leisure of seeking and contemplating
the truth, but instead exercise extremely laborious cares
and offices such as counselling men and busying themselves in the activity of moderating and governing human affairs, they judge themselves to be wise; and
those who do both of these, and live partly in the contemplation of truth and partly in official labors, which
they think they owe to human society, they seem to
themselves to hold the palm of wisdom. I omit innumerable sects of which there is none that does not
place its own sectators above all others and hold them
alone to be wise. Wherefore since it is a question with
us now, not of what we may believe the answer should
be, but of what we are convinced by clear understanding, I shall in no wise be able to answer what you
ask unless I also know by contemplating and by discerning with reason what I hold by believing, and this
is wisdom itself.

26. *A.* Do you think there is any wisdom other than
truth, in which the supreme good is discerned and
known? For all those different sectators whom you
mentioned seek good and avoid evil; but with that in
view they pursue different things because different
things seem good to different people. Therefore he who
desires what should not have been desired, even though
he would not have desired it if it had not seemed good
to him, nevertheless errs. However, neither he who
desires nothing nor he who desires what he should
desire can err. In so far therefore as all men desire
a happy life they do not err. But in so far as any one

does not hold to that way of life which leads to happiness, although he avows and professes himself to wish nothing except to arrive at happiness, he errs to that extent. For error is to follow something which does not lead to that at which we wish to arrive. And the more one errs in the way of life, the less is one wise. For one is that much the further removed from the truth in which the supreme good is discerned and known. When the supreme good, however, is pursued and achieved, every one is made happy because we all without controversy wish the supreme good. As therefore it is certain that we wish to be happy, so it is certain that we wish to be wise, because no one is happy without wisdom. For no one is happy except by the supreme good, which is discerned and known in that truth which we call wisdom. Just as, therefore, before we are happy, a notion of happiness is notwithstanding impressed upon our minds, for through it we know and we say confidently and without uncertainty that we wish to be happy; so too before we are wise, we have a notion of wisdom impressed in our mind, by which each of us, if he were asked whether he wished to be wise, would reply without any obscurity of doubt that he did.

27. Wherefore if it is now clear to us what wisdom is, which perhaps you were not able to explain in words (for if you did not at all discern it by the mind, you would by no means know both that you wish to be wise and that you ought to wish it; which I do not think you will deny), I want you now to tell me whether you think that wisdom too, like the reason and truth of number, exhibits itself in common to all who use reason; or whether you think that, since there are as many minds of men as there are men, whence it is

that I do not discern anything of your mind nor you of mine, there are also as many wisdoms as there could be wise men.

E. If the supreme good is one to all, the truth in which it is discerned and known, that is, wisdom, must likewise be one and common to all.

A. But do you doubt that the supreme good, whatever it is, is one for all men?

E. I doubt it very much, because I see different people enjoying different things as their own supreme goods.

A. I should have wished that no one have doubts of this sort about the supreme good, just as no one doubts that man can be made happy only by securing it, whatever it is. But since this is a great question, and since it calls urgently for a long discourse, let us consider that there are just as many supreme goods as there are different things which are desired by different people as supreme goods: does it not follow therefore that wisdom itself likewise is not one and common to all, because those goods which men distinguish and choose in it are many and diverse? For if you think that, you can doubt too with regard to the light of the sun, whether it is one, since there are many and diverse things which we see in it. From these many, each one chooses by will what he enjoys through the sense of the eyes: and one man willingly looks upon the height of a mountain and enjoys this sight; another the even surface of a field; another the convexity of valleys; another the greenness of woods; another the moving smoothness of the sea; another all of these or whichever of them are beautiful together and contribute to the joy of seeing. Therefore, just as these things are many and diverse which men see and choose for enjoyment in the light of the sun, and still the light itself is one in which the glance of each one who looks sees and knows that which he enjoys: so too, although the goods are many and diverse from which each one chooses that which he wishes and sets it up rightly and truly to be seen and known for his own enjoyment of the supreme good, nevertheless it can happen that the very light of wisdom in which these can be seen and known may be one and common to all wise men.

E. I grant that that can happen, nor is there anything to prevent that there be one wisdom common to all, even though there are many and diverse supreme goods; but I should want to know whether it is so. For if we concede that it can happen that that be so, we do not necessarily concede that it is so.

A. We know meanwhile that there is wisdom: but whether there is one wisdom common to all or whether each wise man has his own as he has his own soul or mind, that we do not yet know.

E. That is so.

CHAPTER X.

There is one light of wisdom common to all wise men.

28. *A.* Where, then do we see this which we know, whether it be the fact that wisdom is or that all men desire to be wise and happy? For I should by no means have doubted that you see it and that it is true. But do you see this truth as your own thought in such wise that if you do not communicate it to me, I ignore it utterly? Or do you understand it in such wise that this truth can be seen by me, even if it is not told to me by you?

E. Certainly in such wise that I do not doubt, it can be seen by you too, even though I were unwilling.

A. Consequently since we both see one truth with separate minds, is it not common to both of us?

E. Most clearly.

A. Again I believe that you do not deny that one must apply oneself diligently to wisdom and that you concede this is true.

E. I do not doubt that in the least.

A. Shall we, further, be able to deny that this truth is one and is common to be seen by all who know it, although each one contemplates it, not in my mind, nor in yours, nor in the mind of any one else; but in his own mind, since that which is contemplated is present in common to all who contemplate?

E. Not at all.

A. Again, will you not grant that this is very true and present in common to me as well as to you and to all who see it, that one must see justly, that the worse must be subordinated to the better, and that equals must be compared with equals, and that to each one must be rendered his due?

E. I agree.

A. Can you deny that any uncorrupted thing is better than a corrupted thing, an eternal thing than a temporal one, an inviolable than a violable.

E. Who can?

A. Can anyone therefore call this truth his own, since it is present immutably to be contemplated by all who are able to contemplate it?

E. No one would say that this truly is his own, since, as it is true, so it is one and common to all.

A. Again, who denies that the mind must be turned away from corruption and turned to incorruption, that is, not corruption but incorruption must be sought out? Or who, when he grants that truth is, does not under-

stand it also as immutable and does not see it to be
present in common to all minds able to contemplate it?

E. That is very true.

A. Then, will any one doubt that that life which is
not turned by adversities from a sure and honorable way
of thinking, is better than that which is broken and
upturned easily by temporal inconveniences?

E. Who would doubt that?

29. *A.* I shall ask no more questions of this sort now:
for it is enough that you see as I do and that you
concede that it is very certain that these, as it were,
rules and certain lights of virtue are true and immutable
and are present in common each or all to be contemplated by those who are able to conceive them, each by
his own reason and mind. But I ask, of course, whether
these seem to you to pertain to wisdom? For I believe
that he seems to you to be wise who has acquired wisdom.

E. Most certainly he does.

A. Well, would he who lives justly be able to live so,
if he did not see the inferior things he subordinates to
the preferable ones, and the equal things he joins to
each other and things due to each which he distributes?

E. He could not.

A. Will you deny then that he who sees these things,
sees wisely?

E. I do not deny it.

A. Then, does not he who lives prudently choose incorruption and does he not perceive that incorruption
is to be placed before corruption?

E. Clearly.

A. Therefore, when he chooses that to which he turns
his mind, which no one doubts should be chosen, could
it be denied that he chooses wisely?

E. I should certainly not deny it.

A. Therefore, when he turns his mind to that which he chooses wisely, he assuredly turns wisely.

E. That is certain.

A. And he who can not be thrust away by terrors and pains from that which he chose wisely and from that to which he turned himself wisely no doubt acts wisely.

E. Beyond any doubt.

A. It is very clear, then, that all these things which we called rules and lights of virtues, pertain to wisdom: seeing that the more any one uses them for the conduct of life and lives his life according to them, the more he lives and acts wisely; anything however which is done wisely can not rightly be said to be separated from wisdom.

E. That is absolutely so.

A. Just as, therefore, there are true and immutable rules of numbers, the reason and the truth of which you said are present immutably and in common to all who see them, so there are true and immutable rules of wisdom, which, you replied a moment ago when you were questioned concerning a few of them one by one, are true and manifest, and you concede that they are present in common to be contemplated by all who are able to consider them.

CHAPTER XI.

Wisdom and number are the same, or else exist one from the other or one in the other.

30. *E.* I can not doubt that. But I should want particularly to know whether these two, namely wisdom and number, are contained in some single genus, because you have pointed out that they have been joined together even in the holy Scriptures; or whether the one

exists dependent on the other or consists in the other,
as if number existed derived from wisdom or in wisdom.
For I should not dare to say that wisdom exists from
number or consists in number: in fact it strikes me
somehow, since I have known many arithmeticians or
numberers or whatever else they may be called, who
compute extremely well and admirably, but only very
few wise men or perhaps none, that wisdom is much
more venerable than number.

A. You say something at which I too always wonder.
For when I consider to myself the immutable truth of
numbers, and the lair, as it were, and innermost part
of it, or the sort of region, or whatever other word can
be found appropriate to name the manner, as it were, of
dwelling place and seat of numbers, I am removed far
from the body: and finding perhaps something which
I can think, but not finding anything which I can set
in words, I return as if wearied to these things of ours
that I may speak, and I talk of things which are located before the eyes, as they are wont to be talked of.
This occurs to me too when, so far as I am able, I
reflect very watchfully and very intently on wisdom.
And because of this I wonder a great deal, since these
two are in the most secret and the most certain truth:
and the testimony of the Scriptures is added too, in
which they are mentioned conjointly, as I have pointed
out; I wonder most of all as I have said, why number
is of trifling value to the multitude of men and wisdom
dear. But doubtless it is this, that wisdom and number
are a certain single and same thing; but yet, since it is
none the less said of wisdom in the divine Books *that it
reaches from end even to the end vigorously and it disposes all things agreeably,*[8] that power by which *it
reaches from end even to the end vigorously* is perchance

[8] *Book of Wisdom* 8:1.

called number: and surely that by which *it disposes all things agreeably,* is then properly called wisdom; since both are of one and the same wisdom.

31. But because he gave numbers to all things even the lowest and to those placed in the end of things (and indeed all bodies have their numbers even though they are most remote in things) yet he did not grant to bodies to be wise nor even to all souls, but only to rational souls, as if he placed in them a seat for himself from which he may dispose all these things, even the lowest, to which he gave numbers: so since we judge easily of bodies, as of things which are ordered beneath us, on which we distinguish numbers impressed beneath us; and because of that we hold them to be of lesser value. But when we began to turn about as if upwards, we found that numbers also transcend our minds, and that they remain immutable in truth itself. And because few can be wise, notwithstanding that it is granted even to the stupid to count, men admire wisdom and despise numbers. The learned, however, and the scholarly, the more remote they are from earthly blemish, the more they look upon both number and wisdom in truth itself and hold both dear: and in comparison with its truth, gold and silver and other things for which men fight, are not for them, but for them grow worthless.

32. Nor should you wonder that numbers have been so little valued by men and that wisdom is so dear, because men can more easily count than be wise, since you see that they hold gold more dear than the light of a lamp, and they would laugh to have gold compared with it. But a thing far inferior is honored more, because even a beggar kindles a lamp for himself, but

few have gold: although wisdom may be absent so that
in comparison with number it is found inferior, despite
that they are the same, still it seeks the eye by which
it can be seen. But just as, to express it thus, brightness and heat are perceived consubstantial in one fire,
nor can they be separated from each other, and yet
heat passes only to such things as are moved close,
whereas brightness is diffused also further and more
broadly: so too by the power of understanding which is
present in wisdom, things which are nearer, such as the
rational souls, grow warm; but those which are more
remote, such as bodies, do not attain to the heat of being
wise, but are steeped in the light of numbers: this perhaps is obscure to you. For no likeness of visible thing
can be fitted to an invisible thing in complete accord.
Consider only this, which is sufficient for the question
which we have taken up and which manifests itself even
to humbler minds, such as we are, that although it can
not be clear to us whether number is in wisdom or from
wisdom or whether wisdom itself is from number or in
number, or whether both can be shown to be the names
of one thing; this certainly is clear, that both are true
and immutably true.

CHAPTER XII.

*There is a single and immutable truth in all understand-
ings and it is superior to our mind.*

33. Wherefore you would certainly not deny that
there is an immutable truth, containing all these things
which are immutably true, which you can not say is
yours or mine or any one man's, but is present and
proffers itself in common to all who discern immutable
truths, as a secret and public light in wondrous ways:

but who would say that all that which is present in common to every one who reasons and understands, pertains properly to the nature of any of them? For you remember, I suppose, what was gone over a little while ago in relation to the senses of the body; namely that those things which we touch in common by the sense of the eyes or the ears, such as colors and sounds, which I and you see at the same time, or hear at the same time, do not pertain to the nature of our eyes or ears, but are common to us to be perceived. So too, therefore, you would never say that those things which I and you each with his own mind perceive in common, pertain to the nature of the mind of either one of us. For you can not say that what the eyes of two people see at the same time, is the eyes of this one or of the other one, but a third something to which the glance of both is turned.

E. That is very apparent and very true.

34. *A.* Do you think then that this truth of which we have been speaking for a long time now and in which, though it is single, we see so many things, do you think it is more excellent than our mind is, or equal to our mind, or else inferior? But if it were inferior we should judge, not according to it, but of it, just as we judge of bodies because they are lower, and we say commonly not only that they are so and not so, but that they ought to be so and not so: so too in regard to our minds, we know not only that the mind is so, but frequently too that it ought to be so. And we judge thus of bodies when we say, It is less white than it should have been, or less square, and many others similarly; moreover, we say of minds, It is less apt than it should be, or less smooth, or less vehement, according as the nature of our customs may have dis-

closed. And we judge these things according to those
interior rules of truth which we discern in common:
of them on the other hand no one in any manner judges.
For although one would say that eternal are greater
than temporal things, or that seven and three are ten,
no one says that they should have been thus, but knowing them only to be so, one does not correct as an
examiner but only rejoices as a discoverer. If, however, this truth of equals were in our minds, it too
would be mutable. For our minds sometimes see it
more, sometimes less, and by this they show themselves
to be mutable: whereas it, continuing in itself, neither
advances when it is seen by us more, nor grows less
when it is seen less, but whole and uncorrupted it rejoices those who are turned to the light and punishes
those who are turned away in blindness. Why is it
that we judge of our minds themselves according to it,
when we can in no way judge of it? For we say of
the mind, It understands less than it should, or it
understands as much as it should. The amount, however, that a mind ought to understand is according as
it has been able to be moved more near to, and to
inhere in, the immutable truth. Wherefore if the truth
is neither inferior nor equal, it remains that it be superior and more excellent.

CHAPTER XIII.

*Exhortation to embracing truth which alone makes men
happy.*

35. However, I had promised, if you remember, that
I should demonstrate to you that there is something
which is more sublime than our mind and reason. Behold it is truth itself: embrace it if you can, and enjoy

it, and delight in the Lord, and he will give you the desires of your heart.[9]   What more, indeed, do you seek than that you be happy?   And who is more happy than he who enjoys the unshaken and immutable and most excellent truth?   But do men cry forth that they are happy when they embrace the beautiful bodies, of wives or even of prostitutes, for which they have lusted with great desire: and do we doubt that we are happy in the embrace of truth?   Do men cry that they are happy when, their jaws arid with heat, they come upon an abundant and healthgiving fountain, or when, hungry, they find a meal or dinner splendidly furnished and plentiful: and will we deny that we are happy when we slacken our thirst and feed on truth?   We are used to hear voices of those crying out that they are happy if they lie down in roses or other flowers or even if they enjoy very sweet smelling unguents: what is more fragrant and what more pleasing than the inspiration of truth?   And do we hesitate to call ourselves happy when we are inspired by it?   Many make for themselves a happy life in the song of voices and of strings and of flutes, and when these are taken from them, they judge themselves miserable; but when they are present they are carried away with joy: and shall we seek some other happy life when, with no crashing, so to speak, of songs, a kind of eloquent silence of truth flows into our minds, and shall we not enjoy the happiness so certain and so present?   Men who are delighted in the light of gold and silver, in the lustre of gems and of other colors, or in the clearness and the joy of the very light which is proper to the eyes, whether in terrestrial fires or in stars or the moon or the sun, seem to themselves happy when they are not recalled from this pleasure by any vexation or by any need, and they

[9] *Psalms* 36 (or 37): 4.

wish to live always for these: and have we feared to place the happy life in the light of truth?

36. By all means, since the supreme good is known and secured in truth, and since that truth is wisdom, let us see the supreme good in truth, and let us secure and enjoy it. He is surely happy who enjoys the supreme good. For this truth reveals all goods which are true, which men of understanding, each according to his capacity, choose singly or together to enjoy. But just as they who choose in the light of the sun that which they look at willingly and are rejoiced by that sight; whereas if perchance there were any among them endowed with very vigorous and healthy and very strong eyes, they would look upon nothing more willingly than the sun itself, which likewise lights up other things by which weaker eyes are pleased: so the keen and vigorous perception of the mind when it has gazed with sure reason on many true and immutable things, directs itself to that truth itself by which all things are shown forth, and inhering in it, as it were, forgets other things, and at once in it enjoys them all. For whatsoever is pleasant in other truths, is pleasant assuredly in the truth itself.

37. This is our freedom when we are subjected to this truth: and it itself is our God, who frees us from death, that is, from the condition of sin. For Truth itself speaking as man with men, says to those who believe in him: *If you have abided by my word, then truly you are my disciples and you will know the truth and the truth will make you free.*[10] For the soul enjoys no thing with freedom except that which it enjoys with security.

[10] *John* 8: 31, 32.

Chapter XIV.

Truth is possessed with security.

But no one is secure in those goods which he can lose while he is unwilling. No one, however, loses truth and wisdom against his will: for no one can be separated from them in space, but what is called a separation from truth and wisdom is a perverse will, by which inferior things are chosen. No one, however, wants any thing when he does not want it. We have therefore what all may enjoy equally and in common: there are no straitnesses, there is no defect in it. All its lovers it receives with none in the least envious of it, and it is common to all and chaste to each. No one says to another: Go back that I too may come near; take away your hand that I too may embrace. All cling to it and all touch it. The food of it is destroyed in no part; you drink nothing of it which I can not. For you do not change anything from its common participation into your private property; but what you take from it remains whole for me. I do not wait that what it inspired you be returned from you, and that thus I may be inspired by it: for there is not anything of it which is ever made the property of one or of several persons, but it is all common at one time to all.

38. Therefore those things which we touch, or which we taste, or which we smell, are less like this truth, but those which we hear and see are more like it: because every word by whomsoever it is heard, is heard whole by all, and at the same time whole by each; and every species which is contiguous to the eyes, is seen at the same time as much by one as by another. But even

these are similar at a very long interval: for no voice sounds wholly at once, because it is stretched out and produced in time, and some of it sounds first, some later; and every visible species spreads out, as it were, through space and is not all everywhere. And certainly all of these are borne away while we are unwilling, and we are hindered by certain difficulties from enjoying them. For even if some one's sweet singing could be eternal, and even if those devoted to him should come earnestly to hear him, they would be crowded together, and they would fight for places according as their number was large that each might be nearer to him who sings, and they would try to remain shut within themselves, hearing nothing else, but they would be touched by all the fleeting voices. Moreover, if I should want to gaze upon this sun, and if I could do that persistently, it could disappear from me by setting, and it could be veiled over by a cloud, and I could lose the pleasure of seeing it by many other obstacles, although against my will. Finally, even if the sweetness, both of seeing light and of hearing a voice, were always there, what great thing would come to me, since it is common to me and to beasts? But that beauty of truth and wisdom, so long as there is a persevering will to enjoy it, does not shut off those who come in a crowded multitude of hearers, nor does it move along in time, nor does it migrate in space, nor is it interrupted by night, nor is it blocked off by shadows, nor does it fall under the senses of the body. Of all the world it is nearest to all those turned toward it who enjoy it, it is eternal to all; it is in no place, it is never away; it admonishes abroad, it teaches within; it changes all who see it to the better, it is changed by none to worse; no one judges of it, no one judges well without it. And it is thereby clear that truth is without doubt more excellent than our minds, which are each made wise by it alone; and of it you may not judge but by it you may judge of others.

Chapter XV.

That God is, is known certainly now from a complete explication of reason.

39. Moreover you had conceded that if I should show you that there is something above our minds, you would confess that it is God, provided there were nothing still loftier. I had said, acceding to this concession of yours, that it would be sufficient to demonstrate this. For if there is something still more excellent, that rather is God: if however there is nothing, then truth itself is God. Whether therefore that more excellent something is or is not, you nevertheless can not deny that God is: which was the question set to be discussed and treated by us. For if this affects you, that in the sacrosanct discipline of Christ we accept in faith the doctrine that God is the Father of Wisdom, remember that we also accept this in faith, that equal to the eternal Father is the Wisdom which is begotten of him. Whence nothing further need be inquired, but only held with unshaken faith. For God is, and he is truly and supremely. This we not only hold now undoubted in faith, as I believe, but we also touch it in a sure, although still very tenuous, form of knowledge; but it suffices for the question which we took up, that we are able to explain some aspects which pertain to the thing: unless you have something which you oppose to this.

E. On the contrary, I accept these things and I am overcome utterly by an incredible joy which I can not explain to you in words, and I cry out that they are most certain. I cry out, moreover, with an interior voice with which I wish to be heard by that very truth and to cling to it: because I concede it to be not only good but the supreme good and the maker of blessedness.

40. *A*. Rightly so, and I too rejoice greatly. But I ask you whether we are now wise and happy? or do we as yet only tend to that, that it may come to be in us?

E. I think we rather tend toward it.

A. Whence then do you understand the things which you cried out that you enjoyed as true and sure; and do you concede that this pertains to wisdom? Or is any fool able to know wisdom?

E. As long as he is a fool he can not.

A. Then you are already wise or else do not yet know wisdom.

E. I am not yet wise, but neither would I say that I am a fool in so far as I know wisdom; since these things which I know are certain and I can not deny that they pertain to wisdom.

A. Tell me, I ask, whether you will not grant that he who is not just is unjust; and he who is not prudent is imprudent; and he who is not temperate is intemperate or can anything be doubted in respect to these?

E. I grant that a man when he is not just is unjust; and I make the same reply too of the prudent and the temperate man.

A. Why then is he not a fool when he is not wise?

E. This too I grant that when any one is not wise he is a fool.

A. Well then which of these are you?

E. Whichever of them you may call me; I do not yet dare to call myself wise; and from the things which I have granted, I see that it follows that I should not hesitate to call myself a fool.

A. Then the fool knows wisdom. For he would not, as has already been said, be sure to wish to be wise, and he would not have to wish it if there did not cling to his mind a notion of wisdom, like the notion of those things, concerning which you replied when questioned one after the other, which pertain to wisdom itself, in the knowledge of which you were rejoiced.

E. It is as you say.

<h2 style="text-align:center">Chapter XVI.</h2>

Wisdom shows itself along the way to its earnest seekers, namely, in numbers impressed in each thing.

41. *A.* What else therefore do we do when we apply ourselves to be wise, except bring in a measure all our soul, with as much alacrity as we can, to that which we touch with the mind, and place it there and fasten it durably, that it may no longer enjoy things private to it which it has involved in passing things, but having removed all the conditions of times and places, it may apprehend what is always one and the same? For just as all the life of the body is the soul, so the happy life of the soul is God. While we do this, even to the time when we may complete it, we are on the way. And consider whether this, that it is granted to enjoy these true and certain goods, even though as yet they flash forth on this dark route, is what has been written of wisdom in respect to what it does to its lovers when they come to it and seek it; for it has been said, *It shows itself to them joyfully along the ways and runs forward to them with all foreknowledge.*[11] Whithersoever you turn it speaks to you by certain marks which it has impressed upon its works, and it recalls you when you

[11] *Book of Wisdom* 6:17.

fall down among exterior things to the very forms of
exterior things which are within: so that you may see
that whatever delighted you in the body and allured you
through the bodily senses, is numbered, and you may
inquire whence it is, and you may return within yourself and understand that you can not approve or dis-
approve of what you perceive by the senses of the
body unless you have in yourself certain laws of beauty,
to which you refer whatever you feel is beautiful without.

42. Look upon the sky and the earth and the sea and
whatsoever flashes in them or above them or crawls beneath them or flies or swims; they have forms, because
they have numbers: take that from them, they will be
nothing. Therefore, from what are they, except from
number: seeing that being pertains to them in so far
as they are numbered? And human artificers too have
numbers of all corporeal forms in art, to which they fit
their works, and they move their hands and instruments
in fashioning, until that which is formed outside is borne
back to that light of numbers which is within, and until
it can receive its consummation, so far as that is possible, and in order that by way of the interpreting sense
it may please that internal judge who gazes upon the
heavenly numbers. Ask in the next place, what moves
the arms of the artificer himself; it will be a number,
for they are moved likewise according to number. And
if you withdraw work from the hands, and the intention of fashioning from the soul, and if the motion of
the limbs be turned to delight, that will be called a
dance. Ask then, what it is that pleases in a dance;
number will answer you: Behold it is I. Now look
upon the beauty of the formed body; numbers are held
fast in place. Look upon the beauty of mobility in

the body; numbers are poured forth in time. Go into the art whence these proceed; seek in it time and space; it never will be; nowhere will it be; nevertheless number lives in it: nor is its region of spaces nor its age of days; and yet when they who wish to make themselves artists apply themselves to learning the art, they move their body through places and times, and even their mind through times: certainly with the passage of time they become more skilled. Transcend then the mind of the artist too that you may see the eternal number; then wisdom will flash forth to you from the very interior seat and from the secret place itself of truth; and if that should beat back your still too languid glance, turn the eye of your mind into that way, where wisdom showed itself joyfully. But remember that you have broken the vision which you may seek forth again when you are stronger and sounder.

43. Alas, those who abandon you as a leader and wander from your footsteps, who love, instead of you, your beckonings and forget what you beckon for, O wisdom, most sweet light of the cleansed mind! For you do not cease to give us the sign of what you are and how much you are; and your beckonings are all the embellishment of creatures. For the artist too in a measure beckons to the spectator of his work from the very beauty of the work, not to remain fixed there wholly, but to run over with his eyes the species of the fabricated body in such wise that he may return in love to him who fabricated it. They however are like men who love instead of you that which you make, who when they hear some eloquent wise man, listen too much to the sweetness of his voice and the structure of the well placed syllables, and lose the high importance of the

thoughts of which these words sound only the signs. Alas, those who turn themselves from your light, and cling in delight to the shadow of it! For, turning their backs, so to speak, to you, they are fastened firmly in carnal work as in their own shadows, and notwithstanding they still, even there, derive what delights them from the circumfulgence of your light. But when the shadow is loved, it makes the eye of the soul too languid and too weak to prefer your sight. Because of this, more and more is man darkened, while he pursues more willingly anything that more tolerably exempts the weak. Wherefore he begins to lack the power of seeing that which is supremely, and he begins to think evil whatever fails unforseen, or attracts him though unworthy, or tortures him when acquired, because such a thing deserves his aversion rightly, and anything that is just, could not be evil.

44. Therefore if you have looked upon anything mutable, you can not grasp it by the sense of the body or by the consideration of the mind, unless it is held firmly by some form of numbers, and if they are removed, it falls back again into nothing; do not doubt that there is some eternal and immutable form in order that these mutable things may not be cut short, but may be, as it were, carried with measured movements and with a separate variety of forms through certain turns of time; and this form is neither contained in and, as it were, diffused through space, nor strengthened and varied in times; by it all mutable things can be formed and fulfill their genus and perform their numbers of places and times.

CHAPTER XVII.

Every good and every perfection is from God.

45. For every mutable thing must also be susceptible of being formed or formable. Moreover, as we call that mutable which can be changed, so we should call that formable which can be formed. But no thing can form itself, because no thing can give itself that which it has not, and assuredly a thing is formed that it may have form. Wherefore if each thing has some form, there is no need that it receive that which it has; but if it does not have form, it can not receive from itself that which it does not have. Therefore no thing, as we have said, can form itself. But what more may we say of the mutability of body and mind? For enough has been said above. It so happens that body and mind are formed by a certain immutable and ever remaining form. To which form it has been said: *You will change them and they will be changed; but you yourself are the same and your years will not end.*[12] The prophetic speech used *years without end* for *eternity.* Of this form it has been said again that, persevering in itself, it renews all things.[13] Hence too it is understood that all things are governed by providence. For if all things which are, will be, provided no form has been taken away, then the immutable form itself, by which all mutable things subsist that they may be fulfilled and governed by the numbers of their forms, is their providence; for things would not be, if it were not. Therefore, whoever, inspecting and considering the whole creation, takes the way to wisdom, he sees wisdom reveal

---

[12] *Psalms* 101:27, 28 (or in some translations 102:26, 27).
[13] *Book of Wisdom* 7:27.

herself to him joyfully along the way and run to him
in all foreknowledge: and he burns the more readily
to go that way, as the way itself is beautiful because
of that which he is consumed to attain.

46. If, however, you should find some other class of
creatures beside that which is and does not live, and
that which is and lives but does not understand, and
that which is and lives and understands, then have the
courage to say that there is some good which is not
from God. These three, in fact, can be designated by
only two names, if they are called body and life, because both that which only lives and does not understand (such is the life of animals) and that which understands (such is the life of men) is very rightly called
life. However these two, namely, body and life, which
surely are classed as creatures (for the life of the
Creator himself is spoken of too, and that is the supreme life): these two creatures therefore, body and
life, since they are *formable,* as the above remarks have
pointed out, and since they would slip back into nothing
should they lose their form entirely, show sufficiently
that they subsist by that form which is always of this
sort. Wherefore no amount of good whatsoever, as great
or as small as you will, could be except from God.
For what can there be in creatures greater than intelligent life or what less than body? Howeversomuch
they are wanting and howeversomuch they incline not
to be, nevertheless something of form remains to them
that they may in some way be. Still whatever form
remains to any deficient thing is from that form which
knows no deficiency, and which does not permit the
motions of deficient or of successful things to go beyond
the laws of their numbers. Whatever therefore is en-

countered praiseworthy in the nature of things, whether it be judged worthy of slight or full praise, must be referred to the most excellent and ineffable praise of the Creator: unless you have something to oppose to this.. . .

ANICIUS MANLIUS TORQUATUS SEVERINUS BOETHIUS (480–525)

After centuries in which logical and metaphysical discussions were grounded on distinctions learned from Boethius, and after further centuries in which only his *Consolation of Philosophy* was remembered and his translations and commentaries were almost forgotten among better attested interpretations of the ancient philosophy, Boethius has come in recent times to suggest problems, rarely to philosophers, but more often to scholars. Whether he is to be classed as an original thinker or as an encyclopedic transmitter of the fragments of an ancient tradition: whether the Boethius of the theological treatises and the Boethius of the philosophic works are one person, are subjects for scholarly inquietude. Yet that such questions should have arisen, itself throws light on the nature of Boethius's contribution to philosophy. Historically, and not a little intellectually, he falls in the line of translators, commentators, and encyclopedists which runs through Chalcidius, Macrobius, Martianus Capella, Cassiodorus, Isidore of Seville, and the Venerable Bede. And for christianity, whether because he was a pagan (which is highly improbable), or because he held to a conviction that faith and reason are independent (which is to attribute to him an almost anachronistic sophistication), or because his pagan philosophy and his christian faith existed unmixed side by side in his thought, his exposition of the aristotelian logic prepared the development of an intellectualist tradition; at the other end of the tradition

65

the opportunity and need might arise to analyse and state faith radically distinct from knowledge; meanwhile reason and understanding could be discussed in logical, metaphysical, and psychological terms.

One important determinant of the career of Boethius was his knowledge of greek which by the sixth century had grown to be a comparatively rare accomplishment. It was his avowed intention to translate the whole of Aristotle and Plato, and comment on them, but how far he succeeded in his enterprise is matter for further controversy. That he completed the translation of the *Isagoge* of Porphyry, and of the *Categories,* and the *on Interpretation* of Aristotle is certain; his translations of the remaining books of the *Organon*—the *Prior* and *Posterior Analytics,* the *Topics* and the *Sophistical Refutations*—seem to have been lost and to have been rediscovered toward the end of the twelfth century, although Abailard knew only of his translations of the *Categories* and the *on Interpretation;* there are some doubtful indications that the *Metaphysics,* the *Physics,* and the *on the Soul* may have been known in a translation by Boethius at the beginning of the thirteenth century. The gap of the missing books of logic, however, was filled for the early middle ages by the commentaries and original works of Boethius: he left two commentaries on the *Isagoge,* one on the *Categories,* two on the *on Interpretation,* one each on the *Prior* and *Posterior Analytics,* and the *Topics* of Aristotle, the *Topics* of Cicero, the *Sophistical Refutations* of Aristotle, and original works on the categorical syllogism, the hypothetical syllogism, on division, definition, topical differences, as well as works on rhetoric, mathematics, and music. It was from Boethius, consequently, that the middle ages learned to discuss universals, the topics, and to form syllogisms according to the rules of Aristotle. On this slight basis and on its neoplatonism, the seven centuries which followed him were to build a philosophy characteristically western-european, without, to be sure, the richness and detail, but still with much the acumen of the philosophy rediscovered in the twelfth and thirteenth centuries from greek moral and metaphysical works in hebrew and arabic translations.

The selection which follows, the First Book of the second *Commentaries* on the *Isagoge,* illustrates the temper and interest, no less than the importance, of Boethius. The entire Book is commentary on not more than a page of text from Porphyry, and a good two-thirds of it is devoted to developing and enforcing in full detail a remark of his concerning the utility of the study of logic. The remaining part is devoted to a penetrating —and startlingly cautious—discussion of the problem of the universal. As in the case of the defense of logic, the discussion grows out of a remark by Porphyry—his refusal to discuss in an introductory work questions concerning the possible existence of genera and species outside our mind; concerning their nature, corporeal or incorporeal; and their relations to sensible objects. To answer such problems in any detail would be to develop an entire philosophy. Particularly, it would necessitate a choice between Plato and Aristotle as Boethius conceived and stated them. Boethius, none the less, with reservations and for reasons which he carefully states, undertakes the discussion of the basic notions of the problem. The later development of scholastic philosophy is based, significantly, upon these questions. It is needless of course to say, as has frequently been said, that Boethius introduced the question to the middle ages and set the twelfth century to discussing the universal: the problem is to be found in Augustine, and it would be difficult to proceed far in philosophy without encountering it.   Yet it is striking that most usually the discussion was introduced in twelfth century writings by a reference to Boethius and to his translation of the questions of Porphyry.

Besides his logical writings, Boethius is known as author of the *Consolation of Philosophy* and of several theological treatises.   From them no theory of knowledge emerges clearly, for the concern is not primarily there with knowing, although distinctions and differentiations relevant to it are frequent.   In conjunction with the logical treatises, indeed, their doctrines give a sense of eclecticism.   The *Consolation of Philosophy* is committed (by way of Proclus's commentary on the *Timaeus,* it has been suggested) to a platonic doctrine of ideas and of reminiscence: the soul is of divine origin and in constant communion with divine elements on which its knowledge depends; it is in need only of the quickening power of sense perception to arouse it to a knowledge of ideas at rest within it.   The developments of that notion bring echoes, one after the other, of pythagoreanism, neoplatonism, stoicism, and augustinism.   Yet, as if these came too near to a dereliction from aristotelian principles, Boethius expounds the Trinity, in the work which shows most clearly the augustinian influence, by applying the ten categories to the persons and their relations.   At the bottom of these diversified philosophic affiliations is the conviction, often explicit, that there was a single philosophy of the greeks, to be grasped best in the reconciliation of Plato and Aristotle.   That, however, was a lesson Boethius had learned from pagan roman philosophers; even before the coming of christianity a change in the attitude toward philosophy had instituted a metaphysical conservatism.   The distinctions by which the greeks thought to have divided themselves into opposed schools are needless subtleties when abstract thought is to be invoked (as it is in the very title of four works of Seneca and one work of Boethius) for refuge, or salvation, or relief, or consolation.

It was as a logician that the middle ages chiefly esteemed Boethius, sometimes to the extreme of preferring him to Aristotle—in translation. Although that preference yielded to others, at least Boethius was for centuries the principal source of aristotelianism in the west. This contribution alone must be estimated considerable, if one remember the despair of Cicero at the rendering of philosophy in the latin language; in the time of Boethius latin had already become a supple philosophic language, and for good or ill many of the terms of later philosophical discussions in it were originated by him.

ANICIUS MANLIUS TORQUATUS SEVERINUS BOETIIIUS

THE SECOND EDITION OF THE COMMENTARIES ON THE ISAGOGE OF PORPHYRY [1]

Book I.

1. This second task of exposition, which I have undertaken, will clarify the course of my translation, for I am afraid I have fallen victim in my translation to the fault of the faithful interpreter, in that I have rendered every word, expressed or implied, with a word. The reason for the present undertaking is that in these writings, in which knowledge of things is sought, there must be expressed, not a charm of translucent style, but the uncorrupted truth. It seems to me that I shall have accomplished a great deal to this end if books of philosophy should be composed in the latin language by painstaking and complete translation, until nothing more were missing from the literature of the greeks. And since the most excellent good of philosophy has been related with human souls, the exposition must begin with the powers of the human soul itself that it may proceed in some sequence and order. There is a triple power of the soul to be found in animated bodies. Of these, one power supports the life for the body, that it may arise by birth and subsist by nourishment; an-

[1] Anicii Manlii Severini Boethii, *In Isagogen Porphyrii Commenta*, in *Corpus Scriptorum Ecclesiasticorum Latinorum*, vol. 48, pp. 135-169, or in J. P. Migne, *Patrologia Latina*, vol. 64, col. 71-86.

other lends judgment to perception; the third is the foundation for the strength of the mind and for reason. Of these, it is the function of the first to be at hand for creating, nourishing, and sustaining bodies, but it will exercise no judgment of reason or of sense. This power is possessed by herbs and trees and anything that is fixed, rooted to the earth. But the second is composite and conjoined: taking over to itself the first and making it part of itself, it is further able to form a varied and multiform judgment of things. For every animal who has the power of sense, is also born, and nourished, and sustained. But the senses are different, and rise in number as far as five; consequently anything that is only nourished, does not also perceive, but anything that can perceive is proved also to have the first power of the soul subject to it, that is, the power to be born and nourished. Moreover, all beings that possess sense grasp not only the forms of things by which they are bombarded, when the sensible body is present, but also retain the images of the forms known by sense even when the sense is withdrawn and when the sensible objects are removed; and they build up memory; and each animal, as he is able to, preserves these images a longer or a shorter time. But they [that is, sensible beings] take on these confused and unevident imaginations, so that they can make nothing from the conjunction and composition of their imaginations. And for this reason they can remember, to be sure, but not all things equally, for when oblivion has come upon the memory they can not recollect or recall it. Moreover, there is no knowledge of the future by these imaginations. But the third power of the soul, which carries with it the prior powers of nourishing and of perceiving, and which uses them as slaves and servants, is constituted completely in reason, and it is occupied in the very firm conception of present things, or in the understanding of absent things, or in the investigation of unknown things. This power is present in the human genus alone, which not only receives sensations and perfect and unconfused imaginations, but also explains and confirms by the full act of understanding, what the imagination has supplied. Consequently, as has been said, those things which it comprehends subject to the senses do not alone suffice this divine nature for knowledge, but besides, it can put names conceived by the imagination on insensible and absent things, and it also opens to the imposition of words that which it comprehends by way of understanding. Moreover, it is proper to that nature to investigate unknown things by means of those known to it and to wish to know of each single thing, not only whether it is, but also what it is, and how it is, and even why it is. Only the nature of man, as has been said, has received this power of the threefold soul. The power of this soul does not lack the movements of intelligence, for it exercises the power of reason itself in the following four respects. It inquires of a thing *whether* it is, or if it has determined that it is, it has doubts concerning *what* it is. But if it has the knowledge of both of these by reason, it searches out *how* any particular thing is, and investigates the other changes of accidents in it; having learned these things, it also inquires and traces out by reason *why* it is thus.

2. Therefore, since the activity of the human soul is such that it is always occupied in the comprehension of present things, or in the understanding of absent things, or in the investigation and discovery of unknown things, there are two problems in which the power of the reasoning soul extends all its care: one, that it know the natures of things by a sure method of inquiry, and the

other, that that which moral gravity may later perform, may come to be known beforehand. In investigating these matters there must necessarily be many things which may lead the inquiring mind not a little from progress along the right road, as happened in many points to Epicurus, who thinks the world consists of atoms and who measures virtue by pleasure. It is clear, moreover, that this happened to him, and to others, because they thought, through inexperience in logical argument, that everything they comprehended in reasoning occurred also in things themselves. This surely is a great error; for in reasoning it is not as in numbers. For in numbers whatever has come out in computing the digits correctly, must without doubt also eventuate in the things themselves, so that if by calculation there should happen to be a hundred, there must also be a hundred things subject to that number. But this does not hold equally in argumentation; nor, in fact, is everything which the evolution of words may have discovered held fixed in nature too. Wherefore it was inevitable that they fall into error who, having cast aside the art of argument, made diligent search into the nature of things. For unless one have learned first the science that shows which reasoning holds to the true path of argument, and which holds to the path like to the truth, and unless one have learned to recognize what is trustworthy and what can be suspected, the uncorrupted truth of things can not be found by reasoning. Therefore, since the ancients often fell into a great many errors and brought together in argumentation many doctrines false and contrary to each other, and since it seemed impossible that this was done in order that, having come to contrary conclusions concerning the same thing, both conclusions which reasoning disagreeing with itself had formed should be true, and since it was ambiguous which line of thought should be believed, it seemed proper to consider the true and whole nature of argumentation itself first, and when that was known, what was discovered or what had been comprehended truly by argument could then be understood too. Hence started the knowledge of the logical discipline, which so contrives the modes of arguing and the ways of distinguishing reasonings themselves, that one can recognize what reasoning is now false, and now again true, what reasoning is always false, what never false. The power of this discipline, moreover, must be considered to be twofold, one in finding, the other in judging. This Cicero, too, expresses clearly in the book whose title is the *Topics,* saying:

> Although all reason suited to discourse has two parts, one of discovering, the other of judging, the prince of both, it seems to me, was Aristotle. The Stoics, however, exerted themselves in only one, for they pursued the ways of judging carefully in the science which they call dialectic, but they left aside the whole art of discovering, which is called topic, and which was more excellent in use and certainly prior in order of nature. But since there is the greatest utility in both and since we think to pursue both if there will be leisure, we shall begin from that which is first.

Since, therefore, the fruit of this consideration is so great, the whole attention of the mind must be given to this so very ingenious discipline, that we may be able, having been made steady in our first steps in the truth of arguing, to come easily to a sure comprehension of things themselves.

3. And since we have already stated what the beginning of the logical discipline is, the next question seems to follow: whether logic is absolutely a definite part of philosophy or, as others hold, an apparatus or instrument by which philosophy seizes on the knowledge and nature of things. I see that these opinions concerning this matter are diametrically opposed. For those who think the logical consideration a part of philosophy, use approximately the following arguments, saying, that philosophy doubtless has speculative and practical parts; the question concerning this third rational part is whether it is to be asserted to be a part; but it can not be doubted that it too is part of philosophy. For just as the investigation of philosophy alone is concerned with natural and other questions which are classed under the speculative part, and again as only philosophy deliberates concerning moral and other questions which fall under the practical part, so too only philosophy judges of this part of the inquiry, that is, concerning these questions which are subjects of logic. But if the speculative and practical are parts of philosophy because philosophy alone treats of them, then by the same reason logic will be part of philosophy, since this matter of arguing falls under philosophy alone. But then they say: since philosophy is concerned with these three, and since the subject matters distinguish the practical and speculative considerations, because the latter inquires concerning the nature of things, and the former concerning morals, there is no doubt that the logical discipline is distinct from the natural and the moral by the characteristic of its subject matter. For the consideration of logic is of propositions and syllogisms and other subjects of this sort, and neither that part of philosophy which speculates, not of discourse, but of things, nor the practical part which watches over morals, can take care

of that too. But if philosophy consists in these three, that is, speculative, practical, and rational, which are set off from each other by their separate and triple ends, since the speculative and the practical are said to be parts of philosophy, there is no doubt that the rational, too, may be demonstrated to be part of philosophy.

Those on the other hand who think it is not a part but an instrument of philosophy, urge approximately the following arguments. They say, there is no end of logic similar to the end of the speculative and practical parts. For each of these is turned to its proper end, the speculative to work out the knowledge of things, and the practical to perfect morals and institutions; nor is the one referred to the other. The end of logic, however, can not be absolute, but is drawn and bound up in a certain manner with the other two parts. For what is there in the logical discipline which should be desired for its own worth; or was not the practise of this art undertaken for the investigation of things? For to know how an argumentation is to be concluded, or what is true, and what similar to the true, tends obviously to this, that this science of reasons is referred either to a knowledge of things or to discovering those things which produce happiness, having led to the exercise of morality. And therefore since the end of the speculative and the end of the practical parts are their own and certain, whereas the end of logic is referred to the other two parts, it is clear that logic is not a part of philosophy but rather an instrument. There are, of course, many more arguments which may be stated on either part, of which it suffices that we have noted strictly these which have been stated.

We settle this controversy, however, with the following reasoning. We say that surely nothing prevents the same logic from serving at the same time the function of part and of instrument. For since it retains its own end, and this end is considered by philosophy only, it must be asserted to be a part of philosophy, but since that end of logic, which philosophy alone contemplates, promises its aid to the other parts of philosophy, we do not deny that it is the instrument of philosophy; but the end of logic is the discovery and judgment of reasons. Obviously it will not seem strange that the same thing should be called a part and a kind of instrument, if we turn our mind to the parts of the body, for something is done by them, so that we use them as a manner of instruments, and yet they hold the place of parts in the whole body. For the hand is for touching, the eyes for seeing, and the other parts of the body seem to have each a proper function. But still if the utility of the whole body be considered, these, which no one would deny are also parts, are judged to be certain instruments of the body. So too the logical discipline is a part of philosophy, since philosophy alone is mistress of it, but it is an instrument too because by it the sought-for truth of philosophy is investigated.

4. But since I have explained, so far as succinct brevity has permitted me, the beginning of logic and what logic itself should be, I must now say a little concerning this book which I have undertaken here to expound. For in the title Porphyry proposes that he write an introduction to the *Categories* of Aristotle. I shall explain briefly what the value of this introduction is, or for what it prepares the mind of the reader. For Aristotle composed the book which is entitled *On the Ten Categories* with this intention, that he might embrace with a small number of genera the infinite diversities (which

could not be encompassed in knowledge) of things, and
so, that which could not come under discipline because
of its number exceeding comprehension, might be made
subject to the mind and to knowledge, as has been said,
by the small number of the genera. Therefore, he considered that there are ten genera of all things, that is,
one substance and nine accidents, which are quality,
quantity, relation, place, time, action and passion, situa-
tion, condition; and since they were the supreme genera
and no other genus could be placed above them, all the
multitude of things must necessarily be found to be
species of these ten genera. These genera are divided
from each other by all differences, nor do they seem
to have anything common except only the name, since all
are predicated to be. Certainly substance is, quality is,
quantity is, and the verb *is* is predicated commonly of
all the others, but that is not their one common substance
or nature, but only their name. Consequently the ten
genera discovered by Aristotle are divided from each
other by all differences. But things which are disjoined by any differences must necessarily have some
peculiar property which maintains them in singular and
solitary form. A property, moreover, is not the same
as an accident. For accidents can appear or disappear, but properties are so implanted that apart from
the things of which they are properties they could not
be. Since these facts are so, and since Aristotle had
found ten genera of things, which the mind seized in
understanding or the disputant brought forth in speaking—for whatever we grasp by the understanding we
divulge to another by word—it came about that he was
led for the understanding of the ten categories to the
treatments of these five predicables, namely, genus,
species, difference, property, accident. Of *genus*, indeed, because we must first learn what genus is, to be

able to recognize that those ten which Aristotle placed before other things are genera; and the knowledge of *species* is extremely valuable for the ability to recognize what the species of any genus is. For if we understand what species is, we are not encumbered by error and thrown into confusion. It can often happen, in fact, that through ignorance of species we may place the species of quantity in relation, and classify the species of some first genus under some other genus, and in this way a promiscuous and indistinguishable confusion of things may be made. Lest this happen it should be known beforehand what the nature of species is. Not only is it important that the nature of species be known, that we may not interchange the species of prior genera with each other, but also that we may know how to choose in any single genus the species proximate to the genus, to the end that we may not say that animal is directly the species of substance instead of body, or man of body instead of animated body. Certainly the knowledge of *differences* holds an extremely important place in these things. For who of us would learn to distinguish quality at all from substance, or the other genera from each other, if we did not see their differences? But how can we distinguish their differences if we do not know what difference itself is? Nor is it only this error which the ignorance of difference spreads over us, but it also takes away all judgment of species. For differences inform all species, and if difference is not known, the species too can not be known. But how can it happen that we be able to recognize any difference at all if we absolutely do not know what the significance of that word is? Moreover, in the next instance, so great is the usefulness of *property* that Aristotle investigated carefully the properties of each of the categories. Who would understand what the properties are before he learns at all what a property is? Nor is this knowledge valuable only in those properties which are stated by single words, as risible of man, but also in those which are employed in the place of definition. For all properties include the subject thing in a certain term of description, which too I shall take up more suitably in its place. Who furthermore can doubt how much the knowledge of *accident* aids, when he sees in ten categories nine natures of accident? How shall we judge that they are accidents, if we absolutely do not know what accident is, since certainly the knowledge of neither differences nor property would be had if we do not hold the nature of accident by most solid consideration? For it could happen that through ignorance accident might be set in the place of difference or property; this, definitions show, is also extremely defective, for although definitions themselves are composed out of differences, and although they are made of any property, nevertheless they do not seem to admit accident.

Since therefore Aristotle brought together the genera of things, which contained under them species truly diverse, which species would never be diverse, if they were not separated by differences, and since he reduced all things to substance and accident, and accident to the other nine categories, and since he followed through for the most part the properties of some of the categories; he taught concerning these categories themselves, what genus was, what species, what difference, what that accident was, of which we have just had to speak, or what property, which he passed by as known. Lest therefore those who come to the *Categories* of Aristotle should be ignorant of what any one of these which have been mentioned above signifies, Porphyry wrote this book on the knowledge of these five predicables that having examined and having considered what each single one of these, which were set forth above, designated, the understanding might learn more easily the things which were set forth by Aristotle.

5. This is the intention of this book, which, Porphyry intimated (as has been said) in the very expression of the title, he had written as an introduction to the *Categories*. But although the intention of this book is turned to this one thing, nevertheless, the utility of it is not simple, but multiplex and extended very broadly. This, too, Porphyry notes in the beginning of this book, saying:

> Since it is necessary, Chrysaor, to know what genus is, and what difference is, and species, and property, and accident, as well for that doctrine of categories which is in Aristotle as for the imposition of definitions and in general for those things which are in division or demonstration, I shall try briefly, in this useful contemplation of such things, to approach as if in an introductory manner those things which have been said by the ancients, making a compendious rendering for you, abstaining from the more lofty questions, but interpreting in an ordinary manner the more simple.

The utility of this book is spread in a fourfold direction. For it is of great use to readers for that to which its intention is directed and also for other things; although these are beyond the intention, a utility no less because of that accrues to readers from them. For by means of this work one has ready knowledge of the categories, and one has the whole imposition of definitions, and the right understanding of divisions, and the most true conclusion of demonstrations. These things, the more difficult and arduous they are, the more they require in the reader a more perspicacious and diligent mind. It must be remarked, however, that this is true of all books. For, if it is known first what the intention is, the amount of utility which can arise thence is judged too; and although many other things besides, as it happens, may follow from a book of this sort, nevertheless, it seems to have that utility nearest, to which its intention is turned, as is shown by the very book which we have taken up. Since its intention is to prepare an easy understanding of the Categories, there is no doubt that this is shown to be its principal utility, although definition, division, and demonstration are no lesser associates, of which certain principles are here suggested to us. The whole meaning, indeed, is of this sort: *Since,* he says, *a knowledge of genus, species, difference, property, and accident is useful to the* Categories *of Aristotle and to its doctrine, and also to the imposition of definitions, to division and demonstration, I shall attempt briefly,* he says, *by making a compendious rendering of the things which have been said broadly and diffusely by the ancients, to lay open that which is the useful and richest knowledge of these things.* Nor, in fact, would it be compendious if the whole work were not bound together by brevity. And seeing that he was writing an introduction, *I shall avoid,* he says, *the more lofty questions willingly, but I shall interpret in an ordinary manner the more simple,* that is, I shall treat the obscurities of the more simple questions by holding to a kind of conjectural reasoning in them.

The whole sentiment of this introduction is such as to attract the mind of the beginner both by an extremely rich utility and by facility. But it seems proper to point out what else there is which the loftiness of the words conceals. The word *necessary* in the latin tongue, like ἀναγκαῖον in greek has several meanings.

For when Cicero says that some one is his relation [*necessarium*], and when we say that it is necessary [*necessarium*] that we go down to the forum, in which word a certain utility is signified, we speak according to different meanings. Still another meaning is the one in which we say that it is necessary that the sun be moved, that is, it is necessary [*necesse esse*]. That first meaning, however, must be passed over, for it is wholly unrelated to this necessary of which Porphyry speaks here. But the last two are of such sort that they seem to war with each other as to which will hold the signification in the place in which Porphyry says: *Since it is necessary, Chrysaor;* for, as has been said, the word *necessary* means both utility and necessity. They seem, moreover, both to fit in this place. For it is both useful in the highest degree for these things which were spoken of above, to investigate genus and species and the others; and the necessity is of the highest, since unless these things are known first, those for which they are prepared, can not be known. For neither can the categories be learned without a knowledge of genus and species, nor does definition ignore genus and difference, and it will appear how useful this treatise is in the others, when the investigation will turn to division and demonstration. But although these five which must be examined here must necessarily be known before those things for which they are prepared, nevertheless the word *necessary* is not used here by Porphyry in a meaning in which he would want necessity and not rather utility to be signified. For the statement itself and the context of words indicate this by the clearest reason to the understanding. Nor indeed does anyone use a reason that he may say that some necessity is referred to something else. For necessity is through itself, but utility is always referred to that for which it is useful,

as is the case here.   He says, in fact, *Since it is necessary, Chrysaor, for that doctrine of categories which is
in Aristotle.*   If, therefore, we understand this necessary
[*necessarium*] as useful, and if we change it to that very
word, saying: since it is useful, Chrysaor, to that doctrine of categories which is in Aristotle, to know what
genus is and the rest, the order of words will be correct;
but if we change it to *necessary* [*necesse*] and if we say:
since it is necessary, Chrysaor, for that doctrine of categories which is in Aristotle, to know what genus is and
the rest, the order of words does not accord with right
understanding.   Wherefore there is no need to delay
longer here.   For although it is of the highest necessity
that, if these things are ignored, one can not arrive at
those things for which this treatise is intended, still the
word necessary is used here not as of necessity, but
rather of utility.

6. Now, although the subject has been touched on
above, still we shall estimate briefly what profit the
knowledge of genus, species, difference, property, and
accident is to the categories.   For Aristotle stated in
the *Categories* ten genera of things which were predicated of all others that whatever could come to have
meaning, if it held full meaning, would be subjected to
each of those genera of which Aristotle treats in the
book which is entitled *On the Ten Categories.*   But for
it to be referred to something as to a genus, is as if
one were to place a species under a genus.   Certainly
this can in no way be done without knowledge of
species, nor assuredly can the species themselves be
understood in respect to what they are, or rather in
respect to the genus of which they are, unless their
differences are known.   But if the nature of differences
is unknown, what the differences of each single species

are, will be ignored completely. Therefore, it must be recognized that if Aristotle treats of genera in the *Categories,* the nature of genera must also be known; an understanding of species also accompanies the knowledge of this. But when this is known, what difference is can not be ignored, since there are many things in the same book which absolutely no understanding will open up unless the reader bring to it a very great learning of genus and species and difference, as when Aristotle himself says: *Things of diverse genera, and not of genera placed subalternately, are diverse as to species and are differences,* which can not be understood if these things are not known. But Aristotle also searches out in most diligent investigation the property of each one of the categories, so that when he says after many questionings, that the *property of substance is that remaining itself the same in number it is susceptible of contraries,* or again that *it is the property of quantity, that only in it may the equal and the unequal be spoken of,* and the *property of quality* similarly *that we state according to it that something is like or unlike something else,* and in the others in the same manner, as, what the property of the contrary is, what the property according to the relation of opposition is, what the properties of privation and condition, of affirmation and negation are. In these he treats, as if for those already learned and scientific, what the nature of property is; if any one should be ignorant of it, he would enter in vain into the questions which are taken up concerning these things. Moreover, it is already clear that accident occupies a very large part of the categories, since it is applied generally as the proper name to nine categories.

7. And it is clear from these considerations how great the utility of this book is in regard to the cate-

gories. What he says concerning the *imposition of definitions* can surely be understood easily, if first a division of the principles [*rationum*] of substance is made. One principle of substance is affirmed in description, and another in definition. But that principle which is in description, brings out a certain characteristic of the thing, the principle of whose substance it brings forth, and it not only informs that which it reveals with a characteristic, but it itself becomes the property which must also enter into definition; if any one wishes to state the principle of quantity, he may properly say: quantity is that according to which equals and unequals are spoken of. Just as, therefore, he placed the character of quantity in the principle of quantity and that whole principle is proper to quantity itself, so the description brings out the characteristic, and the description itself is made proper to it. On the other hand, the definition does not bring out properties, but is itself made proper. For the definition reveals substance, joins genus to differences, and, reducing to one species which it defines those things which are *per se* common and of many, it makes them equal. Consequently, the knowledge of property is useful to description, since only the characteristic is brought out in description, and it is itself made proper: so too in the case of definition, but for definition one needs the genus, which is affirmed first, and the species to which that genus is proper, and differences by which, when they have been joined to genus, the species is defined. But if these things shall seem to any one more precise than the manner of exposition demands, it is fitting that he know that, as was said in the first edition, we had set this present exposition aside in our judgment, that the first edition may suffice for the simple understanding of this book, but that this later edition may speak to the interior speculation

of those already almost established in knowledge and
not hanging upon every word about these things.

8. This book is surely so useful for the making of
division, that, apart from the knowledge of the things
which are investigated one after the other in this book,
partition would be made by chance rather than by reason. This however will be manifest if we divide division itself, that is, if we separate the name of division
into that which it signifies. For there is division of
genus into species, as when we say *of color some is*
white, some black, and some medium. Again there is
division whenever a word signifying many things is
examined, and whenever it is shown how many there
are which are signified by it, as if one were to say *the*
word dog signifies many things, this barking and four-
legged animal, and a celestial constellation, and a ma-
rine beast, which are all separated from each other by
definition. Moreover, a thing is said to be divided
whenever a whole is separated into its proper parts,
as when we say *house is part foundations, part walls,*
part roof. And we call this triple division *substantial*
partition. There is, however, another division which
is said to be *accidental.* This too is done in three ways:
when we divide accident into subjects, as when I
say *of goods there are some in mind and some in body;*
or again when we divide subject into accidents, as
of bodies there are some white, some black, and some of
medium color; or finally when we separate accident
into accidents, as when we say *of liquids some are white,*
some black, and some of medium color, or again *of white*
things some are hard, some liquid, and some soft. Since
therefore all division is either substantial or accidental,
and every partition is made in three ways, and since in
the above triple substantial partition one form of

division is to separate genus into species, this can in no manner be done without a knowledge of genera or without a knowledge of differences, which must be assumed in the division of species. It is manifest therefore how great the utility of this book is for this division which at first approach treats of genus and species and differences. Furthermore, the second substantial division into the meanings of a word, is not unconnected with the utility of this book. For in one way it will be possible to know whether a word whose division we wish to make, seems to be equivocal or a genus, and that is, if the things which it signifies are defined. And if the things which are under the common name are included by a definition, it is necessary that they be species and it be their common genus. But if those things which the stated word designates, can not be brought together in one definition, no one doubts that the word is equivocal or that it is not common to the things of which it is predicated as genus, inasmuch as those things which it signifies subordinate to it, can not be comprehended according to the common word by one definition. If therefore it is made manifest by definition, what is genus and what is equivocal word, and if definition runs through genera and differences, can any one doubt that the authority of this book is equally very valuable in this form of division? In the next place, how is that substantial division, which is into the parts of the whole, distinguished, and how will one avoid thinking it rather to be a division of genus into species, if genus, and species, and differences, and their meanings are not treated before the principle of the discipline? Why, in fact, should one not say that the foundations, walls, and roof are the species of house rather than the parts? But since it happens that the name of the genus can fit wholly in

every single species, whereas the name of the whole
can not accord with every one of its parts, it becomes
clear that the division of genus into species is one thing,
and the division of the whole into parts another. The
name of the genus, however, is shown to accord with
each one of the species by the fact that both man and
horse are individually called animals. But it is not
customary for the roof or the walls or the foundations
to be called singly by the name of house, but when
the parts have been joined, then they take on rightly
the name of the whole. In the next place, concerning
accidental division, no one is unaware that if accident
is unknown, and if the meaning of genus and of differences is unknown, it can easily happen that the accident
may be separated into subjects as genus is divided into
species, and finally ignorance will mix shamefully all
this order of division.

9. And since we have shown of what profit this book
is for division, we shall speak now of *demonstration,*
lest he who has toiled with watchful care and sagacious
labor in this so very great discipline, should be brought
to a standstill because of arduous and difficult obstacles.
For demonstration, that is, a sure inference of reason
concerning any thing inquired about, is made from
things known prior naturally, from agreements, from
first principles, from cause, from necessary things, from
things subsisting through themselves. But genera are
naturally prior to their proper species, for species flow
from genera. Moreover, it is clear that species are
prior naturally to the things subordinate to them,
whether the latter be species or individuals. But whatever things are prior, are known before and are known
better than those which follow naturally. In fact, a
thing is said to be first and to be known in two man-

ners, namely, with respect to us and with respect to nature. For those things are more known to us which are nearest to us, as individuals, next species, finally genera; but by nature, conversely, those things are more known which are least proximate to us. And therefore the more distantly genera are removed from us, the more lucid, and naturally known, they will be. Substantial differences, now, are those which we recognize to be present through themselves in the things which are being demonstrated. A knowledge of genera and differences, however, must come first, that in any particular discipline it may be known what are the appropriate principles of the thing which is demonstrated. That these necessary principles moreover are those which we call genera and differences, no one doubts who understands that without genus and difference species can not be. For genera and differences are the causes of species. Species are, in fact, for this reason, that their genera and differences are, which when placed in demonstrative syllogisms are the causes not only of the thing but also of the conclusion, which the last Resolutorii [2] will state more fully.

Since therefore it is extremely useful to determine all this by definition, and separate it by division, and prove it by demonstration, but since that can not be understood or done without a knowledge of those things which will be examined in this book, who will ever be able to doubt that this book is the greatest aid of all logic, without which the other aids which have great force in logic, can afford no approach to the doctrine?

10. But Porphyry remembered that he was writing an introduction, and he does not depart from the form

[2] i. e. *The Posterior Analytics.*

of treatment which is the manner of instruction. He says in fact that *he abstains from the knots of the more lofty questions, but resolves the simple ones with ordinary interpretation.* Moreover he sets down what the more lofty questions are which he promises to put aside, thus:

> At present, he says, I shall refuse to say concerning genera and species whether they subsist or whether they are placed in the naked understandings alone or whether subsisting they are corporeal or incorporeal, and whether they are separated from sensibles or placed in sensibles and in accord with them. Questions of this sort are most exalted business and require very great diligence of inquiry.

I pass over, he says, the more lofty questions, lest by pouring them intemperately into the mind of the reader I disturb his beginnings and first efforts. But lest he should make the reader wholly negligent, and lest the reader think that nothing more is hidden than what he had said, he adds the very thing whose question he promised he would put off pursuing, that he might spread no confusion before the reader by treating of these things obscurely and completely, and yet that the reader, strengthened by knowledge, might recognize what could be inquired into rightly. The questions, however, concerning which he promises to be silent are extremely useful and secret and have been tried by wise men but have not been solved by many. The first of them is of this sort. The mind, whatever it understands, either conceives by understanding and describes to itself by reason that which is established in the nature of things, or else depicts to itself in vacant imagination that which is not. It is inquired therefore of which sort the understanding of genus and of the rest is: whether we understand species and genera as we understand things which are and from which we derive a true understanding, or whether we deceive ourselves, since we form for ourselves, by the empty cogitation of the mind, things which are not. But even if it should be established that they are, and if we should say that the understanding of them is conceived from things which are, then another greater, and more difficult question would occasion doubt, since the most grave difficulty is revealed in distinguishing and understanding the nature of genus itself. For since it is necessary that everything which is, be either corporeal or incorporeal, genus and species will have to be in one of these. Of what sort then will that which is called genus be, corporeal or incorporeal? Nor in fact can attention be turned seriously to what it is, unless it is known in which of these classes it must be placed. But even when this question has been solved, all ambiguity will not be avoided. For there remains something which, should genus and species be called incorporeal, besets the understanding and detains it, demanding that it be resolved, to wit, whether they subsist in bodies themselves, or whether they seem to be incorporeal subsistences beyond bodies. Of course, there are two forms of the incorporeal, so that some things can be outside bodies and perdure in their incorporeality separated from bodies, as God, mind, soul; but others, although they are incorporeal, nevertheless can not be apart from bodies, as line, or surface, or number, or particular qualities, which, although we pronounce them to be incorporeal because they are not at all extended in three dimensions, nevertheless are in bodies in such fashion that they can not be torn from them or separated, or if they have been separated from bodies, they in no manner continue to be. These questions although they are difficult, to the point that even Porphyry for the time refused to solve them, I shall nevertheless take up, that I may neither leave the mind of the reader uneasy, nor myself consume time and energy in these things which are outside the sequence of the task I have undertaken. First of all I shall state a few things concerning the ambiguity of the question, and then I shall attempt to remove and untie that knot of doubt.

Genera and species either are and subsist or are formed by the understanding and thought alone. But genera and species can not be. This moreover is understood from the following considerations. For anything that is common at one time to many can not be one; indeed, that which is common is of many, particularly when one and the same thing is completely in many things at one time. Howsoever many species indeed there are, there is one genus in them all, not that the individual species share, as it were, some part of it, but each of them has at one time the whole genus. It follows from this that the whole genus, placed at one time in many individuals, can not be one; nor in fact can it happen that, since it is wholly in many at one time, it be one in number in itself. But if this is so, no genus can possibly be one, from which it follows that it is absolutely nothing; for everything which is, is because it is one. And the same thing may properly be said of species. Yet if there are genus and species, but they are multiplex and not one in number, there will be no last genus, but it will have some other genus superposed on it, which would include that multiplicity in the word of its single name. For as the genera of many animals are sought for the following reason, that they have something similar, yet are not the same, so too, since the genus, which is in many and is therefore multiplex, has the likeness of itself, which is the genus, but is not one, because it is in many, another genus of this genus must likewise be looked for, and when that has been found, for the reason which has been mentioned above, still a third genus is to be sought out. And so reason must proceed *in infinitum,* since no end of the process occurs. But if any genus is one in number, it can not possibly be common to many. For a single thing, if it is common, is common by parts, and then it is not common as a whole, but the parts of it are proper to individual things, or else it passes at different times into the use of those having it, so that it is common as a servant or a horse is; or else it is made common to all at one time, not however that it constitute the substance of those to which it is common, but like some theatre or spectacle, which is common to all who look on. But genus can be common to the species according to none of these modes; for it must be common in such fashion that it is in the individuals wholly and at one time, and that it is able to constitute and form the substance of those things to which it is common. For this reason, if it is neither one, because it is common, nor many, because still another genus must be sought for that multitude, it will be seen that genus absolutely is not, and the same conclusion must be applied to the others. But if genera and species and the others are grasped only by understandings, since every idea is made either from the subject thing as the thing is constituted itself or as the thing is not constituted—for an idea can not be made from no subject—if the idea of genus and species and the others comes from the subject thing as the thing itself is constituted which is understood, then they are not only placed in the understanding but are placed also in the truth of things. And again it must be sought out what their nature is which the previous question investigated. But if the idea of genus and the rest is taken from the thing not as the thing is constituted which is subject to the idea, the idea must necessarily be vain, which is taken from the thing but not as the thing is constituted; for that is false which is understood otherwise than the thing is. Thus, therefore, since genus and species neither are, nor, when they are understood, is the idea of them true, it is not uncertain that all this must be set forth relative to the care which is needed for investigating concerning the five predicables aforementioned, seeing that the inquiry is neither concerning the thing which is, nor concerning that of which something true can be understood or adduced.

11. This for the present is the question with regard to the aforementioned predicables, which we solve, in accord with Alexander, by the following reasoning. We say that it is not necessary that every idea which is formed from a subject but not as the subject itself is constituted, seem false and empty. For false opinion, but not understanding, is in only those ideas which are made by composition. For if any one composes and joins by the understanding that which nature does not suffer to be joined, no one is unaware that that is false, as would be the case should one join by the imagination horse and man and construct a centaur. But if it be done by division and by abstraction, the thing would not be constituted as the idea is, yet for all that, the idea is still not in the least false; for there are many things which have their being in others, from which either they can not at all be separated, or if they should be separated they subsist by no reason. And in order that this be shown to us in a well known

example, the line is something in a body, and it owes
to the body that which it is, namely, it retains its being
through body. Which is shown thus: if it should be
separated from body, it does not subsist; for who ever
perceived with any sense a line separated from body?
But when the mind receives from the senses things
confused and intermingled with each other, it distinguishes them by its own power and thought. For sense
transmits to us, besides bodies themselves, all incorporeal things of this sort which have their being in
bodies, but the mind which has the power to compound
that which is disjoined and to resolve that which is
composite, so distinguishes the things which are transmitted by the senses, confused with and joined to bodies,
that it may contemplate and see the incorporeal nature
in itself and without the bodies in which it is concrete.
For the characteristics of incorporeal things mixed with
bodies are diverse even when they are separated from
body. Genera therefore and species and the others are
found either in incorporeal things or in those which are
corporeal. And if the mind finds them in incorporeal
things, it has in that instance an incorporeal understanding of a genus, but if it has perceived the genera
and species of corporeal things, it bears off, as is its
wont, the nature of incorporeals from bodies, and be-
holds it alone and pure as the form itself is in itself.
So when the mind receives these incorporeals intermixed with bodies, separating them, it looks upon them
and contemplates them. No one, therefore, may say
that we think about the line falsely because we seize it
by the mind as if it were outside bodies, since it can
not be outside bodies. For not every idea which is
taken from subject things otherwise than the things are
themselves constituted, must be considered to be false,
but, as has been said above, that only is false which

does this by composition, as when one thinks, joining man and horse, that there is a centaur; but that which accomplishes it by divisions, and abstractions, and assumptions from the things in which they are, not only is not false, but it alone can discover that which is true with respect to the characteristic of the thing. Things of this sort therefore are in corporeal and sensible things, but they are understood without sensible things, in order that their nature can be perceived and their characteristic comprehended. Since genera and species are thought, therefore their likeness is gathered from the individuals in which they are, as the likeness of humanity is gathered from individual men unlike each other, which likeness conceived by the mind and perceived truly is made the species; again when the likeness of these diverse species is considered, which can not be except in the species themselves or in the individuals of the species, it forms the genus. Consequently, genera and species are in individuals, but they are thought universals; and species must be considered to be nothing other than the thought collected from the substantial likeness of individuals unlike in number, and genus the thought collected from the likeness of species. But this likeness when it is in individual things is made sensible, when it is in universals it is made intelligible; and in the same way when it is sensible, it remains in individuals, when it is understood, it is made universal. Therefore, they subsist in sensibles, but they are understood without bodies. For there is nothing to prevent two things which are in the same subject from being different in reason, like a concave and a convex line, which things, although they are defined by diverse definitions and although the understanding of them is diverse, are nevertheless always found in the same subject; for it is the same line which is convex and concave. So too for genera and species, that is, for singularity and universality, there is only one subject, but it is universal in one manner when it is thought, and singular in another when it is perceived in those things in which it has its being.

Once these distinctions are made, therefore, the whole question, I believe, is solved. For genera and species subsist in one manner, but are understood in another; and they are incorporeal, but they subsist in sensible things joined to sensible things. They are understood, to be sure, as subsisting through themselves and not as having their being in others. Plato, however, thinks that genera, and species, and the rest not only are understood as universals, but also are and subsist without bodies; whereas Aristotle thinks that they are understood as incorporeal and universal, but subsist in sensibles; we have not considered it proper to determine between their opinions, for that is of more lofty philosophy. But we have followed out the opinion of Aristotle very diligently for this reason, not in the least because we approved of it, but because this book has been written for the *Categories,* of which Aristotle is the author.

12. *This, however, I shall now try to show you, how the ancients treated probably of the categories and the predicables, and of the ancients most of all the peripatetics.*

Having passed by these questions which he said were too lofty, he seeks an ordinary treatment of this introductory work, but lest the very omission of these questions by him be adduced as a defect, he set down how each of the suggested subjects is to be treated, and he makes announcement beforehand of the authority of every one on whom he relied when he undertook the work. Since he promises a moderateness of treatment, having removed the difficulty of obscurity, he invites the mind of the reader; but that his mind may acquiesce and listen silently to what will be said, he establishes what is said on the authority of the peripatetics. And therefore he says he will treat *probably* of these, that is, of genera and species concerning which he had raised the questions above, and of the predicables, that is, of differences, properties, and accidents. *Probably,* however, means *similarly to the true,* which the Greeks call λογικῶς or ἐνδόξως. For we often find the word λογικῶς meaning *similarly to the true* and *probably* in Aristotle and in Boethus and Alexander. Porphyry too has used that word in many places in that meaning, which we have omitted in translation, because he says that λογικῶς is to be interpreted as if we were to say *rationally.* For the following meaning seemed by far better and more true: that he promised to speak probably, that is, not beyond the imagination of beginners and of readers, which is proper for an introduction. For since the secret of the more lofty doctrine would be remote from the minds of unlearned men, an introduction ought to be such that it is not beyond the imagination of beginners. And therefore we have interpreted it better, it seems to us, as *probably* than as *rationally.* He says, moreover, that the ancients had investigated concerning the same things, but that he followed most of all the treatment which the peripatetics under the leadership of Aristotle left, so that the whole investigation is in accordance with the *Categories.*

JOHN SCOTUS ERIUGENA (800/815–877?)

Following after a period of several centuries during which intellectual effort was devoted chiefly to the perpetuation, in encyclopedic compendia, of scraps of classical information and culture, the middle ages open abruptly with a complete philosophy. John Scotus Eriugena ranged through a diversity of matters with an ordering speculative curiosity and with a doctrinal knowledge which sets his work apart from the works of educational erudition of the eighth and ninth centuries. His translations from the pseudo-Dionysius the Areopagite and Maximus the Confessor permitted him an approach to latin neoplatonism by other questions than those made traditional by Augustine and permitted him also an altered emphasis on the questions Augustine had raised; his familiarity, on the other hand, with Boethius (of whom he wrote a life), Martanius Capella (on whose book he wrote a gloss) and with the fathers of the latin and greek church, particularly Augustine and Gregory of Nyssa, insured that his greek erudition be applied to the organization of materials indigenous to western speculation and civilization.

The *De divisione naturae* is a work of consistent and sustained metaphysical inquiry. Eriugena is concerned throughout its length only with the nature of things and thought; at each turn he pushes aside as irrelevant the accidents of origins and the histories of particular things or species of things, and he refuses, when it is question of what a thing is, to consider the qualities by which it manifests itself at some time or place. On this

100

score he criticizes even the definition of man as a rational animal. To know what a thing is one should examine no individual but the idea. Geometrical figures do not subsist naturally in themselves nor in individual triangles and circles, but in the notions of mathematics; the substantial definition of man is that he is an intellectual idea present in the mind of God. The idea and substance of man resides eternally in God; he is essentially the knowledge which God has of him. Ultimately the knowledge of all things which are, is that which they are; their *esse* is their *intelligi*.

That it is impossible to know or express the idea of man which is present in the mind of God is not the indication of a weakness or lapse in the theory. Rather in the face of that impossibility the theory is recognition and precise statement of the paradox of knowledge and therefore of things. For no man knows essence, nor can any one tell what *ousia* is. But man has an idea of himself, for like other things his essence is his knowledge: and, moreover, what he is, what he can do, and what he does are no different; the trinity of his essence, power, and operation is one. The idea man has of himself is not God's idea of him; but on the other hand they are not totally disparate—rather separate aspects than different things—and if the nature of knowledge is to be examined, the investigation must take the direction which proceeds from God's knowledge to the knowledge of any particular thing. There, in fact, lies the project of the division of nature, of *phusis:* an analysis of the essence, itself incomprehensible, which manifests itself throughout the created universe. The division of nature is first the discovery of a single principle revealed in excellent metaphysical analysis at the foundation of things, and then the passage from that one principle to the innumerable species. The rigor of the method is usually hidden from the modern reader by his familiarity with the more recent tendency to justify all speculation by experience: the explication of principles otherwise than by the elements which they may be supposed to generalize is sufficient to arouse suspicion, and if, instead of analyzing the temporal succession of experience, the inquiry begins with principles as anterior logically or anterior in being, the suspicion seems to be confirmed. For the inheritors of the empirical tradition, in which the intellectual and the dogmatic are confounded, that a work should begin with God is enough to date and to stigmatize it.

None the less, to introduce Eriugena's doctrine of man's knowledge, that is, of the third nature, without examining the two preceding natures is a questionable service and to be justified pedagogically rather than philosophically. Yet it may serve to illustrate how the investigation of thinking or of things must be carried to ideas and to God if the investigation has started elsewhere than with God. Man's knowledge is of three sorts, for the trinity is present in the spirit of man no less than in his being: they are sensation, reason, and intellect. In the operation of the exterior senses images arise in the sensitive organs from the action of exterior things; these external impressions are judged by the interior sense. But the senses know things in their multiplicity and individuality, as phantasies. The essences which are distinguished by the senses as different essences are one to reason. The images of perception are related to the ideas of reason, as the particular figures of geometry to the notions of geometry, or as the examples of a doctrine to the doctrine itself. But ideas are not built out of images; rather images are intelligible by ideas. Reason raises us to a contemplation of Ideas which subsist eternally in God and which are reached without the intermediary of sensible things. These Ideas are of course essences, and they escape us since no man knows the essence of things; but as sensible knowledge is by images, rational knowledge is by theophanies, that is, divine apparitions comprehensible to human intellects. Theophanies are knowledge of first causes by which men may apprehend, not their essence, but their existence and universality in action. It is by reason of them that first principles are discovered and considered. But as the materials of sensation require principles beyond sensation, so the principles of reason are not sufficiently grounded in themselves. That substance is may be known or may be inferred in a variety of ways; what it is can never be known. Reason works with the consequences and manifestations of that which it can not know, but which on the other hand it can not ignore in its contemplation. Ultimately reason, or *logos,* must be supplemented by the more elevated operation of understanding, or *nous.*

This is an insistence, to interpret further what has been said, that since knowledge and being are one, to know a thing perfectly is to be it. Man knows only himself, but knowing himself he knows the essence which manifests itself in different things. Since all things partake of that essence in varying degrees, he knows all existent things. His knowledge of them moreover is developed wholly from within, from the divine apparitions within the mind. Knowledge is essence, and the consideration of essence leads to God, but like essence, the first nature, God, can not be known—not however because of a limitation of knowledge or of finite minds, but because the basis of essence is not itself essence. God himself does not know himself in the sense of knowing what his essence is, because he is not essence. *Deus itaque nescit se, quid est, quia non est quid.* But since the essence of each thing is its knowledge, creation is precisely the manifestation in multitudinous form of the single superessential nature. God may be said even to create himself; by this is meant that he sets up natures; all existent things are founded on God's creation of himself, the manifestation of himself in something. Nothing therefore exists which is not in God, but all exist created at once, coeternal and coessential with him. When God sees the creation, it exists; and seeing only himself he sees all things. The knowledge of all is all, and it alone is all; God who knows all, knows nothing beyond himself. That he is by nature unknowable, signifies that whereas all human thought involves a contrary, God is beyond opposition; in him is a reconciliation of contraries. The principle of contradiction which is the basis of the processes of reason implicates an intellectual realm in which there is no contradiction; all definitions are statements of the effects of a nature which can not be defined. The act of the understanding, therefore, as opposed to the processes of reason, is a simple act, and does not lead to a proper knowledge of the object. The soul turns in understanding to the unknown nature which it recognizes at the center of all its thoughts and which is situated by its excellence above the soul.

In its main outlines this philosophy is in accord with the neoplatonism which the work of Augustine had made familiar in the west. The orientation of its analysis of knowledge is, like Augustine's, platonic: the mind is turned to a reality fundamental to all its activities, single and superessential in itself, diverse only in its manifestations. Even the art of dialectic is not a human device, but is to be found created in the nature of things. The human understanding is not the maker of the natural arts, but their discoverer, and that par-

ticular art which divides genera into species and resolves species into genera is not created by human
machinations, but is established in the nature of things
by the author of all the arts. Moreover this discovery
of the arts is not made outside the soul, but within
the soul itself. Knowledge is possible only because of
the notions of things present in the human mind. Those
notions are not derived from experience nor checked
by sensations because things exist more truly in the notions of man than they exist in themselves. For the
understanding of all things in God is the essence of
all things, and the difference between God's knowledge
and man's knowledge is that God's knowledge is causal,
whereas man's knowledge is as an effect. Therefore
man knows all things, knowing himself, and even material things are to be known only in their immaterial
origins in the primordial causes. The foundations of
certainty, of knowledge, and of philosophy are in the
mind's self-knowledge. But most insistently the first
nature, the nature which creates and is not created, is
present in the thought of man, for though that nature
can not be known it can not be avoided, and each
thought is token of its presence as surely as each
thought involves principles which must be grounded in
turn in something other than themselves or reason;
either they are ungrounded and the whole structure of
thought and the universe falls, or they are grounded
in, and necessarily illustrate, God.

JOHN SCOTUS ERIUGENA

ON THE DIVISION OF NATURE

Book IV, Chapters 7–9 [1]

7. *Disciple.* But still the question remains, why did
God create man, whom he wished to make in his image
and likeness, a creature in the genus of animals? Surely
it would seem more glorious for man, since he had been
elected to be partaker of the supernal sign beyond all
animals, and sharer with the celestial essences in which
no consubstantiality with terrestial animals is permitted, to be created free from all animality. For the
celestial essences are not loaded with terrestial bodies,
nor do they use corporeal senses for knowledge of sensible things. For they do not receive phantasies from
without, but know within themselves the reasons of the
things which they see. So too the soul does not see
outside itself what it perceives, but it sees within by
phantasies which angels do not undergo. Although
Plato defines angel as a rational and immortal animal,
we must not include in the sure speculations on natures
that which we can not prove by the authority of the
holy Scriptures and of the holy fathers, since such
inclusion is rash. On the other hand, the fact that
Saint Augustine does not deny, but asserts that the
highest angels have spiritual bodies in which they appear often, in no way compels us to believe that celestial

[1] JOANNIS SCOTI, *De Divisione Naturae, Liber Quartus,* ch.
7-9, in J. P. MIGNE, *Patrolgia Latina,* vol. 122, col. 762-781.

substances are animals, especially since a harmony and
an inseparable joining of celestial and incorruptible
bodies to angelic spirits does not make an animal, but
a connection of terrestial and corruptible bodies to souls,
rational or irrational, with sense mediating between
body and soul, does. For, if the exterior sense is present in angelic bodies and understandings, what prevents
us from saying, as it pleased Plato to say, that they
are animals composed of body and soul, with sense
mediating and understanding vivifying? And if that
is so, why are they not to be counted in the genus of
animals? But man, even if he had not sinned, would
be animal. Certainly it is not sin but nature which
made an animal of man. For no authority holds that
the transgressing angels are animals. This would follow definitely from such an argument. Yet the future
felicity which is promised to holy men is announced to
be no other than an equality with the angelic nature,
perfect and lacking in nothing. But what wise man
would believe sanely that the future transmutation of
man will be as if from an inferior animal to a superior
one, from a terrestrial animal to a celestial one, from
a temporal to an eternal, from a mortal to an immortal, from a miserable to a happy, rather than that all
the things which in this life are understood or perceived in holy men in common with other animals
are transferred by a certain ineffable mutation into that
essence celestial and incommunicable and lacking in
all animality, because that was to happen to man too
if he did not sin? Wherefore then was man created
in the genus of animals, which were produced of earth,
in which genus he will not remain always? For, when
this world of which man is an animal part shall have
perished, all that is animal in man will perish with it
and in it. For true reason does not permit that the

whole suffer destruction and yet parts of it be saved
from destruction. Besides, if all the world with all its
parts will be destroyed, I do not sufficiently see how
or where man, in so far as he is part of the world, will
remain after the world. And because of this I am in-
sistent in asking that you undo the knots of this question.

Master. You demand a very lofty physical theory
of human creation, and you compel us to draw out
our discussion to much greater length. It would suffice for me to answer you briefly when you ask why
God should have created man, whom he proposed to
make in his own image, in the genus of animals, that
he wished so to fashion him that there would be a certain animal in which he manifested his own express
image. But whoever asks why he wished that, asks the
causes of the divine will, to ask which is too presumptuous and arrogant. *For who hath known the sense of
the Lord?* [2] Yet, if I say this, you will perhaps be
silent ungratefully, and you will think that we can conclude nothing with respect to the pure and the perfect.
I shall not, therefore, say why he willed, because that
is beyond all understanding, but I shall say, as he himself has permitted, what he has willed to do. He has
made all creation, visible and invisible, in man since
the whole spread of created nature is understood to be
in him. For although it is still unknown how much
the first creation of man after the transgression is in
defect of the eternal light, nevertheless there is nothing naturally present in the celestial essences which
does not subsist essentially in man. For there is understanding and reason, and there is naturally implanted
the ground reason [*ratio*] of possessing a celestial and
angelic body, which after the resurrection will appear

[2] *Romans* 11:34.

more clearly than light both in the good and the evil. For it will be common to all human nature to rise again in eternal and incorruptible spiritual bodies. *It is sown, he* [3] *says, an animal body; it is raised a spiritual body.* All this sensible world is fashioned in man. There is no part of it to be found, whether corporeal or incorporeal, which does not subsist created in man, which does not perceive, which does not live, which is not incorporated in him. Do not think of the corporeal size in man; consider rather the natural power, especially since you see even in the human body the pupil of the eye, which subsists with the greatest power although it is the most minute in quantity of all the members. If, therefore, God did not create man in the genus of animals, or certainly, if he did not place the whole nature of all animals in man, how would all creation, visible and invisible, be comprehended in him? And we can therefore say rationally that God wished to place man in the genus of animals for this reason, that he wished to create every creature in him. But, if you ask me why he wished to create every creature in him, I answer that he wished to make him in his image and likness, so that, as the principal example surpasses all by the excellence of essence, so his image would excel all things of creation in dignity and grace. I confess however that I ignore completely why he wished to make man especially in his image before other creatures visible and invisible.

Disc. You have in my judgment answered the question why God wished to make man in the genus of animals sufficiently and reasonably. Nevertheless, I still ask this, how were all things created in man and how do they subsist in him—according to essence alone or according to accidents alone, or according to all things

[3] Paul, *I Corinthians* 15: 44.

that are considered in the whole creation, that is, according to essence, species, difference, and property, and all that is understood concerning them?

Mast. How I shall solve that question reasonably does not occur to me easily. For, if I say according to essence alone, you will reply rightly that then all things are only in so far as they subsist essentially, and the other things which are understood concerning essence or substance are not to be counted in the number of the whole of things, and they are not at all. And if that is so, you will ask me whence those things are, then, which are understood concerning the essence of things. If I answer that they have been made by God, you will say: why, then, are they not included in the whole of things which is made in man? If I say they were not made by God, you will reply that then they are not; for if they were, they would not be from any other cause than from the cause of all things which is God. And if I grant that those things which are understood concerning essences are not in the number of things because they are not from God, you will say forthwith: how, then, are they understood? For everything which is not from God can in no manner be understood because it is not in any manner. If I say that not only the essences but also all things which are understood naturally concerning them are from God and are to be numbered in the parts of the whole, there is no doubt but that I shall be compelled to choose one of the following two alternatives—either that the entire whole of things has not been fashioned in man, if only the essences have been made in him; or the entire whole of things, that is, the essences and whatsoever is perceived about them and in them, has been fashioned in man. And if I say that not a part of the whole, that is, substances, but the complete whole has been set up in man, you will follow after with a most weighty question, saying that then irrationality has been made in him, and bestiality, quadrupedality, volatility, and all the differences of diverse animals and of other things, and the species too, and the properties, and the accidents, and innumerable other things which seem to be far removed from human nature, to such an extent that if it were certain that they are present in man, he would rightly be judged not to be man but a very disgraceful monster.

Disc. You have heaped up the difficulty of the question, and you have with a kind of deliberation opposed to yourself whatever would be opposed by another; and by this means you will either clear up the question or you will pass it by as abstruse and go on to another, which will seem very incongruous indeed.

Mast. Let us try then to examine it in some way, lest it be wholly intact for the time.

Disc. You will not be able to satisfy me otherwise.

Mast. Do you think that everything which is known by the understanding and reason or which is imagined by the bodily sense, can in a certain manner be created and produced in him who understands and perceives?

Disc. It seems to me that it can. Indeed I think that the species of sensible things and the quantities and qualities which I attain by corporeal sense are in a certain way created in me; for, when I imprint the phantasies of them in memory, and when I treat of them within myself, divide, compare, and, as it were, collect them into a kind of unity, I perceive a certain knowledge of things which are outside me being produced in me. In the same way I understand that there arise and are made in me, when I seek them out earnestly, certain ideas like intelligible species, of the intelligibles within, which I contemplate with the mind alone, as, for example, the ideas of the liberal disciplines. But what there is between the knowledge and the things themselves, of which the knowledge is, I do not see clearly.

Mast. What does it seem to you? Are things and the ideas of things, which are made in the soul, of the same nature or different?

Disc. Of different natures. For how can the corporeal species, of, for example, a certain animal, or herb, or tree, and the idea of it which is produced in an incorporeal nature be of one single nature? For the same reason how can the intelligible species of any discipline and the idea of it be made of one single nature?

Mast. If, then, they are of different genera or natures, and not of the same, tell me, I ask, which of them do you judge must be set down as the more excellent of them; are things of a more exalted nature than their own ideas; or are ideas themselves more exalted than things?

Disc. I should have said that visible species are of a better nature than their ideas, if Saint Augustine did not state the following opinion in the ninth book *on the Trinity* in the eleventh chapter:

> Since, he says, we learn bodies through the sense of the body, some likeness of bodies is made in our mind; this is phantasy in memory. For bodies themselves are not at all in the mind when we reflect on them, but only their likenesses. Nevertheless the imagination of the body in the mind is better than the species of the body, inasmuch as it is in a better nature, that is, in vital substance, such as the mind. However I do not dare to say that intel-

ligible things are better than their idea which
is in the soul.

Reason teaches, to be sure, that that which understands
is better than that which is understood. For, if the
knowledge of all things subsists in the divine wisdom,
I should pronounce this knowledge of all things, not
rashly, to be incomparably better than all things of
which it is the knowledge. And if that is so, such an
order, I believe, proceeds from the divine providence
through all creation, that not only every nature which
comprehends the idea of the thing following it, is better and superior, but also, because of the dignity of the
nature in which it is, the idea itself excels greatly that
of which it is the idea. And by this fact I should
say more easily that the idea of intelligible things is
more ancient than the intelligible things themselves.

Mast. You would perhaps be right in saying that if
what is formed is more excellent than what forms.

Disc. Why do you oppose that?

Mast. Because the idea of the arts which is in the
soul seems to be formed from the arts themselves. But
if you established by very sure reason that the idea
was not formed from the arts, but the arts from the
idea, your reasoning would perhaps start out rightly.

Disc. Did we not prove a moment ago that everything which understands is more excellent than that
which is understood?

Mast. That was proved.

Disc. Tell me then, whether the expertness of the
mind understands the discipline or the discipline understands the expertness.

Mast. I do not doubt that the discipline is understood
by the mind. But if I say that the same discipline is
learned by the expertness itself in the same way as it

is learned by the mind of which it is the expertness,
I fear lest I seem to assert that the mind and its expertness are two different outgrowths in ideas of the
discipline, and not one and the same essence in which
the knowledge of the discipline is present naturally.
If, however, the mind and its expertness are not two
different things but one and the same, true reason
teaches (I am forced to admit) that everything which is
understood by the mind is understood too by its expertness, and it follows necessarily that mind and expertness, or certainly the expert mind, is of a more excellent nature than that discipline which it understands,
if understandings are more ancient than things understood. If, on the other hand, I say that the discipline
itself is the expertness of the expert mind, the consequence will be either that the expert mind and the
expert discipline are two particular understandings,
one of the other, and understood one by the other,
and by this attaining to an equal dignity of nature, or
else the mind and its expertness and the discipline,
which it understands and by which it is understood, must
be granted to be of one and the same essence. But
which of these must be held does not yet appear clearly.

Disc. Perhaps it will appear when we enter upon the
right way of reasoning, God leading.

Mast. Let us seek therefore the more carefully; and
first tell me, I pray, whether the nature of the mind
in which there is the expertness of the discipline, is
simple or not.

Disc. I think that it is simple. For it is incorporeal,
intellectual, and for that reason it necessarily lacks all
composition.

Mast. You think rightly. Do you think then that
something is accidental to it which is not naturally
present in its essence?

Disc. I think so. For I see many things are accidental to it. For example, it is moved temporally, although it is not itself time. Expertness of disciplines is accidental to it: for it is now recognized as expert, now as inexpert, now disciplined, now undisciplined, now wise, now foolish, now erring when it considers irrationally, now entering upon the way of reason rightly, and many things of this sort.

Mast. Therefore the expertness of a discipline or the discipline itself is not present in it naturally, but they appear in it extrinsically by accidents.

Disc. I should not dare to say that. For it is not likely that God should have created in his own image and likeness a mind in which there were not implanted naturally expertness and discipline; otherwise it would not be a mind but a kind of brute and irrational life. For, I think, one would not say rightly that man was made in the image of God according to accident and not according to substance, especially since we see that understanding and reason are present in the mind substantially.

Mast. Therefore they are not accidental to it, but are present naturally.

Disc. I should not say that inconsiderately, I believe. For although the mind seems to be born inexpert and unwise, which occurs through the transgression of the divine command, in which it was forgetful both of itself and of its Creator, nevertheless, it is able, when it has been reformed by the rules of doctrine, to find in itself its God and itself and its expertness and discipline and all things which subsist naturally in it, illuminated by the grace of its Redeemer.

Mast. It remains, therefore, to consider in what manner expertness and the discipline are present in the mind: whether as natural qualities, which are called

powers, like species of wisdom and science which it perceives in the repercussion of the divine ray; or whether
as the substantial parts of which the mind consists, so
that it is a kind of trinity of one essence: mind, learning, art.

Disc. I should believe it was what you stated last;
for it seems to me a kind of substantial and connatural
trinity.

Mast. Accordingly the mind understands both its expertness and its discipline, and it is understood by its
expertness and its discipline, not with respect to what
it is, but that it is; for otherwise it will not be a coessential and coequal trinity.

Disc. I would not deny that, since reason compels me
to grant that it is so.

Mast. Consider then whether they are formed by
each other or by some other nature superior to them.

Disc. If the catholic faith did not teach and if truth
did not assent that this trinity is set up and formed
and understood by a superior nature, I should not inconsiderately reply that they are perhaps formed by
themselves or that surely they are their own principal
form; as it is, of course, I do not doubt, since the
superior is itself that from which all things are formed,
by which they begin to be formed, and turned toward
which the things which are or can be turned to it are
formed, that the trinity too of the mind is formed by
the same nature.

Mast. To hesitate about that would be extremely
stupid. Consequently only the divine mind possesses in
itself, formed by itself and to itself, the true idea of
the human mind, of expertness and of discipline.

Disc. Nothing could be considered more true.

Mast. Do you think the human mind is one thing and

the idea of it in the mind of the one forming it and knowing it another?

Disc. That can not be. For I understand the substance of the entire man to be no other than his idea in the mind of the artificer who knew all things in himself before they were made; and that very knowledge is the true and only substance of those things which are known, since they subsist formed most perfectly in it eternally and immutably.

Mast. We can then define man thus: Man is a certain intellectual idea formed eternally in the divine mind.

Disc. That is an extremely true and a very well tested definition of man; and not only of man but also of all things which are formed in the divine wisdom. Nor do I fear them who define man, not as he is understood to be, but by those things which are understood about him, saying that man is a rational mortal animal capable of sense and discipline; and what is more wonderful, they call this definition substantial [*usiadis*], whilst it is not substantial but taken extrinsically about substance from those things which are accidental to substance through generation. But the idea of man in the divine mind is nothing of these. There indeed it is simple, nor can it be called this or that, standing above all definition and collection of parts, for only that it is is predicated of it, but not what it is. For that alone is indeed a true substantial [*usiadis*] definition, which affirms only that it is but negates that it is anything in particular [*quid esse*].

Mast. Does it seem to you that there is a kind of notion in man of all the sensible and intelligible things which the human mind can understand?

Disc. That seems clearly the case; and indeed man is understood to be most of all through the circumstance

that it has been given to him to have an idea of all
things which were either created equally with him or
which he was instructed to govern. For how should the
mastery be given to man of things of which he had no
idea? Indeed his mastery would go astray if he were
ignorant of that which he ruled. The holy Scripture
indicates that to us most clearly, saying: *Therefore having formed out of the ground every beast of the field
and every bird of the heavens, the Lord God brought
them unto Adam to see what he would call them: and
whatsoever Adam called every living soul, that was the
name of it.*[4] It says *to see,* that is to understand what
he would call them. For, if he did not understand, how
would he be able to call them rightly? Whereas each
that he called, is its very name [*nomen*], that is, it is
the idea itself [*notio*] of the living soul.

Mast. What is there astonishing then, if the idea of
things which the human mind possesses because the idea
was created in it, be understood as the substance of
the very things of which it is the idea, that is, in the
likeness of the divine mind in which the idea of the
whole created universe is the incommunicable substance
of that whole? Just as we call the idea of all things
which are understood and are perceived by the corporeal
sense in the whole of things, the substance of the
things which fall under the understanding or the sense,
so shall we also say that the idea of the differences and
properties and natural accidents are the differences
themselves and the properties and the accidents?

Disc. Undoubtedly.

Mast. Irrationality therefore was created in the mind,
and every species, and every difference, and the property of irrationality itself, and all things which are
learned naturally concerning it, since there is an idea

[4] *Genesis* 2: 19.

formed in it of all these and of things similar. I have spoken of things *similar* because of the things which the nature of things contains in addition to animals, such as the elements of the world, the genera and species of grasses too and of woods, the quantities, and qualities, and still others multiplied through innumerable differences. True knowledge of all of these is implanted in human nature, although its presence is as yet concealed from the soul itself until it is restored to its pristine integrity, in which it will understand very purely the magnitude and beauty of the image fashioned in it, and nothing will shut it off from the things which are fashioned in it, encompassed as it will be by divine light and turned to God, in whom it will contemplate all things perspicuously. Or did the magnificent Boethius mean something else to be understood when he says?

> Wisdom is the comprehension of the truth of things which are and which draw as by lot their immutable substance. But we say that those things are which do not grow by any increase, and are not diminished by any withdrawing, nor changed by any variations, but with the endeavor and resources of their own nature preserve themselves always in their own power. These are qualities, quantities, forms, magnitudes, smallnesses, equalities, conditions, acts, dispositions, places, times, and whatever is in any way found joined to bodies: they are themselves incorporeal in nature and thrive by reason of the immutable substance, but they are changed through participation of the body and pass into changeable inconstancy through contact with the variable thing.

And where do you understand these things to subsist except in their ideas in the mind of the wise man? For where they are understood, there they are, and as a matter of fact they are nothing more than their being understood [*imo vero intellectus sui sunt*].

Disc. The solution of the present questions requires a multiple exposition, and an innumerable crowd of different questions do not cease to flow forth on all sides, while it is being resolved, as from a kind of infinite fountain; consequently the figure of herculean hydra may ·with perfect justice be applied to it, of which as many heads grow again as are cut off, so that a hundred bubble forth for one cut off, symbolizing human nature, which is a hydra, that is, a kind of multiplex fountain of infinite profundity, into which who besides Hercules, that is, virtue, is able to look? *For no one knoweth what things are in man, save the spirit of the man which is in him.*[5] Accordingly, if that interior idea which is in the human mind constitutes the substance of the things of which it is the idea, it follows that the very idea by which man knows himself may be considered his substance.

Mast. That follows by all means. For we said that the human mind, its idea by which it knows itself, and the discipline by which it learns itself that it may know itself, subsist as one and the same essence.

Disc. Then what shall we say? Do you remember a little while ago we deduced the pure definition of man, saying, man is a certain intellectual idea formed eternally in the divine mind? And, if that is so, how may that idea by which man knows himself be his substance, if the aforesaid definition has not been made improperly?

Mast. Surely not improperly, for the definition which

[5] *I Corinthians* 2:11.

says that a certain idea eternally made in the divine
mind is the substance of man, is true. And what we
say now, namely, that the knowledge by which the human mind knows itself is substantially in man, is not
stated irrationally. For each creature is considered in
one fashion in the Word of God, in which all things
have been made, and in another fashion in himself.
Therefore Saint Augustine in his *in Hexæmeron* says:

> In one fashion, the things which are made by
> it are under it, in another fashion the things
> which it is are in it. Since the understanding
> of all things in the divine mind is the sub-
> stance of all things, it is, in fact, all things.
> For the knowledge by which an intellectual
> and rational creature understands himself in
> himself is, as it were, a kind of second sub-
> stance of him, by which he knows only that he
> knows, and is, and wills, but not what he is.
> And the former substance, constituted in the
> wisdom of God, is eternal and immutable, but
> the latter is temporal and mutable; the former
> precedes, the latter follows; the former is pri-
> mordial and causal, the latter resulting and
> causative; the former contains all things uni-
> versally, the latter, so far as is allotted by
> the superior, comprehends particularly the
> things subject to it by knowledge; the latter
> was produced from the former and it will re-
> turn again into it.

And I do not speak now of that superessential substance which through itself is God and the unique
cause of all things, but of that substance which in the
beginning was made causally in the wisdom of God,
the effect of which is this substance which we de-

termined, or rather which the natural order of things established, in the second place.

Disc. We must, therefore, comprehend two substances of man, one general in the primordial causes, the other special in the effects of those causes.

Mast. I should not have said two but one understood doubly. For in one fashion, the human substance is perceived through its creation in intellectual causes, in the other by its generation in effects. In the former free from all mutability, in the latter liable to mutability; in the former, simple and absolved from all accidents, it escapes all consideration and understanding, in the latter it puts on a kind of composition of quantities and qualities and other things which are understood of it, and by that composition it has the consideration of the mind. Accordingly one and the same thing is spoken of as double because of the double observation of it, but it still preserves its incomprehensibility on all sides, in causes, I say, and in effects, that is, whether naked in its simplicity or endowed with accidents. For in all these, it comes under no created understanding or any sense, nor with respect to what it is, is it understood by itself.

Disc. Why is it, then, since you have spoken of it for a long time now, that the human mind has the idea by which it knows itself, and the discipline by which it learns itself, and now you assert on the other hand that it can be known neither by itself nor by any other creature?

Mast. Reason teaches that both are true: that the human mind assuredly knows itself and does not know itself. For it knows that it is, but it does not know what it is. And through this circumstance, as we have taught in the previous books, the image of God is shown most of all to be in man. For as God is comprehen-

sible in that one deduces from creation that he is, and
is incomprehensible because what he is can be comprehended by no understanding, human or angelic,
nor even by himself because he is not a *what*, but is
superessential: so it is given to the human mind to
know only this, that it is, but it is in no way granted
to it to know what it is; and, what is even more to be
wondered at and more beautiful to those who contemplate themselves and their God, the human mind is
more to be praised in its ignorance than in its knowledge.   For it is more praiseworthy for it not to know
what it is than for it to know that it is, just as the
negation of the divine nature pertains better and with
greater fitness to the praise of the divine nature than
the affirmation of it: and it is wiser not to know than
to know that, the ignorance of which is true wisdom,
and which is known better by not knowing.   The divine
likeness in the human mind, therefore, is recognized
most clearly in that it is known only to be; but what
it is is not known; and, to put it thus, in it we deny
that it is anything and affirm only that it is.   Nor is
this void of reason.   For if it were known to be some
certain thing, it would be circumscribed certainly in
something and, by that fact, it would not express in itself wholly the image of its Creator who is entirely
uncircumscribed and is understood in nothing because
he is infinite, above all that is said and understood,
superessential.

Disc. How then has every creature been made in the
idea of man, which idea does not know itself with
respect to what it is, and how is this taken for great
praise of it, and as its mark of superiority in that it
is confined by no finite substance?

Mast. On the contrary, that every creature has been
created substantially in man may be deduced likewise

by very cogent argument. For of all things that are, substance can in no way be defined with respect to what it is, according to Gregory, the theologian, who investigates concerning such things, taking issue with those who deny that the Word of God is superessential, and who contend that it is comprised in some substance and therefore is not above all things but is contained within the number of all, and who insist that the substance of the Son be separated from the substance of the Father. Accordingly, just as the divine essence in whose image it was made is infinite, so too that human determination is limited by no certain end. But, from the things which are understood concerning it, that is, from times, places, differences, properties, quantities, qualities, relations, conditions, positions, actions, passions, it is understood only to be, but what it is is never understood. And thence may be understood that there is no other subsistence of any creature than that reason according to which it has been set in the primordial causes in the Word of God, and therefore what it is can not be defined, because it exceeds all substantial definition. It is defined, however, by its circumstances, which occur to it, as it proceeds into its appropriate species by generation, whether intelligible or sensible.

8. *Disc.* The holy Scripture and reason itself both assert that human and angelic nature are either the same or very similar. For both man and angel are called, and are, intellectual and rational creatures. And, if they agree so between them, it must be inquired, not improperly, why every creature is seen created in man but not in the angel.

Mast. Not without cause I believe. For, we see not a few things in man which authority does not teach nor reason understand to subsist in the angel, as this ani-

mal body, which the holy Scripture testifies was joined
to the human soul even before sin, and also the corporeal fivefold exterior sense and the phantasies of
sensible things which are formed in the human soul by
it, and then too the perplexity and fretful difficulty of
ratiocination in inquiring the natures of things, and further the laborious ingenuity in discerning virtues and
vices, and many more of that sort. No man rightly
numbered among the wise would deny that it is clear
that the angelic essence lacks all these and is nevertheless present in the nature of things. For all this,
Augustine would seem to have taught that angels perceive, in the eighth book *on the City of God,* chapter
seven,[6] where he praises the virtue of contemplation of
the great philosophers who

> saw that every species in every mutable thing,
> by which it is whatever it is, in whatever man-
> ner and quality its nature is, can only be from
> him who is truly because he is immutably. And
> because of this, whether we consider the body
> of the whole world, the figures, qualities, and
> the motion ordered and the elements disposed
> from heaven to earth, and whatever bodies are
> in them; or whether we consider all life,
> whether the life which nourishes and main-
> tains, as in trees, or the life which has these
> functions and also perceives, as in animals,
> or the life which has these functions and also
> understands, as in men, or the life which does
> not require the nutritive support, but only
> maintains, perceives, and understands, as in
> angels: all these can only be from him who is
> absolutely.

[6] The reference should be to chapter 6.

I should believe, however, that he spoke of the interior
sense. So, who does not know that the celestial essence does not share in many parts of nature and in
many motions which inhere naturally in human nature?
True reason testifies likewise that it has no knowledge of
things which neither are inherent in it, that is, in celestial substance, as substance, nor happen to it as accident.
For although angels are said to administer this world
and every corporeal creature, they must in no manner
be thought to need corporeal senses, or local or temporal motions or visible apparitions to accomplish that.
Moreover, all the things which are accidental to us because of a deficiency of our nature, subject still to the
variations of places and times, are judged rightly not to
be accidental to angels by a defect of their power. For
when they transmute their spiritual and invisible bodies
into visible forms that they may appear to the senses
of mortals visibly, locally, temporally, this accident does
not occur to them because of themselves but because of
men to whom they are present and declare the divine
mysteries. For they do not see locally by sense nor
is it an accident of theirs to know temporally what will
be done in the administration of things, inasmuch as they
are eternally above all time and place in the contemplation of truth in which they see at once the causes of the
administration of things. And do not think that I
say these things concerning all celestial essences, but
only of the more excellent orders, which are always
about God and to which there is no ignorance save
that of the divine darknesses which exceed all understanding. In fact, the lowest order which is properly
called angelic, through which the higher orders administer whatever the divine providence commands by divine revelations to be done in the human mind or in
other parts of this world, is not yet absolved of all

ignorance, and so, as Saint Dionysius the Areopagite says most subtly in the book *on the Celestial Hierarchy: it is taught by the higher orders, and it is conducted into a knowledge of divine mysteries which are loftier than it*. Moreover, we are commanded, not irrationally, to believe and understand that every visible and invisible creature was created in man alone, since there is no substance created which is not understood to be in him; no species, or difference, or property, or natural accident is found in the nature of things which either is not inherent in him naturally or the knowledge of which can not be in him; and the very knowledge of things, which are contained within him, is better than the things of which it is knowledge to the extent that the nature in which it is formed is better. Every rational nature however is set by right reason before every irrational and sensible nature since it is nearer to God. Wherefore too the things of which knowledge is inherent in human nature are understood not inconsistently to subsist in their ideas. For where they undergo their knowledge better, there they must be judged to exist more truly. Furthermore, if the things themselves subsist more truly in their ideas than in themselves, and if the ideas of them are naturally present in man, then they were created universally in man. The return of all things into man will doubtless prove this in its time. For by what reason would they return into him if they did not possess a certain connatural kinship in him and if they did not proceed in a certain manner from him? Concerning this return we have promised to speak in its proper place.

Disc. Although these things seem extremely difficult since they go beyond the mode of simple doctrine, nevertheless, considered speculatively by reason, they agree wholly with the breadth of understanding of hu-

man creation, and they very usefully establish, as we
may say not inaccurately, that man was not produced
in the genus of animals, but rather every genus of animals was produced in man from earth, that is, from
the solidity of nature, and not only every genus of
animal but indeed the whole created universe was made
in man, so that what Truth said, may be understood
truly of man: *Preach the gospel to the whole creation;* [7]
again the Apostle: *The whole creation groaneth and
travaileth in pain together until now.* [8]   But let him to
whom these things seem too abstruse and deeply incredible, if he is inexpert of all the natural disciplines which
are called liberal, let him either be silent or learn, but
not combat incautiously these things which he is not
able to understand; if he is learned, he will see clearly
(to offer him an example of one of them) that geometrical figures do not subsist naturally in themselves but in
the reasons of that very discipline of which they are
figures.   For since the triangular thing which is seen
by the bodily sense in some matter, is surely a kind of
sensible imagination of that which is present in the
mind, he will understand the triangle itself which subsists in the mind apt to discipline, and he will weigh
with unbiased judgment which is the more excellent,
the figure of the triangle or the triangle itself of which
it is the figure.   And he will find, if I am not mistaken,
that that figure is truly a figure, but a false triangle,
whereas that triangle which subsists in the discipline
is the cause of the figure itself and is the true triangle.
And I do not speak of the triangle of phantasy [i.e.
the triangle perceived by sense] which descends from
the mind through the memory into the senses and
through the senses into sensible figures, nor of that

[7] *Mark* 16:15.   [8] *Romans* 8:22.

triangle which, on the other hand, is imprinted from
the sensible figure through the corporeal sense on the
memory, but that very triangle which remains uni-
formly in the discipline itself where line and angle are
at once and at the same place, nor is the line in one
place, the angle in another, the middle here, the extreme
there, here a sign, there the spaces of sides from the
sign, here the spaces of angles, there a point from which
lines begin and in which, by the junctures of the sides,
angles are formed, but all these things are one, in one
and the same idea aforesaid of the mind of the geom-
eter, and all are understood in each and each in all
and they are united in the understanding itself because
the understanding is the substantial reason of all that
it understands and from it the formulæ of geometrical
bodies are specificated. And what we have said of the
triangle is to be understood of other figures too, angular,
or circular, or oblique, whether in planes or in solids,
inasmuch as all these subsist in one and the same
reason in their ideas in the mind which is expert and
apt to discipline. If, therefore, geometrical bodies,
whether they be formed in phantasies of memory or
in some sensible matter, subsist in their rational ideas,
lacking all phantasy and all matter, above all that
which is perceived by bodily sense or fashioned in memory: what is there astonishing then that natural bodies,
composed from the qualities of the elements of the
world, should subsist in that nature in which there is
the idea of them, especially since all things which are
perceived concerning bodies are incorporeal? For the
species in which they are contained are incorporeal.
That quantities and qualities are similarly intelligible
of nature and proceed from the intellectual reasons of
vital substance seems doubtful to no wise man.

9. *Mast.* Whoever shall have considered the natures of things intently will find immediately that they are so constituted.

Disc. Accordingly, now that these things have been discussed, it may be asked not improperly, how every creature is formed in man, since man is said to have been made after the creation of all. If, therefore, the whole visible and invisible universe was created before him, as the divine story tells, and one reads of the creation of no creature after him, by what reason can we perceive every creature to have been fashioned in man? For, if any one should say that the whole creation was fashioned twice, first specially in itself, but second generally in man, I should not believe that that would accord easily with reason, because if it is so, man will not have a substance proper to him, but will be, as it were, a kind of composition of many things, or rather indeed of the whole creation previously made, and a single multiplex cumulation by different forms. But what is even more grave, if the whole creation whether visible or invisible has been made most perfectly in itself (and indeed since the creator is perfect and more than perfect, it is credible that he should have made no imperfect thing), how could it have taken on a second perfection of its creation, as it were, in man, who was created last in the divine operations? And, if this is so, God did not make man out of nothing in his own image, but he made him of those things which had been made before him. But if any one should say the human body had not been made from nothing but from something earthly, namely mud, what would be said of the more perfect making of man, which was set without doubt in the soul and in the spiritual body in the first creation, which, that is the soul, we believe to have been made from the divine breath, or rather to have been made the divine breath, not from something, but out of nothing?

Mast. I see that this question is involved in a great deal of obscurity and requires a diversified skill for its solution. But lest we pass it over utterly untouched, we shall attempt to contemplate it in some way as the interior beam of the divine light shall have disposed. And first say, I ask, whether intelligible things or sensible things are prior to the mind which understands them or to the sense by which they are perceived.

Disc. I should say, not improperly, that where there is one thing which understands and another which is understood, and where that which understands is of a better nature than that which is understood, the thing understood or perceived is preceded by the understanding soul or the perceiving sense. I should not say, however, that the things which understand themselves are prior to themselves in so far as they can understand themselves. For where the thing and the knowledge of it are one, I do not see what precedence can be made. For I know that I am, nevertheless the knowledge of me does not precede me because I am not one thing and the knowledge by which I know myself another; and, if I did not know that I am, I would not ignore that I do not know that I am: and therefore, whether I shall have known or not have known that I am, I shall not lack knowledge; for it will remain for me to know my ignorance. And, if each being that can know that it does not know itself, can not ignore that it is, in that if it were not at all, it would not know that it does not know itself: it follows that absolutely everything is which knows that it is or knows that it does not know that it is. If any one however is so far sunk in ignorance that he neither

knows that he is nor perceives that he does not know
that he is, I should say that either such an one is
absolutely not a man or is wholly annihilated. We
have sufficiently established likewise in the reasons
which have been given above that the following two
activities are present in the human soul at the same
time and inseparably and always: to know and not to
know. For the soul knows that it is a rational and
intellectual nature; it does not know, however, what
intellect itself and reason itself are.

Mast. Then, were you not, before you knew or did
not know that you were?

Disc. No; for I received at the same time being and
knowledge that I am and understanding that I do not
know myself in the sense of knowing what I am.

Mast. Tell me, when does a man receive knowledge
of himself: in that creation in which all men were
made universally in the primordial causes before secu-
lar times, or in the generation in which in the order
of times, known and predefined by God alone, he proceeds into this life?

Disc. In both, I judge; in one generally and hidden
in causes, but in the other specially and manifestly in
effects. For in that primordial and general creation of
all human nature, no one knows himself specially nor
begins to have proper knowledge of himself; for a
single and general knowledge of all things is there,
and known to God alone. For therein all men are
one and that one assuredly made in the image of God,
in whom all were created. Just as, indeed, all forms
or species which are contained in one genus, do not
as yet fall under the understanding or the sense, known
through differences and properties, but subsist as a
kind of unity not yet divided until each one receives
intelligibly or sensibly its property and difference in

individual species: so in the community of human nature no one discerns by proper knowledge either himself or his consubstantials before he has proceeded into this world at his times appointed in accordance with the eternal reasons.

Mast. Why, then, does not every one know himself as soon as he has arrived through generation into this world?

Disc. I should say, not without justification, that the penalty of the transgression of nature is shown in that. For, if man had not sinned, he would certainly not have fallen into so profound ignorance of himself; just as he would not have suffered the ignominious generation from the two sexes in the likeness of irrational animals, as the wisest of the greek theologians affirm with most certain reasons. For he who alone was born into the world without sin, namely the Redeemer of the world, at no time and at no place endured such an ignorance, but as soon as he was conceived and born, he understood both himself and all things, and he was able to speak and teach, not only because he was the Wisdom of the Father, which nothing escapes, but also because he had taken on uncontaminated humanity in order to purge the contaminated; not because he received another nature beyond that which he restored, but because he alone remained in it uncontaminated and preserved for the remedy of the wound of tainted nature in the most secret reasons of himself. For human nature perished entirely in all men except him in whom alone it remained incorruptible. And, indeed, he is the greatest example of grace, not because he was freed of any part of the guilt of human nature, but because he alone of all men with no antecedent merit was joined in a unity of substance to the Word of God, in whom all the elect, partaking of the plenitude of his grace, are made sons of God and participants of the divine substance.

Mast. There was then present in human nature a power of having most perfect knowledge of itself if it had not sinned?

Disc. Nothing is more probable. The fall of human nature was surely the greatest and the most miserable, to forfeit the knowledge and wisdom implanted in it and to slip into profound ignorance of itself and its creator, even though the desire for the beatitude which it had lost be understood to have remained in it after the fall: this desire would in no way have remained in it, if it had completely ignored itself and its God.

Mast. Therefore the most perfect knowledge, both of itself and its creator, was implanted in it naturally before sin, so far as the knowledge of the creature can comprehend both itself and its cause?

Disc. I think it was no otherwise than that. For how would it be an image if it differed in something from that of which it is an image, except in the relation of subject, concerning which we spoke in the preceding books, when we inquired concerning the prototype, that is, concerning the principal example and its image, saying that God himself is the principal example, subsisting through himself, by himself, in himself, and created or formed or altered by none, but the image of him, which is man, created by him, is not through itself nor does it subsist by itself nor in itself; but from him, whose image he is, man receives being in accordance with nature and divine being [*Deus esse*] by dispensation of grace; and likewise all the rest which are predicated of God, can be predicated of his image, but of God essentially, of the image only by participation? For the image is both goodness and good by participation of the supreme goodness and the supreme good, of which it is the image, and also eternal and eternity by participation of the eternal and the eternity from which it has been formed; and again omnipotence by participation of the omnipotence by which it was fashioned and to which in turn it is specificated. For if human nature had not sinned, and if it had clung immutably to that which formed it, it would assuredly be omnipotent. For whatever it wished to be done in the nature of things, would necessarily be done, as long in any case as it wished nothing other done than that which it understood its creator wished to be done; and in turn, it would understand the will of its creator, absolutely omnipotent and immutable, provided it adhered wholly to him and did not leave him, lest it should be dissimilar to him, and it would understand the other predicates which can be understood or thought or predicated with right reason of God and his image.

Mast. If, therefore, a perfect knowledge was present in human nature before sin, both of itself and of its creator, what is there astonishing that one understood of it reasonably that it had a most full knowledge of natures similar to itself, such as the celestial essences, and of essences inferior to itself, such as this world with its reasons which fall under the understanding, and that at the present time human nature still has this in possibility alone and in actuality in the highest men?

Disc. Clearly that will not be astonishing to those who understand, but true and probable.

Mast. It is great and true praise of human nature and most of all of him who willed to create it thus. Wherefore, in the same way, the following must be accepted too of his understanding and knowledge. For just as the creative wisdom which is the Word of God saw all things which were made in it before they were made,

and the very sight of things which were seen before
they were made is true and immutable and eternal essence, so too the created wisdom which is human nature
knew all things which were made in it before they
were made, and that very knowledge of the things
which were known before they were made is true and
unquestioned essence. Accordingly, the very idea of
the creative wisdom is understood rightly to be the
first and causal essence of all creation and the knowledge of the created wisdom subsists as a second essence
and effect of the higher knowledge. And what we have
said of the first and causal essence, established in the
knowledge of the creative wisdom, and of the second and
effective essence, which is asserted, not improperly, to
subsist in the human soul, must be understood in the
same way without hesitation of all things which are
discerned about the essence of the whole creation. For
the right consideration of nature declares that everything which is established in the human understanding
with respect to the substances of things, proceeds from
that very idea of the creative wisdom through the
created wisdom. And with respect to essences there
are established sensible species, quantities, qualities,
places, times, and such things without which the essence can not be understood. Wherefore all that we
wish to teach may be concluded briefly thus: just as
the understanding of all things which the Father made
in his one-begotten Word is the essence of them and the
determination of all that is understood of essence naturally, so the knowledge of all things which the Word
of the Father created in the human soul is the essence
of them and the subject of all the things which are discerned concerning it naturally. And, just as the divine
understanding precedes all and is all, so the intellectual understanding of the soul precedes all that it

knows and is all that it foreknows, so that all things
subsist in the divine understanding causally and in the
human understanding effectually. Not that the essence
of all things, as we have often said, is one thing in
the Word and another in man, but that the mind ob-
serves one and the same thing in one fashion subsisting
in eternal causes and in another fashion understood
in effects; for in the first it exceeds all understanding,
but in the second it is understood, from the things
which are considered concerning it, only to be; in
neither, however, is it permitted to a created understanding to know what it is. For, if it could be
known, it would not entirely express in itself the image
of its creator who is known only to be from those
things of which he is the principle and cause and
founder, but what he is escapes all sense and understanding.

Disc. Therefore no creature whether visible or invisible precedes the creation of man—not in time, not
in place, not in dignity, not in origin, not in eternity,
and, simply, in no manner of precedence: for in knowledge itself and dignity, but not in time and place,
the creation of man precedes those things which were
created with it and in it and below it; and it was
concreated with those to which it is equal with a con-
dignity of nature, namely, to celestial essences. For
it is itself a partaker of celestial and intellectual essence; assuredly it was written of angelic and human
essence: *Who made the heavens in the understanding,*[9]
as if it were said openly: who made the intellectual
heavens. Wherefore it becomes difficult to understand,
if man were concreated substantially with the angelic
essences, how all visible and invisible things were made

[9] *Psal.* 135:5 (or 136:5); *in intellectu* is usually rendered
in english, *by wisdom.*

in him. For it does not seem to agree with reason that he should have the beginning of his creation together with the celestial powers and that they should have been created in him.

Mast. If you should examine intently the reciprocal joining and unity of intellectual and rational natures, you will find certainly both that the angelic essence is established in the human and the human in the angelic. For in everything that the pure understanding knows very perfectly, it is made and it becomes one with it. So great indeed was the community of human and angelic nature and so great would it be made if the first man had not sinned, that the two would become one. That, even now, begins to be done among the uppermost men of which number are the firstlings in heaven. And the angel, moreover, is made in man through the understanding of the angel which is in man, and man in the angel through the understanding of man constituted in the angel. For he, as I have said, who understands purely, is made in that which he understands. Accordingly, the intellectual and the rational angelic nature was made in the intellectual and rational human nature in the same manner as the human was made in the angelic by the reciprocal knowledge by which angel understands man and man angel. Nor is that strange. For while we discuss, each of us is made into the other. Since, in fact, when I understand what you understand, I am made your understanding and in a certain ineffable way I have been made into you. In the same way, when you understand purely what I understand clearly, you have been made my understanding and from two understandings one has been made, formed from that which we both sincerely and unhesitatingly understand. For instance, to use the example of numbers, you understand that the num-

ber six is equal to its parts, and I understand the same;
and I understand that you understand it, just as you
too understand that I understand it. Our two understandings are made one, formed by the number six,
and by that process I am created in you and you are
created in me. For we are not one thing and our
understandings another, but our true and supreme essence is the understanding made specific in the contemplation of truth. The apostolic word, moreover,
when it forbids our intellectual part to cherish visible
forms, saying: *Be not fashioned according to this
world,*[10] teaches that the understanding can be conformed not only to natures coessential to it, but also to
natures inferior when it understands or perceives them
by loving them. Consequently, by reason of this reciprocal intelligence, it is said, not without foundation in
fact, both that the angel is created in man and man
in the angel, and it can not rightly be believed or understood that the angel precedes man by any law of creation or by any manner of precedence, although, as many
insist, the prophetic narrative pronounces the creation
of the angelic nature first and of human nature later.
For it is not credible as Saint Augustine points out in
the eleventh book of the *City of God* that the holy
Scripture should have been completely silent in the
works of the six primordial and intelligible days concerning the creation of the celestial powers, but either
in the very first line of *Genesis,* where it was written:
*In the beginning God created the heavens and the
earth,*[11] their creation is brought forward under the
name of the heavens, or a little later when it says: *And
God said, Let there be light: and there was light.*[12] For,
in one or the other place, the aforesaid father affirms

[10] *Romans* 12:2.   [11] *Genesis* 1:1.   [12] *Genesis* 1:3.

that the angelic creation was manifested and most particularly in the second. In the first, to be sure, he asserts that under the appellation *the heavens* the making of the whole invisible creation in unformed matter is signified rather than the formation specially of the angelic nature. But in that which was written: *Let there be light: and there was light,* he asserts unhesitatingly that the formation of celestial essences was described; although he introduced the meaning of others who believe that there is in this divine precept the constitution of a certain primitive light, sensible and local in the upper parts of the world; but he attacks this meaning most acutely in his *in Hexæmeron.* When, however, it is said: *And God divided the light from the darkness. And God called the light Day, and the darkness Night,*[13] he wants that to be understood in two ways: for either, by the word *light* the formation of the angelic creature in its proper species, and by the word *darkness* the unshapeliness, preceding in origin not in time, of that nature as yet imperfect, or else by the division of the light from the darkness was signified the segregation and difference of that angelic part which clung immutably to its creator, foreknowing beatitude by virtue of its obedience, from that part which did not stand in truth but was precipitated as a penalty of its pride into the darkness of ignorance of its future fall and eternal misery. But, if anyone wishes to know more fully this double explanation of the most divine master, let him read it carefully in the words of the master himself in his *in Hexæmeron* and in the above mentioned volume *on the City of God:* to insert these explanations in this little discussion of ours seems to me superfluous since they are detailed and clear to all.

Disc. Go on; for the opinions of the holy fathers need

[13] *Genesis* 1:4-5.

not be brought in, especially if they are known to most people, except where the gravest necessity requires that reasoning be fortified for those who, since they are untrained in reasoning, yield to authority more than to reason . . .

SAINT ANSELM (1033-1109)

Much of the work of St. Anselm is dedicated implicitly to a single guiding interest. Indications of it are scattered abundantly through his writings and appear even in their titles: the *Proslogium* was originally known as *Faith Seeking Understanding*. The direction of Anselm's thought, and particularly the emphasis of his arguments for the existence of God (which have been found to be puzzling enough when considered without that emphasis) are intelligently studied consequences to this preoccupation. It is important that faith precede understanding, since of the two sources of human knowledge, reason and faith, faith can exist without reason, but reason can not exist without faith. In rational inquiry there must be a foundation of faith in the principles of the inquiry and in the principles of the understanding itself. Fortunately there is certainty for faith, and therefore for reason, in the Scripture. The authority of every truth which reason may gather is contained there; the Scripture affirms all truths and denies none. The christian may, therefore, proceed to understanding by way of faith; he should not arrive at faith by way of understanding; nor should he, if he can not understand, depart from faith. Even more, no one well established in faith can be weakened by the attempt to understand what he believes. Not to understand what is believed is a weakness, not of faith, but of reason; to understand faith is necessarily to approach God. It is presumptuous therefore to hope, as dialecticians do, to understand without believ-

ing; but on the other hand it is negligent not to appeal
to reason for the explication of faith. One believes in
order to understand; one does not understand in order
to believe.

When the documents of faith are stated, that is obviously the beginning of a specifically christian philosophy. Anselm was concerned with the orthodoxy of
his *Monologium* enough to insist in the preface to it that
it contains nothing inconsistent with the writings of
the fathers, and particularly of Augustine; that, further, his own work could be judged better after the
perusal of Augustine's *on the Trinity*. This recom-
mendation and caution can be extended, with no deroga-
tion from the originality of the work, to the rest of
Anselm's writings. His contribution was largely in
working out the implications of the faith long stated
and, by his time, thoroughly organized; his philosophy
turns about the ontological argument and its subordinate
substantiating doctrines, and the richness of his thought
is in the precise, forcibly reasoned arguments which
grow about the widening implications of the nature
and being of God. In this sense, for its slight concern
with empirical references, it is a limited philosophy;
things and thought enter only as they are relevant to
the central theme of the eternal creator of things. Yet
there is philosophic justification for that, since truth
seemed to Anselm, as to Augustine, so vast and profound that faith and reason could never exhaust it;
reason can proceed safely among its uncertainties only
as faith leads the way.

In another sense this slight concern with the empirical is no limitation of the philosophy, for the
ontological proof involves a theory of knowledge, which
is itself the whole of a philosophy. The criticism of
the scope of the philosophy, no less than the refuta-

tions of the argument with which the history of philosophy from the time of Anselm to the present is studded, can be based on any other theory of knowledge; the decision to ground philosophy in faith is philosophic. Truth is, for Anselm in the tradition already old in philosophy and thought in the eleventh century, the signifying that that which is is. When further questions are asked—how and where such truth is discovered, how far sensation and reason are involved in truth and error, whether truth varies with the objects in which it is found—Anslem moves, in the platonist-augustinian current, away from the experience of empirical physical things to the discovery of one supreme subsistent truth. A thing is never perceived by the senses truly or falsely, but true or false judgments may be based on the sensation; to correct what might seem a perceptual error requires no alteration of the sense organ, but a realization only of its nature and operation.

Truth, therefore, in that it signifies that that which is is, follows as the effect of the very nature of the thing. It is a rightness of the thing signifying its nature. The nature of the thing is a rightness, too, of being; and as the rightness of signifying carries to a rightness of being, so the rightness of being in turn carries to a source of being. For Anselm the fact of truth is significant, not only of the experience from which it is sprung, but of an eternal truth by which it is true. That supreme truth is God; all other truths are the effects of him. It would be a great error, by this analysis, to suppose that besides the supreme truth the only truth is that of signification. There is the truth of the essence of things, for they are what they must by their natures be, and that depends directly on God. On the other hand, the truth of thought and the truth of discourse depend on the existence of things, since man's thought, here (as in all platonist monotheistic creeds), has this difference from God's thought, that whereas the existence of things follows from the truth God thinks, the truth of man is the consequence of the existence of things. Besides these truths, moreover, there is a truth of action and a truth of will. In Anselm's thought once again, the moral and intellectual virtues adumbrate an identical reality and serve to a single end. The rightnesses of understanding and will are involved in the natures of things: truth is rightness perceptible to the mind alone; justice is rightness of the will preserved because of itself alone. They are rightnesses in that the things in which they are, conform in action, thought, speech, will, to one rightness. There is one supreme truth which is the truth of nothing; but only so far as a thing is in conformity with this first truth can one speak of the truth of anything.

Since all things lead so definitely to God, his existence can be proved wherever a well-attested existence is discovered. The *Monologium* offers a variety of such proofs; they can be reduced in general to three. The existence of things which are called good raises the question, whence it is that they are good. To call them all good is to eliminate the possibility that they all have their goodness by separate causes; there must be a single principle in which they all participate. The existence of good things indicates the existence of that which is good through itself; by it all other things are good. The basis of the second argument is the perfection which all things possess in common—that of being. Everything has a cause; the totality of things has either many causes or only one. If they are many, they must (1) be caused by one cause, or (2) exist by themselves (in which case they possess in common the faculty of existing by themselves, which is being), or (3) they may produce each other (but reciprocal causation is contrary to reason). From any of these analyses can be deduced the existence of a being on which all being depends. The third proof follows from the existence of degrees of perfection in things. Either there is an infinite number of things more and less perfect, and therefore no one most perfect being, or else a finite number in which case one must be most perfect. But an infinity of actually existent creatures is absurd; therefore there exists a nature superior to all and inferior to none. If there are several creatures set at the summit of the hierarchy, that which they have in common is either their essence, in which case they are only a single nature, or else if it is not their essence, it is another nature superior to them.

All three proofs of the *Monologium* begin with some real datum, in order to work from the existence of some aspect of nature, from good, or being, or degrees of being, to the existence of God who is necessary for the explication of such aspects of nature. In the *Proslogium* Anselm seeks a single proof which will suffice in itself and from which the others will flow. These requirements he finds fulfilled in the famous argument which has come to be called the ontological proof. We believe that God is something than which a greater can not be conceived. Even the fool who says in his heart there is no God understands in so far as he denies, and therefore the idea exists in his mind. But that than which a greater can not be conceived can not exist in the mind alone, since if it did, a greater, namely one which existed in reality as well, could be conceived; but the existence of such a being would be contradictory. Therefore if God exists at all, even in the understanding, he must exist also in reality since that is a superior existence. The notion with which this proof

begins, unlike the preceding three, is of a special order,
for it is furnished by faith; but to exist at all, even as
an idea, is to exist truly already; therefore, the existence of that notion of God in thought would be impossible if God did not exist really. The passage is made
from faith to reason by the examination of that which
is proposed by faith, since one concludes from that examination that the object of faith is immediately intelligible.

The most persistent argument against the conclusion
of this most characteristic of the anselmian proofs, the
argument which was stated in his own lifetime and
which was repeated by Aquinas in a long line of op-
ponents, insists that the passage from the subjective or
ideal order to the objective or real is unwarranted.
Even if the idea of God be granted to coincide with
the idea of that than which a greater can not be conceived, the conception of God, although it implies necessary existence, would not authorize the affirmation of
God's extra-mental existence. One might assert that
if there were such a being he would exist necessarily,
but from the existence of the idea of him nothing could
be concluded concerning his actual existence. Clearly
this is a cogent argument only if the augustinian-pla-
tonism of Anselm be forgotten. Ideas, by the analysis
Anselm makes of them, are themselves things; and for
them to be is indication of something concerning the
nature of things. The idea of no other thing than
God could be made the basis of a proof of the existence of the thing. But the proof holds in the case of
God precisely because he is that single being on which
all thought, all action, all being depend; whereas, therefore, the idea of no part of being would warrant the
assertion of the existence of that part, still if thought
is itself being, the existence of thought would warrant

the assertion of the existence of being as a whole. The idea of the most perfect being involves us in an order of reality, and the passage from ideas to beings is easy and tempting since ideas are already beings. Beings and ideas, as they approach their source, are identical, since the eternal ideas which may be experienced in thinking are the principles of being.

This explicit and detailed following of the metaphysical implications of christian doctrines constructs a step in the building of a christian philosophy. It makes, of course, important omissions; it encounters significant dangers. The most pertinent of its omissions arises from the program which committed it to an examination of the nature and logic of eternal things; this it does so expertly that the doctrines have continued to be echoed and re-echoed with changes, modifications, ostensible oppositions from the eleventh century to the present; but as a consequence there is no doctrine of time, of changing things, of contingency, for these recall immediately the timeless, the changeless, the necessary on which they depend and by which they must be explained. Obviously they are as irrelevant as the consideration of the origins of knowledge would be in the question of the formal validity of knowledge and of the dependence of ideas on necessary truths. The most important of the dangers is in the suggestion which is made that reason devote itself to understanding faith; the question of how far it should go in the interpretation of faith is not raised. Anselm himself attempts to demonstrate the Trinity and the Incarnation by necessary reasons; these were two mysteries of faith which later writers like Aquinas, Duns Scotus, and Ockham were content to leave for theology. Anselm's faith in the interpretation of reason seems unlimited, as if everything believed were also intelligible, with only one limitation to the exercise of reason —that reason can never attain to complete intelligibility since the data of revelation on which it is employed are inexhaustible.

The progress of philosophy after Anselm is evidenced most strikingly in the analyses to which later writers subjected the requirements of logical demonstration. Under the exigencies of those analyses the vast scope which Anselm confidently assigned to the understanding was steadily lessened. Yet the delimiting of the field of reason by the exclusion of certain problems from its range led again to a heightened confidence (which reached its peak two hundred years after Anselm) in the independent power of thought among its limited problems. Thereafter the items of faith and incredulity in the principles of the understanding have been distributed variously from century to century, but wherever reason figured in the philosophy, the eternal things of Anselm have appeared in some guise.

SAINT ANSELM

DIALOGUE ON TRUTH [1]

PROLOGUE

I have, at various times in the past, written three treatises pertaining to the study of the sacred Scriptures, which have this similarity, that they are presented by question and answer, the person questioning designated by the name of disciple, the person answering by the name of master. I do not wish to number with these (since it pertains to a different study than the other three) a fourth which I published in the same manner, not without its use, I think, as an introduction to dialectic, which begins with the words: *Concerning the Grammarian.* One of these three is *On Truth,* namely, what truth is, and of what things it is ordinarily predicated, and what justice is. Another of the treatises is *On the Freedom of the Will,* what it is, and whether man always has it, and how many diversities of it there are in either having or not having rightness of will, to preserve which is the prerogative of the rational creature. In this treatise I showed only the natural strength of the will for preserving the rightness which was received, and not how necessary it is that grace should follow to that end. The third treatise is on the question in which it is asked in what way the devil sinned by not standing firm in truth: for God

[1] SANCTI ANSELMI, *Dialogus de Veritate,* in J. P. MIGNE, *Patrogia Latina,* vol. 158, col. 467-486.

did not give him the perseverance, which he could not
have unless God gave it to him: and if God had given
it to him he would have had it, just as the good angels
had it because God gave it to them. I entitled this
treatise, although I spoke in it of the confirmation of
the good angels, *On the Fall of the Devil,* since what I
said of the good angels was contingent, but what I
wrote of the bad angels followed from the statement of
the question. Although these treatises obviously do
not hang together by any sequence of presentation, nevertheless their material and the similarity of the investigation demand that they be brought together in
the order in which I have presented them. Consequently, although they have been copied in another
order by certain persons in haste, before they had been
perfected, nevertheless I wish them ordered as I have
here set down.

Chapter I.

That truth does not have a beginning or an end.

Disciple. Since we believe that God is truth, and since
we say truth is in many other things, I would like to
know whether we ought to affirm that wherever truth is
spoken of, God is that truth. For in your *Monologium* [2]
you prove by the truth of discourse that the supreme
truth does not have a beginning or an end, saying,

> Let him who can, think of a time when the fol-
> lowing began to be true, or when it was not
> true, namely, that something was in the future
> to be: or let him think of a time when the
> following will cease to be true, and when it will
> not be true, namely, that something will have
> been in the past. But if neither of these two

[2] Chapter 18.

suppositions can be conceived, and if they can not be true without truth, it is impossible even to think that truth have a beginning or an end. Moreover, if truth had a beginning, or if it will have an end, it was then true before truth began that there was no truth; and after truth will have ceased to be, it will be true that there will be no truth. But nothing can be true without truth: consequently, there was truth before there was truth; and there will be truth after truth will have ceased to be; which is utterly inconsistent. Whether, then, truth be said to have, or whether it be understood not to have, beginning or end, truth can be limited by no beginning or end.

This you said in your *Monologium.* Wherefore I expect to learn a definition of truth from you.

Master. I do not remember to have found a definition of truth, but if you wish, let us inquire what truth is in the diversities of things in which we say truth is.

Disc. If I can do nothing else, I shall help by listening.

CHAPTER II.

On the truth of signification and on the two truths of statement.

Mast. Let us inquire first, then, what is truth in statement, since we most frequently call a statement true or false.

Disc. You inquire, and whatever you find, I shall observe.

Mast. When is a statement true?

Disc. When that is which it states, whether by affirming or denying; for I say that what the proposition states is, even when it denies that that which is not, is, since it states thus in what manner the thing is.

Mast. Does it seem to you then that the thing declared is the truth of the statement?

Disc. No.

Mast. Why not?

Disc. Because nothing is true except by participating in truth, and therefore the truth of what is true is in that which is true; but the thing stated is not in the true statement and therefore it must be called, not the truth of it, but the cause of its truth. Wherefore it seems to me that its truth must be sought only in discourse itself.

Mast. Consider then whether discourse itself or its signification or any of those things which are in the definition [*diffinitione*] of the statement, is what you seek?

Disc. I think not.

Mast. Why not?

Disc. Because if that were the case, it would always be true, since all things which are involved in the definition of a statement remain the same; and whether that which is stated is or is not, the sentence is the same, and the signification is the same, and the others similarly.

Mast. What then does truth in statement seem to you to be?

Disc. I know nothing other than that when it signifies that that which is is, then truth is in it, and it is true.

Mast. To what end is an affirmation made?

Disc. To signify that that which is is.

Mast. Then it should do that?

Disc. Certainly.

Mast. Then when it signifies that that which is is, it signifies as it should.

Disc. That is clear.

Mast. But when it signifies as it should it signifies rightly?

Disc. That is so.

Mast. However, when it signifies rightly, the signification is right?

Disc. There is no doubt of that.

Mast. Therefore, when it signifies that that which is is, the signification is right?

Disc. That follows.

Mast. Likewise when it signifies that that which is is, the signification is true?

Disc. Yes, it is both right and true, when it signifies that that which is is.

Mast. It is the same, therefore, for the affirmation to be right and true, that is, to signify that that which is is?

Disc. Yes, it is the same.

Mast. Consequently, truth, for it, is not other than rightness.

Disc. I see clearly now that truth is this rightness.

Mast. It is the same when the statement signifies that that which is not, is not.

Disc. I understand what you say, but tell me what I can answer if some one should say that likewise when reason signifies that that which is not, is, it signifies as it should. For reason has the power to signify equally that that which is and that which is not, is. For if it had not the power to signify that that which is not, is, it would not signify it. Wherefore, too, since it signifies that that which is not, is, it signifies as it should. But if by signifying what it should, it is true and right, as you have shown, then discourse is true even when it states that that which is not, is.

Mast. It is not ordinarily said to be true when it

signifies that that which is not, is. But it has truth
and rightness in that it does that which it should. But
when it signifies that that which is, is, it does doubly
what it should, since it signifies both what it has the
power to signify and what has happened. But according to this latter rightness and truth, by which it signifies that that which is, is, a statement is called by
usage right and true, and not according to the former
by which it signifies that that which is not, is. For
more is required of it because it undertook signification
than because it did not undertake it. [It has more rightness, its *ought* is greater, in fulfilling a positive than
only a negative task.] For it took on the power of
signifying that a thing is when it is not or that it is
not when it is, only because it could not be made to
signify only at the moment when the thing is that
it is or that it is not only when it is not. Consequently, the one is rightness and truth of statement, in
that it signifies that which it was made to signify; the
other in that it signifies that which it undertook to
signify. So, the latter is the immutable possession
of speech itself, but the former is mutable; for speech
always has the latter, it does not always have the
former; for it has the latter naturally, but it has the former accidently and according to use. For when I say, It
is day, I use the meaning of this sentence rightly to
signify that that which is, is, because it was made for
this, and therefore it is said to signify rightly. But
when I signify by the same sentence that that which is
not, is, I do not use it rightly, for it was not made
for that, and on that account the signification of it is
then said not to be right: although in certain statements these two rightnesses or truths are inseparable,
as when we say, Man is an animal, or, Man is not a
stone. For the affirmation in this case always signifies

that that which is, is, and the negation always signifies that that which is not, is not. Nor can the former be used to signify that that which is not, is, for man is always an animal. Nor can the latter be used to signify that that which is, is not, for man is never a stone. We began therefore to inquire concerning the truth which discourse has according as one uses it rightly, since the common use of speech judges a statement to be true according to that. We shall speak later of the truth which it can not but have.

Disc. Go back then to that with which you began, since you have made sufficiently clear to me the distinction between the two truths of discourse, if you showed it to have some measure of truth none the less even when it lies, as you say.

Mast. Let that suffice for the time for the truth of signification with which we began. For the same principle [*ratio*] and relation of truth which we examined in the proposition of the spoken word, must be taken up in all signs which are used for signifying that something is or is not, among which are written characters and the language of fingers.

Disc. Proceed then to the other.

CHAPTER III.

On the truth of opinion.

Mast. We call thought true when that is which we think is, whether by reason or in some other way, and we call thought false when that is not.

Disc. Usage has it thus.

Mast. What then does truth in thought seem to you to be?

Disc. According to the principle which we saw in the

case of proposition, nothing is more properly called the truth of thought than its rightness. For the power has been given us to think that something is or is not, to the end that we think that that which is, is, and that that which is not, is not. Wherefore whoever thinks that that which is, is, thinks as he should, and consequently the thought is right. If therefore the thought is true and right for no other reason than that we think that that which is, is, or that that which is not, is not, then there is no other truth of thought than rightness.

Chapter IV.

On the truth of will.

Mast. You take the matter up rightly. But Truth himself says that truth is in the will when he says that the devil did not stand in truth.[3] For the devil was not in truth nor did he abandon truth except in will.

Disc. I believe that is so. For if he had always wished what he should have wished, he would never have sinned, since he did not abandon the truth except by sinning.

Mast. Tell me then what you understand by truth here?

Disc. Nothing except rightness. For if he was in rightness and truth as long as he wished that which he should, that, namely, for which he was given will, and if he abandoned rightness and truth, when he wished that which he should not have, then truth can not here be understood to be other than rightness, for truth or rightness was nothing other in his will than to wish that which he should.

[3] *John* 8:44.

CHAPTER V.

*On the truth of natural action and of action which is
not natural.*

Mast. You understand it well. But we must believe truth to be in action, too, as the Lord said. For *he
that doeth evil hateth the light* and *he that doeth the
truth cometh to the light.*[4]

Disc. I follow what you say.

Mast. Consider then, if you can, what truth is here.

Disc. Unless I am mistaken, truth in action must also
be considered according to the same principle by which
we investigated truth above in the others.

Mast. So it is. For if to do evil and to do the truth
are opposed, as the Lord shows when he says: *he that
doeth evil hateth the light,* and *he that doeth the truth
cometh to the light,* it is the same to do the *truth* as to
do good. For doing good is the contrary of doing evil.
Wherefore if to do the truth and to do good are identical because they are opposite to the same thing, they
are not diverse in signification; but the opinion of all
is that he who does as he should, does good and does
rightness. Wherefore it follows that to do rightness
is to do the truth. For it is clear that to do the truth
is to do good and to do good is to do rightness. Wherefore nothing is more apparent than that the truth of
action is rightness.

Disc. I see nothing faltering in your consideration.

Mast. Consider then whether every action which does
what it should, may properly be said to do the truth.
Obviously there is rational action, as alms-giving; and
there is irrational action, as the action of fire which

4 *John* 3: 20-21.

warms. Consider then whether we may properly say
that the fire does the truth?

Disc. If the fire, when it warms, is determined for
warming by that from which it has its being, it does
that which it should when it warms. Therefore I do
not see what impropriety there is that the fire should
do the truth and rightness when it does that which it
should.

Mast. It appears no differently to me. Therefore we
can observe that there are two rightnesses or truths
of action, a necessary one and one which is not necessary. For fire does the truth and rightness of necessity
when it warms, and man does the truth and rightness
out of no necessity when he does good: but the Lord
wanted *to do* to be understood not only for that which
to do properly means, but for every verb, when he said
that *he that doeth the truth cometh to the light.*[5] For
he does not exclude from this truth or light him who
suffers persecution because of justice, or him who is
where he should be and at the time he should be, or
him who stands or sits when he should, or anything of
this sort. For no one says that such persons do not
act well. And when the Apostle says that *each one shall
receive according as he has done* [6] that must be understood to mean whatever we ordinarily call doing good
or doing evil.

Disc. The common usage of the word is to call suf-
fering and many other things which are not *doing,
doing.* Consequently, unless I am mistaken, we can
number among right actions the right will too, to the
truth of which we had turned our attention above before
taking up the truth of action.

Mast. You are not mistaken. For whoever wishes
what he should, is said to do rightly and good, nor is

[5] *John* 3:21.   [6] *II Corinthians* 5:10.

he excluded from the number of those who do the truth. But since we speak of truth in investigating that [the right will], and since the Lord seems to speak especially of that truth which is in the will when he says of the devil that he has not stood in truth,[7] for that reason I wanted to take up separately what truth is in the will.

Disc. I am content that it was so done.

Mast. Since therefore it is clear that the truth of action is in one fashion natural and in another not natural, that truth of discourse which we saw above [8] can not be separated from it, must be classed under the natural. For, just as fire, when it warms, does the truth since it was determined by that from which it has its being, so also this sentence, *it is day,* does the truth when it signifies that it is day, whether it is day or not, since it was determined naturally to do that.

Disc. I see truth now for the first time in false discourse.

CHAPTER VI.

On the truth of the senses, and that the falsity which is thought to be in sense is in opinion.

Mast. Do you think that we have discovered all the places of truth other than the supreme truth?

Disc. I remember now a certain truth which I do not find among these which you have treated.

Mast. What is that?

Disc. Truth is certainly in the senses of the body, but not always, for they sometimes deceive us. For sometimes when I see something through the medium of glass my sight deceives me, in that my body sometimes reports to me that what I see beyond the glass is of

[7] *John* 8: 44.　　　　　[8] Chapter 2, page 155.

the same color as the glass, when it is of another color; and sometimes it makes me think that the glass has the color of the thing which I see beyond it, when it does not have that color. There are many other ways in which sight and the other senses deceive us.

Mast. It does not seem to me that this truth or falsity is in the senses but in opinion. For the interior sense deceives itself; the exterior sense does not lie to it. Sometimes we recognize this easily, sometimes with difficulty. For when a child fears a sculptured dragon with a gaping mouth, it is easy to perceive that it is not sight which brings this about, since it reports nothing more to the child than to adults, but rather it is the childish interior sense which does not yet know how to distinguish clearly between a thing and the likeness of a thing. So it is when, seeing one man like another, we think he is the man he is like, or when some one, hearing what is not the voice of a man, thinks it to be the voice of a man. For the interior sense does this too. What you say of the glass, moreover, is for the following reason, that when sight passes through a body of the color of air it is prevented from taking on the likeness of the color of that which it sees beyond no otherwise than when it passes through air, except in so far as that body through which it passes is thicker and more obscure than air; this is the case when it passes through glass of its own color, that is, a glass to which no other color is added, or when it passes through very pure water, or through crystal, or through something having a like color. But when the same sight passes through another color, as through a glass not of its own color but to which another color is added, it takes on the very color which first it happens on. Wherefore since after it has taken on one color, in so far as it has been affected by it, it takes on any other which

may appear either not at all or less completely: for
that reason it reports the color which it took on first
either alone or with that which appeared later. For
if sight, in so far as it is susceptible of color, is affected very much by the first color, it can not perceive
another color at the same time: but if it is affected by
the first color to a degree less than it is able to perceive color, then it can perceive another. So, if sight
pass through some body such as glass which is so perfectly red that sight itself is wholly affected by its
redness, it can not at the same time be affected by a
different color; but if it finds a redness not so perfect
which comes first, it will be able still, so far as it is
capable of color, to assume, as if not yet full, another
color as far as its capacity is not satiated by the first
color. Any one therefore who is ignorant of this, imag-
ines that sight reports that all things, which it perceives after the first color is taken on, are either
wholly or at least in part of the same color. Whence
it happens that the interior sense imputes its error to
the exterior sense. In the same way, when a whole staff,
of which part is submerged in water and part is out of
water, is thought to be broken, or when we think that
our sight discovers our own faces in a mirror, and when
sight and the other senses seem to report to us many
other things otherwise than they are, it is not the fault
of the senses, which report what they are able to, since
they were given just this potency; but it must be im-
puted to the judgment of the mind, which does not
distinguish clearly what they can or what they ought
to do. But since to demonstrate this is rather more
laborious than fruitful to the inquiry which concerns
us here, I do not think time should be devoted to it.
Let it suffice to say only, that whatsoever the senses
seem to report, whether they do it because of their own

nature or because of some other cause, they do that
which they should, and therefore they do rightness and
the truth, and this truth is contained under the truth
which is in action.

Disc. You have satisfied me with your reply, and I
do not wish to detain you longer in this question of
the senses.

CHAPTER VII.

On the truth of the essence of things.

Mast. Consider now whether, apart from the supreme
truth, truth is to be understood in anything besides these
things which have been investigated above.

Disc. What could that be?

Mast. Do you think that anything could be at any
time or in any place which was not in the supreme truth,
and which did not receive from it that which it is, in
so far as it is, or which could be other than what it is
in the truth?

Disc. That is not to be thought.

Mast. Whatsoever is, therefore, is truly, in so far as
it is that which it is in the supreme truth.

Disc. You can conclude absolutely that everything
which is, is truly, since it is not other than it is in the
truth.

Mast. Truth is therefore in the essence of all things
which are, because they are that which they are in the
supreme truth.

Disc. I see that truth is there in such fashion that
no falsity can be there, for that which is falsely is not.

Mast. You express it well. But tell me whether
any thing should be other than that which it is in the
supreme truth?

Disc. No.

Mast. If therefore all things are what they are there, they are without doubt what they should be.

Disc. Truly they are what they should be.

Mast. But whatever is that which it should be, is rightly.

Disc. It can not be otherwise.

Mast. Therefore everything that is, is rightly.

Disc. Nothing could follow more cogently.

Mast. If therefore truth and rightness are in the essence of things, in that the things are that which in the supreme truth they are, it is certain that the truth of things is rightness.

CHAPTER VIII.

On the different meanings of ought *and* ought not, can *and* can not.

Disc. Nothing is clearer so far as the logical sequence of the argument is concerned. But according to the truth of the thing, how can we say that whatever is, ought to be, since there are many evil deeds which certainly ought not to be?

Mast. Why is it astonishing if the same thing ought to be and not to be?

Disc. How can that be?

Mast. I know that you do not doubt that absolutely nothing is unless God either makes it or permits it.

Disc. Nothing is more certain to me.

Mast. Will you dare say that God does or permits something not wisely or not well?

Disc. On the contrary, I assert that he does and permits nothing except well and wisely.

Mast. Or will you judge that that which so much goodness and so much wisdom does or permits, ought not to be?

Disc. What man of intelligence would dare to think that?

Mast. Therefore that which is done, God doing it, and that which is done, God permitting it, ought equally to be?

Disc. It appears to be as you say.

Mast. Tell me also whether you think that the affect of evil will should be?

Disc. It is the same as if you were to ask whether an evil deed ought to be: a thing which no one gifted with sense would grant.

Mast. Yet God permits some to do evilly that which they wish evilly.

Disc. Would that he did not permit it so often.

Mast. The same thing therefore ought to be and ought not to be. For it ought to be in that it is permitted wisely and well by him, without whom permitting, it could not be done; and it ought not to be with respect to him by whose evil will it is conceived. In this fashion, therefore, our Lord Jesus, since he alone was without sin, ought not to have suffered death nor ought any one to have inflicted it upon him; and yet he ought to have suffered death, in that he himself wisely and benignly and usefully wished to suffer it. So in many ways the same thing takes from different considerations contrary aspects: a thing which happens often in action, as in the case of a stroke. For a stroke is the effect of both agent and patient; consequently it can be called both action and passion, although according to its very name, action or stroke and whatever other words are applied similarly to passive things in an active mean-

ing, seem to be rather of the patient than of the agent.
For in accordance with that which acts they seem to
be more properly called agency or striking [*percu-
tientia*]; and in accordance with that which is passive
they should be called action or stroke. For agency
and striking are derived from agent and striker (just
as providence from provident, and continence from
continent) that is to say, agent and striker, provident,
and continent are active; but action and stroke are
derived from that acted on and struck [*ab acto et per-
cusso*] which are passive. But (to explain in one example that you may understand it in others) just as
there is no striker without a stroke, nor any thing
struck without a striker, so striking and stroke can not
be without each other. Indeed one and the same thing
is signified according to different parts by the different words. Consequently a stroke is said to be of
both the thing striking and the thing struck. Wherefore
according as agent or patient underlies the same judgment or the contrary judgments, the action itself will
also be judged similarly or contrarily from either
part. When therefore he who strikes, strikes rightly
and he who is struck is struck rightly, as, when a
sinner is corrected by him to whom it pertains to
correct, it is right from both parts, for from both parts
there ought to be a stroke. But on the contrary, when
a just man is struck by an unjust man, since neither
the latter should strike nor the former be struck, it is
not right from either part, for from neither part ought
there to be a stroke. But when a sinner is struck by
him to whom it does not pertain to strike, there ought
and there ought not to be a stroke since the former
should be struck but the latter should not strike; and
therefore it can not be denied that it is both right and

not right. But if, from the seat of the judgment of
the divine wisdom and goodness, you consider whether
the blow should not be, either in reference to the striking or the being struck, or to both, that is to say from
the part of the agent and the patient: who will dare
to deny that that ought to be which is permitted by so
much goodness and wisdom?

Disc. Let him deny it who dares; I dare not.

Mast. But again if you consider it according to the
nature of things, would you say that when the iron
nails were inserted into the body of the Lord, the
fragile flesh ought not to have been penetrated or that
having been penetrated by the sharp iron, it ought not
to have pained?

Disc. I should say that was contrary to nature.

Mast. It can happen, therefore, that an action or a
passion ought to be according to nature which according to the agent or the patient ought not to be, in that
the former ought not to act nor the latter suffer.

Disc. I can deny nothing of this.

Mast. You see then that it can happen very frequently that the same action ought to be and ought not
to be, according to different considerations.

Disc. You show that so clearly that I could not fail
to see it.

Mast. Yet I want you to know that *ought* and *ought
not* are sometimes used improperly, as when I say that
I ought to be loved by you. For if I truly ought, I
am a debtor to return what I owe; and I am to be
blamed if I am not loved by you.

Disc. That follows.

Mast. But since I ought to be loved by you, that is
not to be required of me but of you.

Disc. I must own that it is so.

Mast. Consequently when I say that I ought to be loved by you, it is not said as if I owed something, but that you ought to love me. Similarly when I say that I ought not to be loved by you, it is not to be understood otherwise than that you ought not to love me. This is also the manner of speaking in reference to power and impotence, as when it is said that Hector could be conquered by Achilles, and Achilles could not be conquered by Hector. For it was not power in him who could be conquered but in him who could conquer, nor impotence in him who could not be conquered, but in him who could not conquer.

Disc. I am pleased by what you say, inasmuch as I think it useful to know this.

CHAPTER IX.

That all action signifies either a truth or a falsity.

Mast. You think rightly; but let us return to the truth of signification with which I started that I might lead you from the better known to the less known. For every one speaks of the truth of signification but very few consider the truth which is in the essence of things.

Disc. It has been of great benefit to me that you have led me by this order.

Mast. Let us see then how broad the truth of signification is. For signification is true or false not only in those things which we are accustomed to call signs but also in all other things which we have spoken of. For since nothing must be done by any one except that which he ought to do, by the very fact that any one does anything, he says and signifies that he ought to do that, but if he ought to do that which he does, he tells the truth, but if he ought not to do it, he lies.

Disc. Although it seems clear to me, nevertheless, since I have never before heard it, please expound more fully what you say.

Mast. If you were in a place in which you knew there were salubrious herbs and deadly herbs, but were not able to tell them apart, and if there were some one in that place who, you did not doubt, was able to distinguish them, and if he said to you, when you asked him which were wholesome and which deadly, that some were wholesome and yet ate the others, which would you believe more, his word or his action?

Disc. I should not believe his word as much as his act.

Mast. He would therefore tell you more by act than by word which were wholesome.

Disc. That is so.

Mast. And so, too, if you did not know that one must not lie, and some one lied in your presence, even though he told you that he ought not lie, he would tell you more by his act that he ought to lie than by his word that he ought not. In the same way, while some one thinks or wishes something, if you did not know whether he ought to wish that or think it, if you should perceive his will and thought, he would signify to you by his act itself that he should think it and wish it. But if that were what he ought to do, he would tell the truth; if not, he would lie. There is similarly true or false signification in the existence of things too, since by the very fact that the thing is, it pronounces that it should be.

Disc. This had never before occurred to me, but I see it clearly now.

CHAPTER X.

On the supreme truth.

Mast. Let us proceed to that which remains.

Disc. Proceed and I shall follow.

Mast. You will not, then, deny that the supreme truth is rightness?

Disc. On the contrary, I can say that it is nothing other than that.

Mast. Consider that since all the abovementioned rightnesses are rightnesses in that the things in which they are either are or do that which they ought to: but the supreme truth is not rightness because it has any obligation. All owe it, but it owes nothing to anything, nor is it what it is for any other reason than that it is.

Disc. I understand.

Mast. You see likewise how this rightness is the cause of all other truths and rightnesses, and how nothing is the cause of it?

Disc. I see, and I observe further that among the others some are only effects, whereas others are causes as well as effects, as the truth which is in the existence of things, although it is the effect of the supreme truth, is also the cause itself of the truth which is of thought and of that which is in proposition; and these two latter truths are the cause of no truth.

Mast. You turn it over very well; consequently you can now understand how I proved by the truth of discourse in my *Monologium* [9] that the supreme truth has no beginning or end. In fact, when I said *when it was not true that something was in the future to be,* I did not say it as if the sentence, which asserted that some-

[9] Chapter 18.

thing was to be, was without beginning, or that this truth was God; but since no time could be understood when, if there were this statement, the truth of it would be lacking, so that by the fact that we could not conceive a time when it was possible for this truth not to be, provided there were the means to express it, we may understand that that truth (which is the first cause of this other truth) was without beginning. Certainly the truth of discourse could not always be, if its cause were not always. For discourse which says that something will be, is not true, unless something will in very fact be, nor will anything be unless it is in the supreme truth. The same must be understood of the statement which says *that something has been in the past.* For if truth will in no possible sense be lacking to that statement once the thing has been, it follows necessarily that no end of that truth which is the supreme cause of this truth can be conceived. For something is said truly to have been for this reason, that it is thus in fact, and a thing is past for this reason, that it is thus in the supreme truth. Consequently if it never could not be true that something future will happen, and if it will never possibly not be true, that something which occurred did take place, it is impossible that there should have been a beginning of the supreme truth, or that there will be an end of it.

Disc. I see nothing that can be opposed to your reasoning.

CHAPTER XI.

On the definition of truth.

Mast. Let us return to the investigation of truth which we began.

Disc. All this pertains to investigating truth; however, return to what you wish.

Mast. Tell me then whether there seems to you to be some rightness other than these which we have considered.

Disc. There is no other rightness than these except that which is in corporeal things and which is very much different from these, such as the rightness and straightness of a rod.

Mast. In what does that rightness seem to you to differ from these others?

Disc. In that it can be perceived by the corporeal sight, whereas the others are seized by the contemplation of reason.

Mast. Is not that rightness of bodies understood and known by reason over and beyond the actual subject? Or if it be doubted whether or not the line of some absent body were right and straight or not, and if it can be demonstrated that it is bent in no part, is it not inferred by reason that it must necessarily be right?

Disc. It is. But this same rightness or straightness which is understood thus by reason, is perceived by sight in the subject; whereas these others can be perceived only by the mind.

Mast. We can, therefore, if I am not mistaken, state as definition, that truth is rightness perceptible to the mind alone.

Disc. You seem to me not in the least mistaken in saying that. Certainly this definition of truth contains neither more nor less than is expedient, since the name rightness distinguishes it from every other thing which is not called rightness. And that it is said to be perceived by the mind alone, separates it from visible rightness.

CHAPTER XII.

On the definition of justice.

But since you have taught me that all truth is rightness, and since rightness seems to me to be the same as justice, teach me too what I am to understand that justice is. For it seems that whenever a thing is right, it is also just: and conversely whenever it is just, it is right. For it seems just and right that fire be warm; and that every man requite with love whosoever loves him. For if anything ought to be, it rightly and justly is; nor is anything rightly and justly, except what ought to be. So I think justice can not be other than rightness. For in the supreme and simple nature, although it is not right and just because it has some obligation, nevertheless there is no doubt that rightness and justice are the same.

Mast. Then you have the definition of justice, if justice is nothing other than rightness. And since we speak of truth as rightness perceptible to the mind alone, truth and rightness and justice define each other, so that whoever knows one of them and does not know the others, is able to attain by means of the known to a knowledge of the unknown. Nay rather, he who knows one of them can not be ignorant of the others.

Disc. Why is that? Shall we say a stone is just, when from higher places it seeks the lower, in that it does what it should, just as we call a man just who does what he should?

Mast. We do not ordinarily call a man just because of that kind of justice.

Disc. Why then is a man more just than a stone, if they both act justly?

Mast. Do you yourself not think that the action of a man differs in some way from the action of a stone?

Disc. I know that a man acts voluntarily, a stone naturally and not voluntarily.

Mast. Consequently a stone is not called just, since that is not just which does as it should, if it does not wish that which it does.

Disc. Shall we then call a horse just when he wishes to feed, because wishing it he does what he should?

Mast. I have not said that he who voluntarily does what he should is just; but I said that he is not just who does not do voluntarily what he should.

Disc. Tell me then who is just?

Mast. You seek, as I understand it, a definition of the justice, to which praise is due, just as censure is due its opposite, injustice.

Disc. That is what I seek.

Mast. It is obvious that that justice is not in any nature which does not perceive rightness. For whatsoever does not wish rightness does not merit praise for maintaining it even though it does maintain it. But whatever is ignorant of it, is not able to wish it.

Disc. That is true.

Mast. The rightness therefore which brings praise to one maintaining it, is only in the rational nature which alone perceives the rightness of which we are speaking.

Disc. That follows.

Mast. Therefore since all justice is rightness, the justice, which brings praise to the one who preserves it, is in nowise in any except rational beings.

Disc. It can not be otherwise.

Mast. Where then does it seem to you that this justice is in man since it is rational?

Disc. It is only in his will, or in his knowledge, or in his action.

Mast. But if a person understands rightly, and acts rightly, but does not wish rightly, will any one praise him for justice?

Disc. No.

Mast. Therefore this justice is not rightness of knowledge, or rightness of action, but rightness of will.

Disc. Either it will be this or nothing.

Mast. Does the justice which we seek seem to you to be sufficiently defined?

Disc. It is for you to decide.

Mast. Do you think that he who wills what he should, wills rightly and has rightness of will?

Disc. If any one without knowing it wills what he should, as when he wills to close the door against him who, without the former knowing it, wishes to kill some one else in the house, whether or not he has some rightness of will, he does not have that rightness which we seek.

Mast. What do you say of him who knows that he should will what he wills?

Disc. It can happen that with understanding he wills what he should, and yet would rather not have that obligation. For when a robber is compelled to return stolen money, it is clear that he does not will that he should, although he is compelled to will to return it because he should; but he is in nowise to be praised for this rightness.

Mast. He who feeds the hungering poor for inane glory, is willing to have the obligation which he has accepted; for he is therefore praised, because he wills to do what he should. What do you say about him?

Disc. His rightness is not to be praised, and therefore it does not suffice for the justice which we are seeking. But now show me what does suffice.

Mast. Every will, inasmuch as it wills something, wills as it does because of something. For just as what it willed must be considered, so too must it be seen why it willed. Certainly the will has no more rightness when considered in relation to its object than when considered in relation to its end. Wherefore every will has a *what* and a *why,* for we will absolutely nothing unless there be a reason why we will.

Disc. We recognize all these things in ourselves.

Mast. But what is the end which makes any one's will when it aspires to a proper object a praiseworthy will? As for the object of the will, that is clear: for whosoever wills what he ought not will, that one is not just.

Disc. It seems to me no less clear that just as each one must will what he should, so he must will because he should, in order that his will be just.

Mast. You understand clearly that these two are necessary to the will for justice, namely, that it will *what* it should and *because* it should. But tell me whether these suffice.

Disc. Why not?

Mast. When any one wills *what* he ought to because he is compelled, and is compelled *because* he ought to will it, does he not in a certain sense will *what* he should *because* he should?

Disc. I can not deny that, but he wills in one way whereas the just man wills in another.

Mast. Distinguish between these ways.

Disc. The just man truly preserves the rightness of his will when he wills what he should, not because of something else, so far as he is just, but because of rightness itself. But he who wills what he should only as he is compelled or is led by extraneous reward (if he must be said to preserve rightness) does not preserve it because of itself, but because of something else.

Mast. Therefore that will is to be called just which preserves its rightness because of rightness itself.

Disc. Either that or no will is just.

Mast. Justice is therefore rightness of the will preserved because of itself.

Disc. That is the definition of justice which I sought.

Mast. Nevertheless, consider whether perchance something should be corrected in it.

Disc. I see nothing in it to be corrected.

Mast. Nor I. For there is no justice which is not rightness, nor is any other rightness than that of the will called justice because of itself. For rightness of action is called justice, but only if the action is done with a just will. But rightness of the will, even if it is impossible to do that which we rightly will, by no means loses the name of justice. But since it is said to be preserved, perhaps some one will say, if rightness of the will is to be called justice only when it is preserved, it is not justice as soon as it is had, nor do we receive justice when we receive it, but by preserving it we make it to be justice. For we receive it and have it before we preserve it; we surely do not receive it, nor do we in the first instance have it because we preserve it; but we begin to preserve it because we receive it and have it. But to this we can reply that we begin at the same time both to will and to have it, for we do not have it except by willing; and if we will it, by that very fact, we have it. But as we have it and will it at the same time, so we will it and preserve it at the same time; for just as we do not preserve it except when we will it, so there is no time when we will it and do not preserve it; but so long as we will it, we preserve it; and while we preserve it, we will it. Since therefore it results

that we will it and have it at the same time, and that we
do not will it and preserve it at different times, of
necessity we began at the same time both to have it and
to preserve it. And just as we have it as long as we
preserve it, so, we preserve it as long as we have it;
nor does any inconsistency arise from this. For surely
just as the receiving of this rightness is prior in nature
to having or willing it, since to have it or to will it is
not the cause of receiving it, but receiving it makes the
willing and having it; and nevertheless the receiving,
and the having, and the willing are together in time;
for we begin at the same time to receive it, and to have
it, and to will it; and as soon as we receive it, it is in
us and we will it; so the possession of it and the willing
of it, although they are prior in nature to the preservation of it, are together in time. Wherefore we receive
justice from that from which we receive simultaneously
the having, and the willing, and the preserving of the
rightness of the will, and it must be called justice as
soon as we have and will the same rightness of will.
But we have added *because of itself,* so that it follows
necessarily that that same rightness, unless it is preserved because of itself, is in no wise justice.

Disc. I can think of nothing contrary to that.

Mast. Does it seem to you that this definition can be
fitted to the supreme justice, in so far as we can speak
of that thing concerning which nothing or scarcely anything can properly be said?

Disc. Even though will is one thing and rightness
another only to you, yet, just as we say the power of
divinity, or the divine power, or powerful divinity
(since in divinity power is no different from divinity),
so here we say, not inconsistently, rightness of the will,
or voluntary rightness, or right will. But if we say that
that rightness is conserved because of itself, it seems

that it can be said of no other rightness so aptly. For just as something else does not preserve it, but it preserves itself, and just as it does not preserve itself through something else, but through itself, so it does not preserve itself because of something else, but because of itself.

Mast. And certainly therefore we can say that justice is rightness of the will, which rightness is preserved because of itself. And since we have no passive participle of the present tense of the verb which I use [is preserved, *servatur*], we can use instead of the present the past passive participle of the same verb.

Disc. It is a very common usage to use past passive participles for the present participles which latin does not have. So too there is no past participle to active and neuter verbs, and the present participles are used for the past which are lacking, as when it is said of some one: He teaches only when he is compelled that which, studying and reading, he learned, that is to say, he teaches only when he is compelled, that which he learned when he studied and read.

Mast. Consequently we have been right in saying that justice is rightness of the will preserved because of itself, that is, which is preserved because of itself. And hence it is that the just are sometimes called the right in heart, that is, the right in will; and sometimes the right, without the addition of heart, since the right means no other than him who has a right will. So it is said, *Shout for joy all ye that are right in heart* [10] and also it is said, *The right shall see it and be glad.* [11]

Disc. You have made the definition of justice clear even for children; let us proceed to the other.

[10] *Psalms* 31:11 (or 32:11).
[11] *Psalms* 106:42 (or 107:42).

Chapter XIII.

That truth is one in all true things.

Mast. Let us return to rightness or truth. By these two words (since we speak of rightness perceptible to the mind alone) one single thing is signified, which is the genus of justice. Let us inquire whether there is one single truth in all things in which we say truth is, or whether there are many truths as there are many things in which truth is said to be.

Disc. I desire very much to know that.

Mast. It is clear that in whatever thing it be, truth is no other than rightness.

Disc. I do not doubt that.

Mast. Therefore if there are many truths as there are many things it follows also that there are many rightnesses.

Disc. That too is no less certain.

Mast. If it is necessary that there be a diversity of rightnesses according to the diversity of things, certainly these same rightnesses have their being according to the things themselves, and as the things in which they are vary, so too are the rightnesses necessarily various.

Disc. Show me, in one thing in which we say rightness is, what I am to understand of the others.

Mast. I say that if the rightness of signification is other than the rightness of will because the latter is in the will and the former in signification, then rightness has its being because of signification and changes according to it.

Disc. That is so. For when that which is, is signified to be, or when that which is not, is signified not to be, the signification is right, and it is clear that there is that rightness without which signification can not be right. But if that which is not should be signified to be, or that which is, not to be, or if nothing at all is signified, there will be no rightness of signification which rightness is bound up with signification. Wherefore the rightness of signification has its being through signification and varies according to it, just as color has its being and non-being through body. For when the body exists, its color must necessarily be, and when the body perishes, it is impossible that its color remain.

Mast. Color is not related to body in the same way as rightness to signification.

Disc. Show me the difference.

Mast. If no one should wish to signify by any sign that which must be signified, will there be any signification by sign?

Disc. None.

Mast. Will it on that account not be right that that be signified which should be signified?

Disc. It will not on that account be less right, nor will rightness exact it less.

Mast. Therefore when the signification does not exist, the rightness does not perish, by which it is right and by which it is required that that be signified which must be signified.

Disc. If the rightness had ceased to exist this signification would not be right nor would rightness require it.

Mast. Do you think that when what should be signified, is signified, the right signification is then because of and according to this rightness itself?

Disc. Indeed I can not think otherwise. For if signification were right by some other rightness, then, if that perished there would be nothing to prevent signification being right. But there is no right signification which signifies what it is not right to signify or what rightness does not demand.

Mast. Consequently no signification is right by any rightness other than that which remains when the signification perishes.

Disc. That is clear.

Mast. And so, do you not see that rightness is not in signification because it begins to be at that moment when that which is, is signified to be, or when that which is not, is signified not to be, but because at that moment the signification was made according to the rightness which is always: nor is rightness lacking in a signification because the rightness perishes when the signification is not as it should be, or when there is no signification, but because the signification is then deficient from a rightness which is never deficient?

Disc. I see that so definitely that I can not escape seeing it.

Mast. The rightness therefore by which signification is called right does not acquire being, or any change, through signification, howsoever the signification itself may be changed.

Disc. Nothing is clearer to me now.

Mast. Can you prove that color is related to body in the same way as rightness is related to signification?

Disc. I am more prepared now to prove that they are very much different.

Mast. I think you understand now what should be known concerning the will and its rightness, and concerning other things which should have rightness.

Disc. I see that it has been proved without doubt by this argument that, in whatsoever manner they be, the rightness itself remains immutable.

Mast. And therefore what do you think should be inferred concerning the rightnesses themselves? Are they different one from the other, or is there one and the same rightness for them all?

Disc. I granted above that if there are many rightnesses because there are many things in which they are considered, it is necessary that these exist and vary according to the things themselves, which was demonstrated never to have been the case. Wherefore there are not many rightnesses because there are many things in which they are.

Mast. Do you have any other reason why they seem to you to be many? other than the plurality itself of things?

Disc. As I know that this is no reason, so likewise I think that no other reason could be found.

Mast. Consequently the rightness of all things is one and the same.

Disc. That I must say.

Mast. But further, if rightness is in those things which have rightness only when they are as they should be, and if for them to be right means this alone, it is clear that there is only one rightness for all of them.

Disc. That can not be denied.

Mast. There is consequently only one truth in all these.

Disc. And it is impossible to deny that; but still tell me why we speak of the truth of this and of that thing, as if to distinguish differences of truths, if they take on no diversity from the things themselves? For there are many who will hardly concede that there is no difference between the truth of the will, and that which is spoken of in regard to action, or any of the others.

Mast. Truth is improperly said to be of this or that thing, since truth does not have its being in things, or out of things, or because of things in which it is said to be, but when things are according to that which is always present in those things which are as they should be, then the truth of this or that thing is spoken of, as the truth of word, of action, of will, just as one speaks of the time of this or that thing, although time is one and the same for all things which are together in the same time. And if there were not this or that thing, the same time would none the less be: for one speaks of the time of this or that thing not because time is in the things themselves, but because they are in time. And just as time considered in itself is not said to be the time of anything, but we speak of the time of this or that thing when we consider the things which are in it, so too the supreme truth subsisting in itself is the truth of no thing, but when something is according to truth, then it is called the truth or the rightness of that thing.

PETER LOMBARD (c. 1100-1160/64)

From the thirteenth to the sixteenth century perhaps no single book exercised an influence in education and in the development of philosophical and theological sciences comparable to that of the *Four Books of Sentences* of Peter Lombard. Criticized in his own lifetime, attacked after his death by John of Cornwall, by Joachim of Flora, by Walter of St. Victor (who numbered him among the labyrinths of France), object of an unsuccessful attempt at the Lateran Council in 1215 to condemn his doctrines, little read in the time of Alexander of Hales, his work had become virtually the center of university education by the middle of the thirteenth century. It was usual then and thereafter for a doctor of theology to start on his career with a course on the *Sentences* of Peter Lombard, and most of the outstanding philosophers for centuries to come, Bonaventura, Thomas Aquinas, Duns Scotus, William of Ockham to mention only a few, have left notable statements of their thought in commentaries on the *Four Books of Sentences*. So pervasive was the domination of Peter that Roger Bacon lists among the seven sins of the study of theology the preference of the *Book of Sentences* over the Bible; at Paris, Bacon says, a bachelor who reads the Bible must yield to the reader of the *Sentences*. With the passing of time the domination increased rather than diminished; Gerson would have us believe that in the fifteenth century the Bible was almost forgotten in universities.

None the less, although it became the text book of

185

universities, attempts, which have not been lacking, to
state the doctrine of the *Book of Sentences* have en-
countered little success, since the work is almost entirely
a work of compilation. The very lack of originality
indeed, and the circumstances that the questions are not
always resolved or the opposed authorities reconciled,
may in part account for the rapidly extended adoption
of the work as the basis for courses in theology. The
selection from the *Sentences* which follows, Distinction
III of Book I, on man's knowledge of God and the
Trinity, should indicate sufficiently the method employed by Peter and the manner of his conclusions; the
later selections from Bonaventura and Duns Scotus,
which are commentaries on this distinction, will illustrate the manner of scholastic interpretation of the *Sentences*. The question is announced; then the Scriptures, the fathers and sometimes scholastics are quoted
in solution of the question. The germ of the scholastic
method is in the *Sentences*, although there is lacking the
manipulation of authorities, the acuteness of philosophic
perception, and the sense of systematic philosophy
which might have anticipated the philosophic constructions worked by later scholastics from these materials.

It has been insisted that there is no originality in the
method, the philosophy, or the theology of Peter; that
Walafrid Strabo had anticipated his treatment of
patristic materials in the *Ordinary Gloss* and that Peter
borrows his patristic and conciliar texts from Gratian;
that in the third Book the first three distinctions depend
on John Damascenus so suddenly and so heavily that
they suggest that Peter had come, at the time of their
composition, on the *De fide orthodoxa* of John, newly
translated by Burgundius of Pisa into latin; that the
method, not to say whole passages of text, are copied
from Yves of Chartres, Alcher of Liège, Hugo of St.

Victor and Peter Abailard, (John of Cornwall adds that
Peter was an assiduous student of Abailard, and since
John of Salisbury testifies that Abailard was teaching
again in Paris in 1136, it is not impossible that Peter
attended his courses). Naturally the bulk of material
and doctrine in the work is stated in the words of other
men. Of the church fathers Augustine is quoted by far
the most frequently and extensively; indeed from the
mass of quotations of Augustine in Peter Lombard, as
well as from other indications, such as the manner in
which Aquinas makes use of his doctrines, the role
which Augustine played in the formation of scholastic
thought is inescapably clear. Others of the Fathers
have their place, notably Hilary, Ambrose, Jerome,
Gregory the Great; of the Greeks there are few apart
from John Damascenus and of the antenicenes, few
apart from Origen; Cassiodorus, Isidore of Seville, the
Venerable Bede, Boethius figure importantly but to a
lesser degree.

The *Four Books of Sentences* cover in their scope
the chief problems of theology and range them in a
sequence which was by this time customary. Book I
treats of God: the Trinity, God's attributes, providence,
predestination, evil; Book II of the creation: the work
of the six days, angels, demons, the fall, grace, sin;
Book III of the Incarnation, Redemption, the virtues, the
ten commandments; Book IV of the sacraments, first in
general, then the seven in particular, and the four last
things, death, judgment, hell, heaven. Besides the *Sentences* Peter is known only as the author of commentaries on the Psalms and the Pauline epistles and of
some sermons. But it was as the Master of the Sentences that he achieved fame in the middle ages, and for
all the criticisms of his lack of originality it was a fame
well deserved, for his selections are of rare pertinence,

and his book of quotations reveals often greater force and power of analysis than the extended works of the authors he cites. Not a little, therefore, despite his hesitation to state doctrines of his own and sometimes even to resolve contradictions, he achieves in his presentation, by setting excellent statements of doctrine in support of each other or in opposition, better dialectical demonstrations and better syntheses of doctrines than more exclusively dogmatic theologies have achieved. However that may be, few books have been studied by so many students over so long a period, and speculation returns unavoidably, none the less that the details are impossibly obscure, to the consequences in the formation of later european thought that might depend on some aspect of its long domination in the schools.

PETER LOMBARD

THE IV BOOKS OF SENTENCES

Book I, Distinction III [1]

CHAPTER I.

On knowledge of the Creator through creatures, in whom the trace of the Trinity appears.

For the Apostle says [2] that *the invisible things of God, even his everlasting power and divinity, are clearly seen by the creation of the world, being understood through the things which have been made.* By *creation of the world* man is understood "because of the pre-eminence by which he excels among other creatures or because of the agreement which he has with all creation." [3] Man, therefore, has been able to look on the invisible things of God with the understanding of the mind, or rather he has looked upon them *through the things which have been made,* that is, through creatures visible or invisible. For he was aided by two means, namely, by nature which was rational and by works performed by God that truth might be manifested to man. Therefore the Apostle says,[4] *for God manifested it unto them,* that is, when he performed the works in which the evidence of the artifex in some measure shines forth.

[1] PETRI LOMBARDI, *Libr. IV Sententiarum, studio et cura. PP. Collegii S. Bonaventurae,* Quaracchi, 1916; vol. 1, pp. 30-39.　　　　[2] *Rom.* 1:20.
[3] According to the *Ordinary Gloss.*　　　　[4] *Rom.* 1:19.

For as Ambrose says,[5] "That God, who is invisible
by nature, may be known even by visible things, he
performed work which manifested the worker in its own
visibility that the uncertain may be known through the
certain, and that that God of all, who has done this
which can not be done by man, might be believed to
be." Therefore, they have been able to learn, or they
have known, that beyond all creation there is he who
made what no creature is able to make or destroy. Let
any strength whatever be added to him and let the creature make such a sky and such an earth, and I shall
say that God is. But because no creature is able to
make such things, it follows that above all creation
there is he who made these things; and by that circumstance the human mind has been able to know that he
is God.

In another manner, too, they have been able to learn
and they have known the truth of God by the guidance
of reason.

For, as Augustine says in the book *on the City of
God*: [6] "The greatest philosophers saw that no material
body is God, and therefore when they sought God they
transcended all bodies; they saw likewise that whatever is mutable is not the supreme God and principle
of all things, and therefore they transcended every soul
and the mutable spirits; finally, they saw that whatever
is mutable can be only from him who is immutably and
simply. . . They understood, therefore, both that he
had made all these things and that he could have been
made by none of them.

"They considered, likewise, that whatever is in substances is either body or spirit, and that spirit is some-

[5] *In Epist. ad Rom.*, cap. 1: 19.
[6] Augustinus, *De Civit. Dei*, lib. VIII, cap. 6.

thing better than body, but that that which made spirit
and body is far better.

"They understood, too, that the species of body is
sensible and the species of spirit intelligible, and they
esteemed intelligible species above sensible species. We
call those things sensible which can be perceived by the
sight or touch of the body; those intelligible which can
be understood by the sight of the mind. . . Since,
therefore, in their view both body and mind were more
or less specious [i.e., present in knowledge] and since,
if they should lack all species, absolutely none of them
would be, they saw that there was something by which
those specious [i.e., known] things were made, in which
there is the first and immutable and, therefore, incom-
parable species; and they believed very rightly that that
is the principle of things, which was not made, and from
which all things have been made."

Therefore, the truth of God could be known in a great
many ways. Although, then, God is a single and simple
essence, which consists of no diversity of parts or of
accidents, still the Apostle says in the plural: *the invisible things of God,* because the truth of God is known
in many ways through things which have been made.
For the eternal Author is understood from the perpetuity of creatures; the omnipotent Author from the
magnitude of creatures; the wise Author from their
order and disposition; the good Author from their
governance. But all these relate to revealing the unity
of Deity.

It remains now to show whether any vestige or slight
evidence of the Trinity could be had through things
which have been made.

Concerning this Augustine says in the VIth book *on
the Trinity:* [7] "When with the understanding we look

[7] AUGUSTINUS, *De Trinit.,* cap. 10, n. 12.

upon the Creator by way of things which have been made, we must understand the Trinity. Indeed, the trace of this Trinity appears in creatures. For the things which have been made by the divine art, show in themselves a certain unity and species and order. For each of these created things is at once a single something, such as the natures of bodies and of souls; and is also formed by some species, such as the figures or qualities of bodies and the doctrines or arts of souls; and each of them seeks or preserves some order, such as the weights or locations of bodies and the loves or delights of souls; and so in creatures the trace of the Trinity shines forth. For in that Trinity is the supreme origin of all things and the most perfect beauty and the most blessed delight."

"However, the supreme origin," as Augustine shows in the book *on True Religion* [8] "is understood as God the Father, from whom all things are, from whom the Son and the Holy Spirit are. The most perfect beauty is understood as the Son, that is, the truth of the Father, unlike in no part to him; this truth we venerate with the Father himself and in the Father; it is the form of all things that are made from one and are returned to one; they all, however, would not have been made by the Father through the Son, nor would they have been preserved to their ends, if God were not supremely good, and if he were not one who begrudged no nature that it should be good because of him, and if he were not one who granted that it should remain in the good itself, sometimes as much as it wished, sometimes as much as it was able; this goodness is understood as the Holy Spirit who is the gift of the Father and the Son. Wherefore it is fitting that we love and hold the gift of God equally, immutably with the Father

[8] Augustinus, *De Vera Religione,* cap. 55, n. 113.

and the Son. From the consideration of creatures, therefore, we understand the Trinity of one substance, to wit, one God, the Father, from whom we are, and the Son, through whom we are, and the Holy Spirit, in whom we are, that is the principle to which we return, and the form which we follow, and the grace by which we are reconciled; that is, one by whom as author we are created, and the likeness of him, through which we are reformed to unity, and the peace, by which we adhere to Unity: that is, God who said: *let it be made;* and the Word, by which all that is substantially and naturally is made; and the Gift of his benignity, by which it has pleased him that what was made by him through the Word and was reconciled to its author, should not perish."

It has been shown, then, how the image of the Trinity is revealed in a certain manner in creatures; to be sure no sufficient knowledge of the Trinity can be had, nor could it be had by the contemplation of creatures without the revelation of doctrine or of inward inspiration. Wherefore, those ancient philosophers saw truth as if through a shadow and from a distance, failing in the sight of the Trinity as did the magicians of Pharaoh in the third sign.[9] We are aided, none the less, in the faith of invisible things by the things which have been made.

CHAPTER II.

Concerning the image and likeness of the Trinity in the human soul.

"Now, however, let us proceed to the consideration of where in the human mind, which knows God or can know him, we find the image of the Trinity."[10]

[9] *Exod.* 8:18.
[10] AUGUSTINUS, *De Trinit.*, lib. XIV, cap. 8, n. 11.

For, as Augustine says in the XIVth book *on the Trinity:* [11] "Although the human mind is not of the same nature as God, nevertheless the image of him than whom nothing is better, must be sought and found in that, than which our nature has nothing better, that is, in the mind. For in the mind itself even before it is a partaker of God, his image is found; for, even when the mind is deformed, when it has lost the participation of God, the image of God still remains. Indeed, the mind is the image of God in that by which it is capable of him and by which it can be partaker of him. Therefore, let us seek in it now the Trinity which is God. The mind, then, remembers itself, understands itself, loves itself; if we are aware of this, we are aware of a trinity, not yet God to be sure, but an image of God." A certain trinity appears here of memory, understanding, and love. "These three, therefore, we shall treat principally—memory, understanding, will." [12]

"These three, therefore," as Augustine says in the Xth book *on the Trinity* [13] "are not three lives but one life; not three minds, but one mind, one essence. Memory, of course, is called memory with reference to something, and understanding and will or love are similarly spoken of with reference to something; but life and mind and essence are spoken of with reference to themselves. These three, therefore, are one in that by which they are one life, one mind, one essence; and whatever else they are called severally with reference to themselves, they are also called together, not plurally, but singularly. And they are three in that by which they are referred to each other.

"Equal things likewise are equal not only each to each,

[11] *Ibid.*
[12] Augustinus, o. c., lib. X, cap 11, n. 17.
[13] Augustinus, De Trinit., lib. X, cap. 11, n. 18.

but also each to all; otherwise they would not comprehend each other mutually; but they do comprehend each other. For each is comprehended in each and all in each. For I remember that I have memory and understanding and will; and I understand that I understand and will and remember; and I will that I will and remember and understand, and I remember at the same time my whole memory and understanding and will. Whatever, indeed, of my memory I do not remember, is not in my memory; but nothing is so much in memory as memory itself: therefore, I remember it whole. Again, whatever I understand, I know that I understand, and I know that I will whatever I will; but whatever I know, I remember. Therefore, I remember my whole understanding and my whole will.

"In the same way, when I understand these three, I understand them as a whole at the same time. Nor, indeed, is there any intelligible which I do not understand except that which I do not know. But I neither remember nor will what I do not know. Whatever intelligible therefore I do not understand, I likewise as a consequence neither remember nor will. Whatever intelligible, therefore, I remember and will, I consequently understand.

"My will, too, comprehends my whole understanding and my whole memory, when I employ all that I understand and remember. Since, therefore, all of them and the whole of them are embraced by each of them, each as a whole is equal to each as a whole and each as a whole is equal to all at the same time as wholes; and these three are one, one life, one mind, one essence."

"The human mind, although inadequate, is the image," [14] "then, of this supreme Unity and Trinity, in

[14] AUGUSTINUS, *De Trinit.*, lib. X, cap. 11, n. 18.

which there is one essence and three persons." [15] Mind,
however, is taken here for the soul itself, in which that
image of the Trinity is; "properly, of course," as Augustine says [16] "not the soul itself, but that which is most
excellent in it," as the word is often taken. It should
likewise be known that memory is not only of things
absent and past, but also of present things, as Augustine
says in the XIVth book *on the Trinity*,[17] otherwise it
would not comprehend itself.

In what sense that which has been stated above
should be taken, must be considered very earnestly here,
namely, that these three, memory, understanding, and
will are one, one mind, one essence. Certainly this does
not seem to be true according to the proper meaning of
the words. For mind, that is, rational spirit, is a spiritual and incorporeal essence. But, these three are
natural properties or powers of the mind itself and
differ from each other, because memory is not understanding or will, nor is understanding will or love.

"And these three are also referred to themselves," [18]
as Augustine says in the IXth Book *on the Trinity*: [19]
"for the mind can not love itself or remember itself
unless it also knows itself: for how is it to love or remember what it does not know?" Consequently these
three are in a wondrous way inseparable from each
other; and each of them and all together are still one
essence, even when they are also spoken of relatively to
each other.

But in what way these three are called one substance
must be seen now; clearly, because they exist substan-

[15] Augustinus, *De Trinit.*, lib. XV, cap. 7, n 11.

[16] Augustinus, *De Trinit.*, lib. XV, cap. 7, n. 11.

[17] Augustinus, *De Trinit.*, lib. XIV, cap. 11, n. 14.

[18] Augustinus, *De Trinit.*, lib. X, cap. 11, n. 18.

[19] Augustinus, *De Trinit.*, lib. IX, cap. 3, n. 3.

tially in the very soul or mind, not as accidents in subjects, which can be present or absent.

Whence Augustine in the IXth book *on the Trinity* says: [20] "We are admonished that, if we can see in any way at all, these [i.e. love and knowledge] exist in the mind substantially, not as in a subject, as color in body, because, even though they are spoken of relatively to each other, each of them is nevertheless substantially in its substance."

Consider, then, in what sense these three are said to be one or one substance. "Whoever perceives distinctly," as Augustine says in the XVth book *on the Trinity* [21] "these three instituted by nature divinely in the mind and whoever remembers by memory, contemplates by understanding, embraces by love, how great that is in the mind by which even the eternal and immutable nature can be recalled, conceived, desired, he assuredly finds the image of that supreme Trinity."

CHAPTER III.

On the likeness of the creating and the created Trinity.

"Nevertheless he should take care, lest he so compare to that same Trinity this image made by it, that he judge it wholly similar, but rather he should discern in that likeness, of whatever sort it be, a great unlikeness too." [22]

"This can be shown briefly. One man, who is not memory, nor understanding, nor love, but who has them, remembers, understands, loves by the three of them. There is, therefore, one man who has these three, but

---

[20] AUGUSTINUS, *De Trinit.*, lib. IX, cap. 4, n. 5.
[21] AUGUSTINUS, *De Trinit.*, lib. XV, cap. 20, n. 39.
[22] *Ibid.*

is not himself the three. In the simplicity, however, of that supreme nature which is God, although God is one, nevertheless there are three persons, the Father, the Son, and the Holy Spirit," [23] and these three are one God. "The thing itself, then, the Trinity, is one matter, the image of the Trinity in some other thing is another; on account of this image, that in which the three are, is likewise called an image, to wit, man. In the same way both the panel and the picture which is on it are called an image; but the panel is called by the name of the image because of the picture which is on it." [24]

"Again that image which is man and which has these three is one person. But that Trinity is not one person, but three persons, the Father of the Son and the Son of the Father and the Spirit of the Father and the Son. Consequently, in the image of the Trinity these three are not one man but of one man. But in that supreme Trinity, of which this is the image, these three are not of one God, but one God; and they are three persons, not one." [25] "The former three, indeed, are not man, but they are of man or they are in man. But can we say that the Trinity is so in God that it is something of God and it is not itself God?" [26] May we be preserved from such belief! Let us say, rather, that the image of the Trinity is in our mind, but a poor one of some sort, which bears the likeness of the supreme Trinity in such a fashion that it is for the greatest part unlike it.[27] But it must be known that "this Trinity of the mind," as Augustine says in the XIVth book *on the Trinity* [28] "is not the image of God so much because the mind remembers and understands and loves itself, but rather be-

[23] AUGUSTINUS, *De Trinit.*, lib. XV, cap. 22, n. 42.
[24] *Ibid.*, n. 43.   [25] *Ibid.*
[26] AUGUSTINUS, *De Trinit.*, lib. XV, cap. 7, n. 11.
[27] Cf. *Ibid.*, cap. 22, n. 43.
[28] AUGUSTINUS, *De Trinit.*, lib. XIV, cap. 12, n. 15.

cause it can also remember and understand and love him by whom it was made."

Furthermore the Trinity can be distinguished in another way and by other names in the soul, which is the image of that supreme and ineffable Trinity.

As, indeed, Augustine says in the IXth book *on the Trinity*: [29] "The mind and its knowledge and its love are three things. For the mind knows itself and loves itself; and it can not love itself unless it also knows itself. The mind and its knowledge are two things; again, the mind and its love are two things." "When, therefore, the mind knows itself and loves itself, the Trinity continues, to wit, mind, love, and knowledge." [30] "But the mind is not taken here as the soul, but as that which is most excellent in the soul." [31] These three, however, although they are distinct from each other, are nevertheless said to be one, because they exist substantially in the soul.

And the mind itself is, as it were, the parent, and its knowledge is, as it were, its offspring. "The mind, indeed, when it knows itself, gives birth to the knowledge of itself and is the sole parent of its knowledge. . . The third is love, which proceeds from the mind itself and from knowledge, when the mind knowing itself loves itself; for it could not love itself if it did not know itself. Furthermore, it loves its pleasing offspring, that is, its knowledge; and so love is a certain embrace of parent and offspring. Nor is the offspring less of the parent since the mind knows itself as much as it is; nor is the love less than the parent and the offspring, that is, than the mind and knowledge, since the mind only loves itself, as much as it knows itself and

---

[29] AUGUSTINUS, *De Trinit.*, lib. IX, cap. 4, n. 4.

[30] *Ibid.*, cap. 5, n. 8.

[31] AUGUSTINUS, *De Trinit.*, lib. XV, cap. 7, n. 11.

as much as it is." [32] "Moreover these are each in themselves, because the mind loving is in love, and love is in the knowledge of the mind loving, and knowledge is in the mind knowing." [33]

Therefore, in these three a kind of trace of the Trinity appears.

Consequently, the rational mind considering these three and that one essence in which they are, extends itself to the contemplation of the Creator and sees unity in trinity and trinity in unity. For it understands that there is one God, one essence, one principle. It understands, also, that if there were two, either both would be insufficient or one would be superfluous; because if something were lacking to one, which the other had, there would not be supreme perfection in it; but if nothing were lacking to one which the other had, since all things would be in one, the other would be superflous. The rational mind has understood, therefore, that there is one God, one author of all things, and it has seen that he is not without wisdom, as if a senseless thing; and therefore it has understood that he has wisdom, which was born of him; and because he loves his wisdom, it has understood too that love is there.[34]

CHAPTER IV.

On the Unity of the Trinity.

"Wherefore, in accordance with that consideration," as Augustine says in the IXth book *on the Trinity*,[35] "let us believe that the Father and the Son and the

---

[32] AUGUSTINUS, *De Trinit.*, lib. IX, cap. 12, n. 18.
[33] AUGUSTINUS, *De Trinit.*, lib. IX, cap. 5, n. 8.
[34] Cf. HUGO SANCT. VICT. *Summa Sent.* tr. 1, cap. 6.
[35] AUGUSTINUS, *De Trinit.*, lib., IX, cap. 1, n. 1.

Holy Spirit are one God, maker and ruler of all creation; and that the Father is not the Son, nor is the Holy Spirit either the Father or the Son, but a Trinity of persons related to each other."

As, moreover, he says in the book *on Faith to Peter*: [36] "There is one nature or essence of the Father and the Son and the Holy Spirit, not one person. For if there were one person, as there is one substance of the Father and the Son and the Holy Spirit, it would not truly be called a trinity. Further, if in the way that the Father and the Son and the Holy Spirit are distinct from each other by the propriety of persons, they had likewise been discrete by a diversity of natures, the trinity would have been true, but the Trinity itself would not have been one God. The faith, however, of the Patriarchs, of the Prophets, and of the Apostles proclaims that one God is the Trinity." "In that holy Trinity, therefore, one God is the Father who alone gave birth of himself essentially to one Son; and one Son who alone was born essentially of one Father; and one Holy Spirit who alone proceeded essentially from the Father and the Son. One person, however, can not do all this, that is, give birth to himself and be born of himself and proceed from himself." [37] For as Augustine says in the Ist book *on the Trinity*: [38] "There is no thing which, in order that it be, gives birth to itself."

[36] AUGUSTINUS, *De Fide ad Petrum,* cap. 1, n. 4.
[37] *Ibid.,* n. 6.
[38] AUGUSTINUS, *De Trinit.,* lib. I, cap. 1, n. 1.

PETER ABAILARD (1079-1142)

The name of Abailard and some traits and incidents of his life are perhaps most known of the current lore concerning medieval thinkers. The interest in him, however, is limited in its accuracy, and its scope usually includes no more than the romantic episodes of his career. It is possible that popular interest indicates accurately that his significance is as a personality rather than as an original philosopher. He was a penetrating spirit, a vigorous dialectician, a great professor; the efforts to make him out an initiator, the founder of a system, the discoverer of the scholastic method encounter serious historical and philosophical difficulties. There are indications to suggest that his personal influence was greater and broader than his remaining works could show; and for corroborating emphasis, it should be added that not all his works have been published. As late as 1919 a hitherto unpublished treatise which added considerably to his philosophic stature (and from which the following selection was translated) appeared. It is incontestable, in any case, that his work was important preparation for the thirteenth century, and his acute analyses are valuable testimony of the problems that agitated the masters of the twelfth century; his teaching was among the most powerful forces preparing in his century for the aristotelianizing of philosophy.

The characteristics of Abailard's thought may, indeed, be accounted for by the times in which he lived. Had he possessed the philosophical materials which

were to become available in the thirteenth century by
translations from the greek, arabic and hebrew, he
might conceivably have elaborated a system comparable
to those of the great aristotelians who followed after
Thomas Aquinas. One has the impression of slight philosophic scope for all the penetration that his philosophy displays, and yet despite the paucity of his materials he was able to reconstruct aristotelian doctrines
with a nice sense of intellectual fitness. But even for
his own century his philosophic erudition was slighter
than it need have been; the contemporary masters of
the school of Chartres were, for example, better versed
in Aristotle and in the sciences than he was. His interests and his doctrines seem to have been determined
by the masters under whom he successively studied. He
learned something of dialectic under Roscelin; later he
attacked in three of his works Roscelin's nominalistic
doctrine of the universal and his supposed tritheistic
doctrine of the trinity, and in final defense of himself
he wrote a letter to the Bishop of Paris defaming Roscelin's doctrine and person. He studied under William
of Champeaux, and by his repeated criticisms forced
William to modify his realist position on the doctrine
of the universals and eventually to retire from his chair.
He studied theology under Anselm of Laon; while
studying under him he attempted a commentary to show
how theology might be presented and wrote of Anselm
that he was a tree burdened with leaves but no fruit, a
fireplace from which came a great deal of smoke but no
light. Yet one may hazard that his own position on
the universal was not uninfluenced by the doctrine of
Roscelin, and that the celebrated method of the *Sic et
non* was not unrelated to that employed in the *Sentences*
of William and Anselm.

The doctrine of the universal which Abailard finally

states in his commentary on Porphyry may be said to
be the solution with which the twelfth century closed
its acute and isolated discussion of the problem. For
the thirteenth century it was only one among many
problems in the context of a rounded philosophy. Abailard's discussion of the universal naturally derives much
from Boethius, for the selection which follows, although
it is from a work which is designated a gloss on Porphyry, could more properly be called a commentary
on the selection from Boethius which is translated above.
It is interesting indication of the change of philosophic
emphasis in six centuries that Boethius should have
devoted two-thirds of his discussion to the utility of the
study of logic while Abailard spends four-fifths of his
commentary on that discussion in the intricacies of the
problem of the universal. He adds a fourth to the
three questions of Porphyry which opened the problem
to Boethius, whether the reality of genera and species
is dependent upon the existence of individuals belong-
ing to them; but apart from that, his additions are in
the subtleties implied in and dependent on the answers
to the questions suggested, rather than in the discovery
of new questions. The solution of Abailard is an
aristotelian moderate realism; in its essential features
his statement of the doctrine is not much different from
the statement of Hugo of Saint Victor; John of Salisbury too agrees in this resolution, and in it numbers
Abailard among his friends.

Universals are words, not *voces* (the doctrine of
Roscelin which John of Salisbury says had practically
disappeared with its author) but *nomina*. There are,
strictly, no universal things, for only individual things
exist. Human language however is composed of con-
ventional words which are general in form. Such words
(*voces*) cover general and abstract notions; nouns

(*nomina*), according to Boethius, are words set in the relation of signified content. *Nomen est vox significativa.* The difference between a universal and a particular is reduced to the difference between an appellative and a proper noun. The appellative noun, the universal, is susceptible of being predicated of many individuals, whereas the proper noun can be predicated of only one. Yet the universal word does not indicate a universal thing, rather it forms a certain conception which is common to the individuals it names. Its universality consists in the multitude of individuals named by it in that common likeness. The conception which is formed in the universal is faithful but inadequate to particular existences; each element of the conception is true, but things do not exist as they are conceived. Spirit works *divisim* but does not affirm concerning *divisa.* The difference therefore between the proper and the universal is the difference between sensible, imaginative knowledge and abstractive knowledge. Yet the content of abstract perception is based on the data of sensation, much as the design of a painting is seen by means of colors.

In the case of Àbailard's doctrine of the universal as in the case of his other doctrines it is difficult to estimate the place and importance of his thought either in his age or as a contribution to philosophy. The acumen, pertinence, insight of his criticism of doctrines (and his criticism of contemporaries is frequent and acrimonious) has tended to give an importance to his own views in the eyes of investigators; his letters and his *History of Calamities,* which have furnished autobiographical details such as are relatively unusual in the middle ages, have tended to give his personality an unwonted prominence. His *Scito te ipsum, seu Ethica,* one of the rare ethical treatises of the century, has seemed to enforce the originality of his turn of mind, particularly since grave errors were discovered in it by St. Bernard of Clairvaux. The fragments of his theological treatises, the *De unitate et trinitate divina,* the *Theologica christiana,* the *Introductio ad theologiam,* the *Epitome,* since they probably represent the doctrines for which he was condemned by two councils, have furthered the reputation which he sometimes enjoys of an original and free thinker. And the *Sic et non* has been read usually to contribute verisimilitude to that reputation as well as to lend color to the contention that he originated the scholastic method. Yet his doctrine of the Trinity, his attitude toward authority, his method, were not peculiar to him, save in the sense that controversy with some one opponent may have forced him to defend an opposed ancient doctrine and in the sense that a keen logical perception sharpened in his use the customary mode of argumentation and presentation. The *Sic et non* is thus a compilation, like the early *Quaestiones* or *Sententiae,* of texts from the Scriptures and the church fathers on 158 important questions of religion. The arrangement has this much of novelty, that the texts are apparently contradictory texts, and the problems they present are not resolved. They were not collected, however, as is frequently supposed, to ruin the principle of authority, but rather to raise the questions and to stir the mind to solve them. Abailard does not presume to substitute reason for faith, for he seems never to have varied from the principle that authority passes before reason, and that the chief use of reason is to clarify the truths of faith and to refute the infidels. To be sure he ridicules frequently the fervor of faith which leads some to believe before they understand of what it is question, without even inquiring whether such things should be

admitted or should be submitted to discussion according
to one's power. But he ridicules too the presumption
of professors of dialectic who are easily drawn into
heresy where, believing themselves well-armed with
reason, they permit themselves to attack or defend anything. His own statement to Héloïse is accurate estimation of the freedom of his thought: that he would not
wish to be a philosopher if it were necessary to contradict St. Paul; that he would not wish to be an Aristotle if it were necessary to separate himself from
Christ, for in no other name under heaven could he be
saved; the stone, he concludes, on which he founded his
conscience was the stone on which Christ had built his
Church and he was founded on a firm stone.

Abailard's condemnation by the Church was not as a
radical or as an innovator. He was influential over a
legion of thinkers, and the danger was that his
thoughts seemed to lead to paganism. Apart from the
particular errors his prosecutors named, they never for-
got that he thought the christian truth and the pagan
truth were essentially one, that Plato was nearer, for
example, to a knowledge of the trinity than was Moses,
for Plato's knowledge of nature and the revelations
vouchsafed him from God left only a few of the
mysteries of Christianity beyond his grasp. The horror
of this was clearly present in the mind of Bernard when
he wrote his treatise *On the Errors of Abailard,* for he
complains that when Abailard sweats blood and water
to make Plato a christian, he proves only that he is
himself a pagan. It was another battle than that of
rational skepticism that Abailard fought, and doubtless
the justice that led to his condemnation in the twelfth
century would have procured the same effect today.

PETER ABAILARD

THE GLOSSES OF PETER ABAILARD ON PORPHYRY [1]

We may open our introduction to logic by examining something of the characteristic property of logic in its genus which is *philosophy*. Boethius says that not any knowledge whatever is philosophy, but only that which consists in the greatest things; for we do not call all wise men philosophers, but only those whose intelligence penetrates subtle matters. Moreover, Boethius distinguishes three species of philosophy, *speculative,* which is concerned with speculation on the nature of things, *moral,* for the consideration of the honorableness of life, *rational,* for compounding the relation of arguments, which the greeks call logic. However, some writers separated logic from philosophy and did not call it, according to Boethius, a part of philosophy but an instrument, because obviously the other parts work in logic in a manner, when they use its arguments to prove their own questions. As, if a question should arise in natural or moral speculation, arguments are derived from logic. Boethius himself holds, against them, that there is nothing to prevent the same thing from being both an instrument and a part of a single thing, as the hand is both a part and an instrument of the human

[1] PETER ABAELARDS *Philosophische Schriften, herausgegeben von Dr. Bernhard Geyer, I Die Logica "Ingredientibus,"* in *Beiträge zur Geschichte der Philosophie des Mittelalters, Band XXI,* Heft I, pp. 1-32.

body. Logic moreover seems itself often its own instrument when it demonstrates a question pertaining to itself by its own arguments, as for example: *man is the species of animal.* It is none the less logic, however, because it is the instrument of logic. So too it is none the less philosophy because it is the instrument of philosophy. Moreover, Boethius distinguishes it from the other two species of philosophy by its proper end, which consists in compounding arguments. For although the physicist compounds arguments, it is not physics but only logic which instructs him in that.

He noted too in regard to logic that it was composed of and reduced to certain rules of argumentation for this reason, namely, lest it lead inconstant minds into error by false inferences, since it seems to construct by its reasons what is not found in the nature of things, and since it seems often to infer things contrary in their conditions, in the following manner: *Socrates is body, but body is white, therefore Socrates is white.* On the other hand: *Socrates is body, but body is black, therefore Socrates is black.*

Moreover in writing logic the following order is extremely necessary that since arguments are constructed from propositions, and propositions from words, he who will write logic perfectly, must first write of simple words, then of propositions, and finally devote the end of logic to argumentations, just as our prince Aristotle did, who wrote the *Categories* on the science of words, the *On Interpretation* on the science of propositions, the *Topics* and the *Analytics* on the science of argumentations.

Porphyry himself moreover as the very statement of the title shows, prepares [2] this introduction for the *Categories* of Aristotle, but later he himself shows that

[2] See above, p. 77.

it is necessary to the whole art. The *intention* of it, the *matter*, the *manner of treatment*, the *utility* or *the part of dialectic to which the present science is to be subordinated*, will now be distinguished briefly and precisely.

The *intention* is particularly to instruct the reader in the *Categories* of Aristotle, that he may be able to understand more easily the things that are there treated. This makes necessary the treatment of the five subjects which are its materials, namely genus, species, difference, property, and accident. He judged the knowledge of these to be particularly useful to the *Categories* because the investigation is concerning them in almost the whole course of the *Categories*. That which we spoke of as five, however, can be referred to the words, genus, species and the others and also in a certain sense to the things signified by them. For he appropriately makes clear the significance of these five words which Aristotle uses, lest one be ignorant, when one has come to the *Categories,* of what is to be understood by these words; and he is able, moreover, to treat of all the things signified by these words, as if of five things, since, although they are infinite taken singly, inasmuch as genera are infinite and likewise species and the others, nevertheless as has been said, all are considered as five, because all are treated according to five characteristics, all genera according to what constitutes genera, and the others in the same way, for in this same way the eight parts of speech are considered according to their eight characteristics, although taken singly they are infinite.

The *manner of treatment* here is the following: having first distinguished the natures of each singly in separate treatments of them, he proceeds then for further knowledge of them to their common properties and characteristics.

Its *utility,* as Boethius himself teaches, is principally

as it is directed to the *Categories*. But it is spread in
four directions which we shall disclose more carefully
later when he himself takes it up.[3]

If the parts of logic have first been distinguished
carefully, it is seen at once what is the part through
which the science of the present work leads to logic.
On the authority of Cicero and Boethius [4] there are two
parts of which logic is composed, namely, the science of
discovering arguments and of *judging* them, that is, of
confirming and proving the arguments discovered. For
two things are necessary to one who argues, first to find
the arguments by which to argue, then if any should
criticize the arguments as defective or as insufficiently
firm to be able to confirm them. Wherefore Cicero says
that discovery is by nature prior. The present science,
however, is concerned with both parts of logic, but most
of all with discovery. And it is a part of the science
of discovering. For how can an argument be deduced
from genus or species or the others, if the things which
are here treated are not known? Wherefore Aristotle
himself introduces the definition of the predicables into
the *Topics,* when he treats of their places, as Cicero
likewise does in his *Topics.* But since an argument is
confirmed from the same considerations from which it
is discovered, this science is not unrelated to judgment. For, as an argument is derived from the nature
of genus and species, so, once derived, it is confirmed
from the nature of genus and species. For considering
the nature of species in man, so far as it is related to
animal, I find at once from the nature of the species the
argument for proving animal. But if any one should
criticize the argument, I show that it is suitable immediately by indicating the nature of the species and
the genus in both, so that from the same conditions of

[3] See above, p. 81.   [4] See above, p. 74.

the terms the argument may be found and when it has
been found it may be confirmed.

There are some nevertheless who separate this science
[i.e. the *Isagoge*] and the science of the categories and
of the divisions and of definitions and even of propositions completely from discovery and judgment, nor do
they count it in any sense among the parts of logic,
although, for all that, they think such subjects are necessary to the whole of logic. But authority as well as
reason seems contrary to them. For Boethius *On the
Topics of Cicero* asserts a double division of dialectic,
both parts of which so include each other reciprocally
that they each comprise the whole of dialectic. The
first part is through the science of discovery and judgment; the second through the science of division, definition and collection. He reduces each of these to the
other so that in the science of discovery (which is one
of the two divisions of the above classification) he includes also the science of division or definition, for the
reason that arguments are deduced from divisions as
well as from definitions. Wherefore the science of genus
and of species or of the others may also be adapted for a
similar reason to discovery. Boethius himself says that
the treatise on the *Categories* comes first among the
books of Aristotle for those beginning logic. From this
it is apparent that the *Categories,* in which the reader
has his introduction to logic, are not to be separated
from logic, particularly since the distinction of the categories supplies the greatest strength to the argumentation, since the nature, to which each thing pertains or
does not pertain, can be established by it. The peculiar
study of propositions [i.e. the *On Interpretation*] likewise is not unrelated to that of arguments, since it proves
now this, now that, as contrary or contradictory or
opposed in any other manner whatever. Therefore,

since all treatises of logic converge to the end of logic, that is to argumentation, we separate the knowledge of none of them from logic.

Having examined these things let us begin the literal commentary.

Since it is necessary, etc.[5] He places first an introduction concerning the subject matter of which he will write, in which he indicates the subject matter itself and gives assurance of the utility of the book and promises that he will write in an introductory manner concerning that which philosophers have judged rightly of these things. There are however three accustomed meanings of the word *necessary,*[6] since it is sometimes used to mean *inevitable,* as, *it is necessary that substance is not quality,* sometimes to mean *useful,* as, *to go to the forum,* sometimes to mean *determined,* as, that *man will die some time.* The first two meanings of necessary obviously are of such sort that they seem to contend with each other with respect to which of them can be taken more properly here. For it is both the highest necessity to know these things first that one may proceed to others, since without the former the latter can not be known, and it is an obvious utility. If however any one should consider seriously the context, he will decide that *useful* is meant more properly than *inevitable.* For since Porphyry supplies the thing for which he says it is necessary, as if intending some sort of relation to something else, he suggests the meaning of utility. For useful, has reference to something else; inevitable is so called because of itself.

Construe it thus: it is necessary, that is, useful, to know what genus is, etc., that is, what the characteristics of each are. This is shown in their definitions which are assigned not according to their substance but ac-

[5] See above, p. 81.   [6] See above, p. 82.

cording to their accidental properties, since the name of genus and the name of the others do not designate substance but accident. Wherefore we interpret that *what* according to property rather than substance. *As well for that,* etc. He brings forward four points in which he shows a fourfold utility, as we noted above, namely, categories, definitions, divisions, demonstrations, that is, arguments, which demonstrate the question proposed. *Which,* that is, the knowledge of categories, *is in Aristotle,* that is, is contained in his treatise. For a book is sometimes designated by the name of its author, as for example Lucian. *And for the imposition of definitions,* that is, for imposing and compounding definitions. *And in general.* Likewise these five predicables are useful *for those things which are in division and demonstration,* that is, in argumentation. And since it is necessary, that is, it is useful to so many things to know these things, *I shall try to approach what has been said by the ancients, making a rendering for you,* that is, a treatise, *concerning the contemplation of such things,* that is, concerning the consideration of these five predicables, I say a *compact* rendering, that is, moderately short. This he explains immediately, saying: *briefly* and *as in an introductory manner.* For too much brevity may introduce too great obscurity, according to that saying of Horace: *I labor to be brief, I become obscure.* Therefore lest the reader be distrustful because of brevity or lest he be confused because of prolixity, he promises to write in an introductory manner. But, how this work may be of use as well to the categories as to the other three subjects, Boethius himself states carefully enough,[7] but still let us touch on it briefly.

And first let us show how each of the treatments of these five predicables is proper to the categories.

[7] See above, p. 84

Knowledge of *genus* pertains to the categories because
Aristotle there sets forth the ten supreme genera of all
things, in which categories he comprehends the infinite
meanings of the names of all things: but how they are
the genera of other things can not be known, unless it is
preceded by a knowledge of genera. The knowledge of
species likewise is not unrelated to the categories; without that knowledge there can be no knowledge of genus;
for since they are relative to each other they draw their
essence and knowledge from each other. Wherefore it
is necessary to define one by the other, as Porphyry
himself states.[8] *Difference,* too, which when joined to
the genus completes the species, is necessary to distinguishing species as well as to distinguishing genus: in
stating the division of the genus, the difference shows
the signification of that which the species contains.
Many things, moreover, are brought forth by Aristotle
in the *Categories* where these three, genus, species, difference, are taken up; if they were not first known those
further conclusions could not be understood. One of
these is the rule: *Things of diverse genera* etc.[9] The
knowledge of *property* too is of help because Aristotle himself speaks of the properties of the categories,
as when he says that the property of substance is that
since it is one and the same in number, etc. Therefore,
lest the nature of property be ignored at that later point,
it must be demonstrated now. Still this must be noted,
that Porphyry treats only of the properties of the most
special species, whereas Aristotle investigates the properties of genera; but nevertheless the nature of those
properties [of genera] is made clear through the similarity of these [of the most special species], for the
properties of genera are described in the same way as
the properties of species, namely, that the property be-

[8] See above, pp. 84-85.   [9] See above, p. 85.

longs only to that one species, to every individual of that species, and at all times. Who will doubt the extent to which the knowledge of *accident* is valuable to the categories, when he finds in nine of the categories only accidents? Besides Aristotle frequently and earnestly seeks out the properties of those things which are *in the subject,* that is, of accidents, to which especially pertains the treatment of accident. The knowledge of accident is also profitable to the distinguishing of difference or property, because difference and property will not be known perfectly if the distinction of accident is not had.

Now, however, let us show how the same five predicables are valuable for *definitions*. Definition, of course, is either substantial or it is description. Substantial, on the one hand, which is only of species, uses genus and differences, and therefore the treatment of genus as well as of difference or species is valuable to it. But description is frequently derived from accidents. Wherefore knowledge of accident is particularly valuable to it. Knowledge of property moreover is generally present in all definitions which have a likeness to property in this respect, that they too are converted with that which is defined.

The five predicables also are so necessary to *divisions* that without a knowledge of them division is made by chance rather than by reason. This assertion must be tested in connection with the several divisions. There are three kinds of essential division, namely, division of genus, of whole, and of word; again, three kinds of accidental division, namely, when the accident is divided into subjects, or the subjects into accidents, or the accident into accidents. The division of genus is sometimes made into species, and sometimes into differences asserted for species. Wherefore genus as well as species and difference is needed for that division; and the same three contribute to the distinction of the division of whole and of word, which might be confused with the divisions of genus, if the nature of the genus were not first known, as e.g. that the entire genus is predicated univocally of each species, whereas the whole is not predicated singly of the parts composing it, and the word which has multiplex applications is not adapted to its divisions univocally. The predicables are therefore also extremely useful for the division of equivocal words for the following reason, that they were useful for definitions, for from definitions it is known what is equivocal or what is not. For the accidental division likewise, the knowledge of accident, by which such division is constituted, is necessary, and the other predicables too are valuable for making the distinction of that division, otherwise we should divide genus into species or difference, as we divide accident into subjects.

The knowledge of the five predicables, as we have stated above, is obviously valuable too for discovering *argumentations* or for confirming them once they have been discovered. For we find arguments and we confirm them, when they have been found, according to the nature of genus and of species or the others. Boethius moreover in this place calls them the five seats of syllogisms,[10] against which statement it might be said that we do not accept places [*topoi*] in the perfect combination of syllogisms. But certainly that special word is used loosely instead of the genus, that is, speaking of syllogism instead of argumentation, otherwise Boethius would lessen the utility if he directed this knowledge only to syllogisms and not generally to all argumentations, which are similarly called demonstrations by Porphyry. Moreover, in a certain sense it is

[10] See above, p. 90.

possible to assign places in the perfect combination of syllogisms, not that they belong to syllogisms *per se,* but because they too can be adduced as evidence of syllogisms in that they afford confirmation of enthymemes which are deduced from syllogisms. Now, however, that these things have been stated concerning utility, let us return to the literal interpretation.

From the more lofty questions.[11] He states further how he will preserve the introductory manner, namely, by abstaining from difficult questions and from questions involved in obscurity and by treating in an ordinary way the more simple ones. Nor is it without meaning that he says *in an ordinary way:* for a thing may be easy in itself and still not be treated lucidly.

At present concerning genera.[12] He states definitely what those more lofty questions are, although he does not resolve them. And the cause is stated for both actions, namely, that he should pass over inquiring into them and nevertheless should make mention of them. For he does not treat of them for this reason, because the uncultivated reader is not able to inquire into them or perceive them. But on the other hand he mentions them lest he make the reader negligent. For if he had ignored them entirely, the reader, thinking there was absolutely nothing more to be inquired concerning them, would disdain altogether the inquiry into them. There are then three questions, as Boethius says,[13] secret and very useful and tried by not a few philosophers, but solved by few. The *first* is as follows, namely, whether genera and species subsist or are placed in the naked understandings alone, etc., as if he were to say: whether they have true being or whether they consist in opinion alone. The *second* is, if they are conceded to be truly,

---

[11] See above, p. 81.   [13] See above, p. 91.
[12] See above, p. 91.

whether they are corporeal essences or incorporeal, and
the *third* is whether they are separated from sensibles
or are placed in them. For the species of incorporeal
beings are two,[14] in that some incorporeal beings, such
as God and the soul, can subsist in their incorporeality
apart from sensibles, and others are in nowise able to
be beyond the sensible objects in which they are, as
line cannot be found except in a body. These questions, however, he passes over in this fashion, saying:
*At present I shall refuse to say concerning genera and
species this, whether they subsist*, etc., *or whether subsisting they are corporeal or incorporeal, or whether,*
when they are said to be incorporeal, they should be
separated *from sensibles,* etc., *and in accord with them.*
This last can be taken in different ways. For it can be
taken this way, as if to say: I will refuse to make the
three assertions stated above concerning them and certain other statements in accord with these, that is, these
three questions. In the same way, other questions which
are difficult can be brought up concerning them, such as,
the question of the common cause of the imposition of
universal nouns, namely, what is that cause in virtue
of which different things agree, or again the question
of the understanding of universal nouns, in which no
particular thing seems to be conceived, nor does the
universal word seem to deal with any such particular
thing, and many other difficult questions. We are able
so to expound the words, *and in accord with them* that
we may add a fourth question, namely, whether genera
and species, so long as they are genera and species,
must have some thing subject to them by nomination,
or whether, if the things named were destroyed, the
universal could still consist of the meaning only of the
conception, as this noun *rose* when there is not a single

[14] See above, p. 92.

rose to which it is common. But we shall investigate these questions more carefully later.

Now, however, let us follow the introduction literally. Note that when Prophyry says: *at present,* that is, in the present treatise, he intimates in a way that the reader may expect these questions to be solved elsewhere. *Most exalted business.* He states the reason for which he abstains here from these questions, namely, because to treat them is very exalted with respect to the reader who may not be able to attain to them in order to determine this business now. *And requiring greater diligence of inquiry,* for although the author is able to solve it, the reader is not able to inquire into it. Greater diligence of inquiry, I say, than yours. *This, however.*[15] Having stated these things concerning which he is silent, he states those which he does treat of, namely, that which *the ancients,* not in age but in comprehension, *concluded probably,* that is, with verisimilitude, that is in which all have agreed and there was no dissension, *concerning these things,* to wit, genus and species *and of the* other three *things mentioned.* For in resolving the aforesaid questions some are of one opinion and others of another. Wherefore Boethius[16] records that Aristotle held that genera and species subsist only in sensibles but are understood outside them, whereas Plato held not only that they were understood without sensibles but that they actually were separate. *And of these the ancients,* I say, and *most of all the peripatetics,* that is, part of these ancients; he calls dialecticians or a kind of argumentators the peripatetics.

Note likewise that the functions which are proper to introductions can be distinguished in this introduction. For Boethius says *on the Topics of Cicero: Every introduction which is intended to compose the reader, as*

[15] See above, p. 98.   [16] See above, p. 98.

is said in the Rhetoric, *seizes on benevolence or prepares attention or produces docility.* For it is proper that any one of the three or several at the same time be present in every introduction; but two are to be noted in this introduction, docility when he sets forth the material, which is those five predicables, and attention when he commends the treatise for a fourfold utility in that which the ancients advanced as the doctrine of these, or when he promises the style of an introduction. But benevolence is not necessary here where there is no knowledge hateful to one who seeks the treatment of it by Porphyry.

Let us return now, as we promised, to the above stated questions, and inquire carefully into them, and solve them. And since it is known that genera and species are universals and in them Porphyry touches on the nature of all universals generally, let us inquire here into the common nature of universals by studying these two [genus and species], and let us inquire also whether they apply only to *words* or to *things* as well.

In the *On Interpretation* Aristotle defines the universal as *that which is formed naturally apt to be predicated of many;* Porphyry moreover defines the particular, that is, the individual as *that which is predicated of only one.* Authority seems to ascribe the universal as much to things as to words; Aristotle himself ascribes it to things since he asserted immediately before the definition of universal: *However, since of things some are universals, and others are singulars, I call that universal which is formed to be predicated of many, and that singular which is not,* etc. Likewise Porphyry himself, when he said species are made of genus and difference, located them in the nature of things. From which it is manifest that things themselves are contained in the universal noun.

Nouns too are called universals. Wherefore Aristotle says; *Genus determines quality with respect to substance; for it signifies how each thing is.* And Boethius in the book *on Divisions* says: *It is, however, extremely useful to know this, that the genus is in a certain manner the single likeness of many species, and that likeness displays the substantial agreement of them all.* Yet *to signify* or *to display* pertains to words; but *to be signified* applies to things. And again he says: *The designation of a noun is predicated of many nouns, and is in a certain manner a species containing under itself individuals.* However, it is not properly called species since a noun is not substantial but accidental, but it is decidedly a universal since the definition of the universal applies to it. Hence it follows that words are universals whose function it is to be predicates of propositions.

Since it would seem, then, that things as well as words are called universal, it must be inquired how the universal definition can be applied to things. For it seems that no thing, nor any collection of things, is predicated of many things taken one by one, which [predication] is required as the characteristic of the universal. For although this people or this house or Socrates may be predicated of all their parts at the same time, still no one says that they are universals, since the predication of them does not apply to each of the several individuals or parts. And one thing is predicated of many much less properly than a collection of things. Let us hear therefore how either one thing or a collection of things is called universal, and let us state all the opinions of all thinkers.

Certain philosophers, indeed, take the universal thing thus: in things different from each other in form they set up a substance essentially the same; this is the mate-

rial essence of the individuals in which it is, and it is
one in itself and diverse only through the forms of its
inferiors. If these forms should happen to be taken
away, there would be absolutely no difference of things,
which are separated from each other only by a diversity
of forms, since the matter is in essence absolutely the
same. For example, in individual men, different in
number, [i.e. in the different individuals of the species
man] there is the same substance of man, which here is
made Plato through these accidents, there Socrates
through those. To these doctrines Porphyry seems to
assent entirely when he says: *By participation in the
species many men are one but in particulars the one
and common is many.* And again he says: *Individuals
are defined as follows, that each one of them consists
of properties the collection of which is not in another.*
Similarly, too, they place in the several animals different in species one and essentially the same substance of
animal, which they make into diverse species by taking
on diverse differences, as if from this wax I should first
make the statue of a man, then the statue of a cow, by
accommodating the diverse forms to the essence which
persists wholly the same. This however is of importance, that the same wax does not constitute the statues
at the same time, as is possible in the case of the universal, namely, that the universal is common, Boethius
says,[17] in such a way that the same universal is at the
same time entirely in the different things of which it
constitutes the substance materially; and although it is
universal in itself, the same universal is individual
through forms advening, without which it subsists naturally in itself; and apart from them it in no sense exists
actually; for it is universal in nature but individual in
actuality, and it is understood incorporeal and not

[17] See above, p. 94.

subject to sense in the simplicity of its universality, but the same universal subsists in actuality, corporeal and sensible through accidents: and according to the same authority, Boethius, individuals subsist and universals are understood.

This is one of two opinions. Although authorities seem to agree very much upon it, physics is in every manner opposed to it. For if what is the same essentially, although occupied by diverse forms, exists in individual things, it is necessary that one thing which is affected by certain forms be another thing which is occupied by other forms, so that the animal formed by rationality is the animal formed by irrationality, and so the rational animal is the irrational, and thus contraries would be placed in the same thing at the same time; but they are in no wise contrary when they come together in the same essence, just as whiteness and blackness would not be contrary if they occurred at the same time in this one thing, although the thing itself were white from one source and black from another, just as it is white from one source and hard from another, that is, from whiteness and from hardness. For things that are diverse by contrariness can not be inherent at the same time in the same thing, like relatives and most others. Wherefore Aristotle in his chapter on *Relativity* [in the *Categories*] demonstrates that great and small, which he shows to be present at the same time in the same thing in diverse respects, can not be contraries because they are present in the same thing at the same time.

But perhaps it will be said according to that opinion that rationality and irrationality are no less contrary because they are found thus in the same thing, namely, in the same genus or in the same species, unless, that is, they be joined in the same individual. That too is shown thus: rationality and irrationality are truly in the same individual because they are in Socrates. But since they are in Socrates at the same time, it is proved that they are in Socrates and in an ass at the same time. But Socrates and the ass are Socrates. And Socrates and the ass are indeed Socrates, because Socrates is Socrates and the ass, since obviously Socrates is Socrates and Socrates is the ass. That Socrates is the ass is shown as follows according to this opinion: whatsoever is in Socrates other than the forms of Socrates, is that which is in the ass other than the forms of the ass. But whatever is in the ass other than the forms of the ass, is the ass. Whatever is in Socrates other than the forms of Socrates, is the ass. But if this is so, since Socrates is himself that which is other than the forms of Socrates, then Socrates is himself the ass. The truth of what we assumed above, namely, that whatever is in the ass other than the forms of the ass is the ass, we may indicate as follows, for neither are the forms of the ass the ass, since then accidents would be substance, nor are the matter and the forms of the ass taken together the ass, since then it would be necessary to say that body and not body were body.

There are those who, seeking an escape from this position, criticize only the words of the proposition, *the rational animal is the irrational animal,* but not the opinion, saying that the animal is both, but that that is not shown properly by these words *the rational animal is the irrational animal,* because clearly although it is one and the same thing, it is called rational for one reason and irrational for another, that is, from opposite forms. But surely, then, there is no opposition in those forms which would adhere absolutely in these things at the same time, nor do critics criticize the following propositions, *the rational animal is the mortal animal* or *the white animal is the walking animal,* because the animal is not mortal in that it is rational, nor does it walk in that it is white, but these propositions they hold as entirely true because the same animal has both forms at the same time although under a different aspect. Otherwise they would say that no animal is man since nothing is man in that it is animal.

Furthermore according to the position of the above-stated doctrine there are only ten essences of all things, that is, the ten generalissima, because in each one of the categories only one essence is found, and that is diversified only through the forms of subordinated classes, as has been said, and without them the essence would have no variety. Therefore, just as all substances are the same at bottom, so all qualities are the same, and quantities, etc. through the categories. Since, therefore, Socrates and Plato have in themselves things of each of the categories, and since these things are at bottom the same, all the forms of the one are forms of the other, which are not essentially different in themselves, just as the substances in which they inhere are not different, so that, for example, the quality of the one is the quality of the other for both are quality. They are therefore no more different because of the nature of qualities than because of the nature of substance, because the essence of their substance is one as is likewise that of qualities. For the same reason quantity, since it is the same, does not make a difference nor do the other categories. For which reason there can be no difference because of forms, which are not different from each other, exactly as substances are no different from each other.

Moreover, how should we explain the plurality of things under substance if the only diversity were of forms while the subject substance remained at bottom the same? For we do not call Socrates many in number because of the imposition of many forms.

That position can not stand, moreover, by which it is held that individuals are made up by the accidents of themselves. For if individuals draw their being from accidents, obviously the accidents are prior naturally to the individuals, as differences are prior to the species they draw into being. For as man is made distinct by the formation of difference, so they speak of Socrates from the imposition of accidents. Whence Socrates can not be without accidents, nor man without differences. Therefore, Socrates is not the basis of accidents as man is not the basis of differences. If, however, accidents are not in individual substances as in subjects, surely they are not in universals. For whatever things are in second substances as in subjects, he shows are likewise universally in first substances as in subjects. Whence, consequently, it is manifest that the opinion in which it is held that absolutely the same essence subsists at the same time in diverse things, lacks reason utterly.

Therefore others are of another opinion concerning universality, and approaching the truth more closely they say that individual things are not only different from each other in forms, but are discrete personally in their essences, nor is that which is in one in any way to be found in another whether it be matter or form; nor even when the forms have been removed can things subsist less discrete in their essences because their personal discreteness (according to which of course this is not that) is not determined by forms but is the diversity itself of essence, just as the forms themselves are diverse one from the other in themselves; otherwise the diversity of forms would proceed *in infinitum,* so that it would be necessary that still other forms be made the basis of the diversity of any forms. Porphyry noted such a difference between the most comprehensive genus and the ultimate species, saying: *Further, species would never become the highest genus and genus would never become the ultimate species,* as if he were to say: this is the difference between them, that the essence of the one is not the essence of the other. So too the distinction of categories is not effected through some forms which make it, but through the diversification of their very essence. But since they hold all things are so diverse from each other that none of them participates with another in either the same matter essentially or the same form essentially, and yet, they cling to the universality of things, they reconcile these positions by saying that things which are discrete are one and the same not *essentially* but *indifferently,* as they say individual men, who are discrete in themselves, are the same in man, that is, they do not differ in the nature of humanity, and the same things which they call individual according to discreteness, they call universal according to *indifference* and the agreement of similitude.

But here too there is disagreement. For some hold that the universal thing is only in a collection of many. They in no manner call Socrates and Plato species in themselves, but they say that all men collected together are that species which is man, and all animals taken together that genus which is animal, and thus with the others. Boethius seems to agree with them in this.[18] *Species must be considered to be nothing other than the thought collected from the substantial likeness of individuals, and genus from the likeness of species.* For since he says the *collected likeness* he indicates a collecting of many. Otherwise they would not have in the universal thing a predication of many things or a

[18] See above, p. 97.

content of many things, nor would universals be fewer than individuals.

There are others, moreover, who say that the species is not only men brought together, but also the individuals in that they are men, and when they say that the thing which is Socrates is predicated of many, it is to be taken figuratively as if they were to say: many are the same as he, that is, agree with him, or else he agrees with many. According to the number of things they posit as many species as there are individuals and as many genera, but according to the likeness of natures they assign a smaller number of universals than individuals. Certainly all men are at one time many in themselves by personal discreteness and one by the similitude of humanity; and with respect to discreteness and with respect to likeness the same are judged to be different from themselves, as Socrates, in that he is a man, is divided from himself in that he is Socrates. Otherwise the same thing could not be its own genus or species unless it should have some difference of its own from itself, since things that are relatives must at least in some one respect be opposed one to the other.

Now, however, let us first invalidate the opinion which was set down above concerning collection, and let us inquire how the whole collection of men together, which is called one species, has to be predicated of many that it may be universal, although the whole collection is not predicated of each. But if it be conceded that the whole is predicated of different things by parts, in that, namely, its individual parts are accommodated to themselves, that has nothing to do with the community of the universal, all of which, as Boethius says,[19] must be in each individual, and it is in this point that the universal is distinguished from the type of com-

[19] See above, p. 94.

munity which is common by its parts, as for example a
field of which the different parts belong to different
men. Further, Socrates would in the same way be
predicated of many because of his many different parts,
so that he would himself be a universal. Even more,
it would be proper that any group of many men taken
together be called universal, and the definition of the
universal or even of the species would be adapted to
them in the same way, so that the whole collection of
men would then include many species. In the same way
we should call any collection of bodies or spirits one
universal substance with the result that, since the whole
collection of substances is one generalissimum, if any
one substance be removed and the others remain, we
should have to maintain that there are many generalissima in substances. But perhaps it should be said that
no collection which is included in the generalissimum, is
generalissimum. But I still object that when one substance has been taken from substances, if the residual
collection is not the generalissimum and nevertheless
remains universal substance, it is necessary that this be
a species of substance and have a coequal species under
the same genus. But what can be opposite to it, since
either the species of substance is contained entirely in
it, or else it shares the same individuals with it, as
rational animal, mortal animal? Even more. Every
universal is naturally prior to its own individuals. But
a collection of any things is an integral whole to ·the
individuals of which it is composed and is naturally
posterior to the things from which it is composed. Further. Between the integer and the universal Boethius
sets up this difference in the *on Divisions,* that the part
is not the same as the whole, but the species is always
the same as the genus. But how will the whole collection of men be able to be the multitude of animals?

It remains for us now to attack those who call single individuals, in that they agree with others, universal, and who grant that the same individuals are predicated of many things, not as they may be the many essentially, but because the many agree with them. But if it is the same to be predicated of many as to agree with many, how do we say that an individual is predicated of only one, since clearly there is no thing which agrees with only one thing? How too is a difference made between universal and particular by *being predicated of many,* since in exactly the same way in which man agrees with many, Socrates too agrees with many? Surely man, in so far as he is man and Socrates in so far as he is man agree with others. But neither man, in so far as he is Socrates nor Socrates in so far as he is Socrates agrees with others. Therefore, that which man has, Socrates has and in the same way.

Further, since the thing is granted to be absolutely the same, namely, the man which is in Socrates and Socrates himself, there is no difference of the one from the other. For no thing is itself different from itself at the same time because it has whatsoever it has in itself and in absolutely the same manner. Whence Socrates, at once white and a grammarian, although he has different things in himself, is not nevertheless by that fact different from himself since he has the same two and in absolutely the same manner. Indeed he is not a grammarian in another manner from himself nor white in another manner, just as white is not other than himself nor grammarian other than himself. Moreover how can this, which they say, be understood, that Socrates agrees with Plato in man, since it is known that all men differ from each other as well in matter as in form? For if Socrates agrees with Plato in the thing which is man, but no other thing is man except

Socrates himself or another, it is necessary that he agree with Plato either in himself or in another. But in himself he is rather different from him; with respect to another it is concluded likewise that he is not another. There are, however, those who take *agree in man* negatively, as if it were said: Socrates does not differ from Plato in man. But this likewise can be said, that he does not differ from him in stone, since neither of them is stone. And so no greater agreement between them is noted in man than in stone, unless perchance some proposition precede it, as if it were stated thus: They are man because they do not differ in man. But this can not stand either, since it is utterly false that they do not differ in man. For if Socrates does not differ from Plato in the thing which is man, he does not differ from him in himself. For if he differs in himself from Plato, but he is himself the thing which is man, certainly he differs from him also in the thing which is man.

Now, however, that reasons have been given why things can not be called universals, taken either singly or collectively, because they are not predicated of many, *it remains to ascribe universality of this sort to words alone.* Just as, therefore, certain nouns are called appellative by grammarians and certain nouns proper, so certain simple words are called by dialecticians *universals,* certain words *particulars,* that is, individuals. A *universal* word, however, is one which is apt by its invention to be predicated singly of many, as this noun *man* which is conjoinable with the particular names of men according to the nature of the subject things on which it is imposed. A *particular* word is one which is predicable of only one, as *Socrates* when it is taken as the name of only one. For if you take it equivocally, you make it not a word, but many words in signification,

because according to Priscian many nouns obviously
may coincide in a single word. When, therefore, the
universal is described to be that which is predicated of
many, the *that which,* which is used, indicates not only
the simplicity of the word as regards discreteness of
expression but also the unity of meaning as regards
discreteness of equivocals.

Having shown, however, what is accomplished by the
phrase *that which* above in the definition of the universal, we should consider carefully two more phrases
which follow, namely, *to be predicated* and *of many.*

To be predicated is to be conjoinable to something
truly by the declarative function of a substantive verb
in the present [tense], as *man* can be joined truly to
different things by a substantive verb. Verbs such as
he runs and *he walks* likewise when predicated of many
have the power of substantive verbs to join as a copula
joins. Whence Aristotle says in the second section of
the *on Interpretation: These verbs in which 'is' does
not occur, as to run or to walk do the same when so
affirmed as if 'is' were added.* And again he says: *There
is no difference in the expressions, man walks and man
is walking.*

That he says, *of many,* however, brings together
names according to the diversity of things named.
Otherwise Socrates would be predicated of many when
it is said: *this man is Socrates, this animal is, this white,
this musician.* These names although they are different
in the understanding, nevertheless have precisely the
same subject thing.

Note, moreover, that the conjoining involved in *construction* to which *grammarians* direct their attention is
one thing, the conjoining of *predication* which *dialecticians* consider another: for as far as the power of
construction is concerned, *man* and *stone* are properly

conjoinable by *is,* and any nominative cases, as *animal* and *man,* in respect to making manifest a meaning but not in respect to showing the status of a thing.   The conjoining involved in *construction* consequently is good whenever it reveals a perfect sentence, whether it be so or not.   But the conjoining involved in *predication,* which we take up here, pertains to the nature of things and to demonstrating the truth of their status.   If any one should say *man is a stone,* he has not made a proper construction of man and stone in respect to the meaning he wished to demonstrate, but there has been no fault of grammar; and although so far as the meaning of the proposition is concerned, this stone is predicated of man, to whom clearly it is construed as predicated (as false categories too have their predicated term), still in the nature of things stone is not predicable of man. We merely note here the great force of this predication while defining the universal.

It seems, then, that the universal is never quite the appellative noun, nor the particular the proper noun, but they are related to each other as that which exceeds and that which is exceeded.   For the appellative and proper contain not only the nominative cases but also the oblique cases, which do not have to be predicated, and therefore they are excluded in the definition of the universal by *to be predicated;* these oblique cases, moreover, because they are less necessary to the proposition (which alone, according to Aristotle, is the subject of the present speculation, that is, of dialectic consideration, and assuredly the proposition alone compounds argumentations), are not taken by Aristotle himself in any sense into the nouns, and he himself does not call them nouns but the cases of nouns.   But just as it is not necessary that all appellative and proper nouns be called universals or particulars, so also conversely. For the universal includes not only nouns but also verbs and infinite nouns, to which, that is, to infinite nouns, the definition of the appellative which Priscian gives does not seem to apply.

However, now that a definition of universal and of particular has been assigned to words, let us inquire carefully into the property of universal words especially. Questions have been raised concerning these universals, for there are very grave doubts concerning their meaning, since they seem neither to have any subject thing nor to constitute a clear meaning of anything. Universal nouns seemed to be imposed on no things whatsoever, since obviously all things subsisted in themselves discretely and, as has been shown,[20] did not agree in anything, according to the agreement of which thing the universal nouns could be imposed. Consequently, since it is certain that universals are not imposed on things according to the difference of discreteness of things, for they would then be not common, but particular; and again since universals could not name things as they agree in some thing, for there is no thing in which they agree, universals seem to derive no meaning from things, particularly since they constitute no understanding of any thing. Wherefore in the *on Divisions* Boethius says that the word *man* gives rise to doubt of its meaning because when it has been heard, *the understanding of the person hearing is carried off by many changing things and is betrayed into errors. For unless some one define the word, saying: 'all men walk' or at least 'certain men,' and should characterize this man if he happens to walk, the understanding of the person hearing does not have anything to understand reasonably.* For since *man* is imposed upon individuals for the same reason, because namely they are rational

[20] See above, p. 232.

mortal animals, that very community of imposition is
an impediment which prevents any one man being understood in it, as on the contrary in this name *Socrates*
the proper person of only one man is understood, and
therefore it is called a particular. But in the common
name which is *man,* not Socrates himself nor any other
man nor the entire collection of men is reasonably understood from the import of the word, nor is Socrates
himself, as certain thinkers hold, specified by that word,
even in so far as he is man. For even if Socrates alone
be sitting in this house, and if because of him alone
this proposition is true: *A man sits in this house,* nevertheless in no wise is the subject transferred by the name
of man to Socrates, except in so far as he is also man,
otherwise sitting would rationally be understood from
the proposition to inhere in him, so that it could be inferred clearly from the fact that a man sits in this
house, that Socrates sits in it. In the same way, no
other man can be understood in this noun *man,* nor can
the whole collection of men since the proposition can
be true of only one. Consequently, man or any other
universal word seems to signify no one thing since it
constitutes the meaning of no thing. But it seems that
there can not be a meaning which does not have a subject thing which it conceives. Whence Boethius says
in the *Commentary:* [21] *Every idea is made either from
the subject thing, as the thing is constituted or as it is
not constituted. For an idea can not be made from
no subject.* Wherefore universals seem wholly unrelated to signification.

But this is not so. For they signify in a manner
different things by nomination, not however by forming
a conception arising from different things but only pertaining to each of them. Just as this word *man* names

[21] See above, p. 94.

individual things for a common reason, namely that they
are men, because of which it is called universal, and
also forms a certain conception which is common, not
proper, that is, pertaining to the individuals of which
it conceives the common likeness.

But now let us inquire carefully into these things
which we have touched upon briefly, namely, *what that
common cause by which the universal word is imposed
is, and what the conception of the understanding of the
common likeness of things is, and whether the word is
called common because of a common cause in which the
things agree or because of a common conception or because of both at once.*

And first we should consider the *common cause.* Individual men, discrete from each other in that they
differ in respect to properties no less in essences than
in forms (as we noted above when we were inquiring
into the physics of a thing) are united nevertheless in
that they are men. I do not say that they are united in
man, since no thing is man except a discrete thing, but
in being man. But *to be man* is not the same as man
nor any thing, if we should consider it very carefully,
as *not to be in the subject* is not any thing, nor is it
any thing *not to undergo contrariety* or *not to undergo
more and less;* in these nevertheless Aristotle says all
substances agree. For since, as we have demonstrated
above, there can be no agreement in fact, if that by
which there is an agreement between any things, be
taken in this way, that it is not any thing, so Socrates
and Plato are alike in being man as horse and ass are
alike in not being man, in which way both horse and
ass are called non-man. Consequently for different
things to agree is for the individuals to be the same or
not to be the same, as to be man or white or not to be
man and not to be white. It seems, however, that we

must avoid considering the agreement of things according to that which is not any thing (as if we were to
unite in nothing things which are) since we say, in fact,
that this and that agree in the status of man, that is, in
that they are men. But we understand nothing other
than that they are men, and in this they do not differ
in the least, in this, I say, that they are men, although
we appeal to no essence. We call it the status itself of
man to be man, which is not a thing and which we also
called the common cause of imposition of the word on
individuals, according as they themselves agree with
each other. Often, however, we call those things too
by the name of cause which are not any thing, as when
it is said: he was lashed because he does not wish to
appear in court. He does not wish to appear in court,
which is stated as cause, is no essence. We can also
call the status of man those things themselves, established in the nature of man, the common likeness of
which he who imposed the word conceived.

Having shown the signification of universals, namely,
relative to things by nomination, and having set forth
the cause of their common imposition, let us now show
what are the understandings of universals which they
constitute.

And let us first distinguish generally the nature of all
understandings.

Although, then, the senses as well as the understandings are of the soul, this is the difference between them,
that the senses are exercised only through corporeal instruments and perceive only bodies or what are in
bodies, as sight perceives the tower and its visible qualities. The understanding, however, as it does not need
a corporeal instrument, so it is not necessary that it
have a subject body to which it may be referred, but it
is satisfied with the likeness of things which the mind

constructs for itself, into which it directs the action of its intelligence. Wherefore if the tower should be destroyed and removed, the sense which acted on it perishes, but the understanding remains in the likeness of the thing preserved in the mind. However, just as the sense is not the thing perceived to which it is directed, so neither is the understanding the form of the thing which it conceives, but the understanding is a certain action of the soul by which it is called intelligent or understanding, but the form to which it is directed is a certain imaginary and fictive thing, which the mind constructs for itself when it wishes and as it wishes, like those imaginary cities which are seen in dreams, or that form of the projected building which the artist conceives as the figure and exemplar of the thing to be formed, which we can call neither substance nor accident.

Nevertheless, there are those who call that form the same as the understanding, as they call the building of the tower, which I conceive while the tower is not there and which I contemplate, lofty and square in the spacious plain, the same as the understanding of the tower. Aristotle seems to agree with them, when he calls, in the *on Interpretation,* those passions of the soul which they call the understandings, the likenesses of things.

We, on the other hand, call the image the likeness of the thing. But there is nothing to prevent the understanding also being called in a sense a likeness, because obviously it conceives that which is properly called the likeness of the thing. But we have said, and well, that it is different from the image. For I ask whether that squareness and the loftiness is the true form of the understanding which is formed to the likeness of the quantity and the composition of the tower. But surely true squareness and true loftiness are present only in bodies, and neither an understanding nor any true essence can be formed from a fictive quality. It remains, therefore, that just as the quality is fictive, a fictive substance is subject to it. Perhaps, moreover, the image in a mirror too, which seems to be the subject of sight, can be said truly to be nothing, since obviously the quality of a contrary color appears often in the white surface of the mirror.

The following question, however, can be raised, when the soul perceives and understands the same thing at the same time, as when it discerns a stone, whether then the understanding too deals with the image of the stone or whether the understanding and the sense at the same time have to do with the stone itself. But it seems more reasonable that the understanding has no need of the image when there is present to it the truth of the substance. If, moreover, any one should say where there is sense there is no understanding, we should not concede that. For it often happens that the mind perceives one thing and understands another, as is apparent to those who study well, who, while they look at the things present to the open eyes, nevertheless think of other things concerning which they write.

Now that the nature of understandings has been examined generally, let us distinguish between the understandings of universals and particulars. These are separated in that that which is of the universal noun, conceives a common and confused image of many things, whereas that which the particular word generates, holds to the proper and as it were the particular form of one thing, that is, restricts itself to only one person. Whence when I hear *man* a certain figure arises in my mind which is so related to individual men that it is common to all and proper to none. When, however, I hear *Socrates* a certain form arises in my mind, which expresses the likeness of a certain person. Whence by this word *Socrates,* which generates in the mind the proper form of one person, a certain thing is specified and determined, but by *man,* the understanding of which rests in the common form of all men, that very community leads to confusion, lest we should not understand any one in particular. Wherefore *man* is rightly said to signify neither Socrates nor any other man, since none is specified by the meaning of the word, although nevertheless it names particulars. *Socrates,* on the other hand, must not only name a certain particular, but also determine the subject thing.

But the question is raised, then, since we said above [22] that according to Boethius every idea has a subject thing, how this applies to the ideas of universals. But it must be noted surely that Boethius introduces this statement in the sophistical argument by which he shows that the idea of universals is vain. Whence there is nothing to prevent that the statement is not proved in truth; whence avoiding falsity he shows the reasons of other writers. We can, moreover, refer to, as the thing subject to the understanding, either the true substance of the thing, as when it is at one with the sense, or else the conceived form of any thing whatsoever, that is, when the thing is absent, whether that form be common as we have said or proper; common, I say, with respect to the likeness of many which it retains although it is still considered in itself as one thing. For thus, to show the nature of all lions, one picture can be made representing what is proper to no one of them, and on the other hand another can be made suitable to distinguish any one of them, which would bring out certain individual characteristics, as if it were painted limping or mutilated or wounded by the spear of Hercules. Just

[22] See above, p. 236.

as, therefore, one figure of things is painted common, another particular, so too, are they conceived one common, another proper.

However, with respect to that form to which the understanding is directed, it is a matter of doubt, not unintelligently, whether the word too signifies the form. This seems to be firmly established by authority as well as by reason.

For Priscian in the first book of *Constructions,* after he had stated first the common imposition of universals on individuals, seemed to have a certain other meaning of universals, namely, a meaning of common form, saying: *with respect to the general and special forms of things, those which are constituted in the divine mind intelligibly before they were produced in bodies, are suited to demonstrate the genera or species of the nature of things.* For the question in this place is of God, as of an artist about to compose something, who preconceives in his mind the exemplary form of the thing to be composed; he works to the likeness of this form which is said to go into the body when the true thing is composed in its likeness. This common conception, however, is well ascribed to God, but not to man, because those general works or special states of nature are proper to God, not to the artist; as man, soul, or stone are proper to God, but house or sword to man. Whence the latter, house or sword, are not works of nature, as are the former, nor are words of them of substance, but of accident, and therefore they are neither genera nor are they species. Therefore, conceptions of this sort by abstraction are ascribed well to the divine mind but not to the human mind, because men who learn things only through the senses, scarcely ever or never ascend to simple understanding of this sort, and the exterior sensuality of accidents prevents

them from conceiving the natures of things purely.
God, however, to whom all things which he created are
known through themselves and who knows them before
they are, distinguishes the individual states among
them, and sense is no impediment to him who alone has
only true understanding. Whence it happens that men
have, in those things which have not been touched by
the sense, opinion rather than understanding as we
learn from experience itself. For, when we have
thought of some city which we have not seen we discover when we have come to it that we had thought it
to be otherwise than it is.

So likewise I think we have opinion of the intrinsic
forms which do not come to the senses, such as rationality and mortality, paternity, sitting. Any names of
any existent things, on the other hand, generate, so far
as is in them, understanding rather than opinion, because their inventor intended that they be imposed according to some natures or properties of things, although even he was not able to think out thoroughly
the nature or the property of the thing. Priscian, however, calls these common conceptions general or special,
because general or special nouns describe them in one
way or another to us. He says that the universals
themselves are as proper nouns to these conceptions,
which, although they are of confused meaning with
respect to the essences named, direct the mind of the
auditor to that common conception immediately, just as
proper nouns direct the attention to the one thing which
they signify. Porphyry, too, when he says that some
ideas are constituted from matter and form, and some
to the likeness of matter and form, seems to have understood this conception, since he says to the likeness
of matter and form, of which more will be said in its
proper place. Boethius likewise, when he says that the

thought collected from the likeness of many things is genus or species, seems to have understood the same common conception. Some insist that Plato was of this opinion too, namely that he called those common ideas which he places in *nous,* genera or species. In this perhaps Boethius records that he dissented from Aristotle when he says [23] that Plato wanted genera and species and the others not only to be understood universals, but also to be and to subsist without bodies, as if to say that he understood as universals those common conceptions which he set up separated from bodies in *nous,* not perhaps taking the universal as the common predication, as Aristotle does, but rather as the common likeness of many things. For that latter conception seems in no wise to be predicated of many as a noun is which is adapted singly to many.

That he says Plato thinks universals subsist without sensibles, can be resolved in another manner so that there is no disagreement in the opinions of the philosophers. For what Aristotle says to the effect that universals always subsist in sensibles, he said only in regard to actuality, because obviously the nature which is animal which is designated by the universal name and which according to this is called universal by a certain transference, is never found in actuality except in a sensible thing, but Plato thinks that it so subsists in itself naturally that it would retain its being when not subjected to sense, and according to this the natural being is called by the universal name. That, consequently, which Aristotle denies with respect to actuality, Plato, the investigator of physics, assigns to natural aptitude, and thus there is no disagreement between them.

Moreover, now that *authorities* have been advanced

[23] See above, p. 98.

who seem to build up by universal words common concepts which are to be called forms, *reason* too seems to assent. For what else is it to conceive forms by nouns than to signify by nouns? But certainly since we make forms diverse from understandings, there arises now besides thing and understanding a third thing which is the signification of nouns. Although authority does not hold this, it is nevertheless not contrary to reason.

Let us, then, set forth what we promised above to define, namely, whether the community of universal words is considered to be because of a common cause of imposition or because of a common conception or because of both. There is nothing to prevent that it be because of both, but the common cause which is taken in accordance with the nature of things seems to have greater force.

Likewise we must define that which we noted above, namely, that *the conceptions of universals are formed by abstraction, and we must indicate how we may speak of them alone, naked and pure but not empty.*

And first concerning *abstraction*. In relation to abstraction it must be known that matter and form always subsist mixed together, but the reason of the mind has this power, that it may now consider matter by itself; it may now turn its attention to form alone; it may now conceive both intermingled. The two first processes, of course, are by abstraction; they abstract something from things conjoined that they may consider its very nature. But the third process is by conjunction. For example, the substance of this man is at once body and animal and man and invested in infinite forms; when I turn my attention to this in the material essence of the substance, after having circumscribed all forms, I have a concept by the process of abstraction. Again, when

I consider only corporeity in it, which I join to substance, that concept likewise (although it is by conjunction with respect to the first, which considered only the nature of substance) is formed also by abstraction with respect to other forms than corporeity, none of which I consider, such as animation, sensuality, rationality, whiteness.

Conceptions of this sort through abstraction seemed perhaps false and vain for this reason, that they perceive the thing otherwise than it subsists. For since they are concerned with matter by itself or form separately, and since none the less neither of these subsists separately, they seem obviously to conceive the thing otherwise than it is, and therefore to be empty. But this is not so. For if one understands otherwise than the thing is constituted, in such manner that one considers it manifestly in such a nature and property as it does not have, certainly that understanding is empty. But that is not what is done in abstraction. For, when I consider this man only in the nature of substance or of body, and not also of animal or of man or of grammarian, obviously I understand nothing except what is in that nature, but I do not consider all that it has. And when I say that I consider only this one among the qualities the nature has, the *only* refers to the attention alone, not to the mode of subsisting, otherwise the understanding would be empty. For the thing does not have only it, but it is considered only as having it. And still in a certain sense it is said to be understood otherwise than it is, not in another state than it is, as has been said above,[24] but otherwise, in that the mode of understanding is other than the mode of subsisting. For this thing is understood separately from the other, not separated from it, although it does

[24] See above, p. 238.

not, notwithstanding, exist separately; and matter is
perceived purely and form simply, although the one is
not purely and the other is not simply, so that manifestly that purity or simplicity is reduced to the understanding and not to the subsistence of the thing, so that
they are of course modes of understanding and not of
subsisting. The senses, moreover, often operate in different ways with composite things, so that if a statue
is half of gold and half of silver, I can discern separately the gold and the silver which are joined together, that is, examining now the gold, now the silver
by itself, looking separately upon things which are conjoined, but not looking upon them as separated, in that
they are not separated. So too the understanding considers separately by abstraction, but does not consider
as separated, otherwise it would be empty.

Nevertheless, perhaps such a conception too could be
good which considers things which are conjoined, as
in one manner separated and in another manner conjoined, and conversely. For the conjunction of things
as well as the division can be taken in two ways. For
we say that certain things are conjoined to each other
by some likeness, as these two men in that they are
men or grammarians, and that certain things are conjoined by a kind of apposition and aggregation, as form
and matter or wine and water. The conception in question conceives things which are so joined to each other
as divided in one manner, in another conjoined. Whence
Boethius ascribes the following power to the mind, that
it can by its reason both compound that which was
disjoined and resolve that which is composite, departing
nevertheless in neither from the nature of the thing, but
only perceiving that which is in the nature of the thing.
Otherwise it would not be reason, but opinion, that is,

if the understanding should deviate from the state of the thing.

But the following question arises concerning the *providence* of the artist, whether it is empty when he holds in mind the form of a work still future, seeing that the thing is not yet constituted so. But if we grant that, we are forced to say that likewise the providence of God is empty, which he had before the creation of his work. But if one says this with respect to the effect, namely, that what he foresees would not eventuate actually as he foresees, then it is false that the providence was empty. If on the other hand one says that it was empty for this reason, that it did not yet agree with the future state of the thing, we are disinclined to the evil words but we do not object to the opinion. For it is true that the future state of the world was not yet materially, when he disposed it intelligibly as future still. Nevertheless, we are not accustomed to call empty the thought or the providence of any thing except that which lacks effect, nor do we say that we think in vain except those thoughts which we will not accomplish actually. Consequently, modifying the words we should say that the providence is not empty which does not think in vain, but conceives things which are not yet materially as if they subsisted, which is natural to all providences. Obviously thought concerning future things is called providence; thought concerning past things memory; concerning present things understanding proper. If, however, any one says that he is deceived who thinks of providing for the future state as for the one now existing, he is rather himself deceived in thinking that such an one must be said to be deceived. For, to be sure, he who foresees for the future is not deceived, unless he should think it is already as he foresees. Nor, in fact, does the con-

ception of a non-existent thing lead to deception, but
rather the faith added to it. For even though I think
of a rational crow, if I do not believe it, I am not deceived. So too the provident person is not deceived, in
that he does consider that that which he thinks as existing does not now exist thus, but as he thinks of it now
he sets it as present in the future. Surely every conception of the mind is as of the present. So if I should
consider Socrates in that he was a boy or in that he
will be an old man, I join boyhood or old age to him,
as it were in the present, because I consider him at
present in a past or future property. Nevertheless, no
one says that this memory is empty because what it conceives as present it considers in the past. But there
will be a fuller investigation of this in relation to the
on Interpretation.

In the case of God it is decided even more rationally
that his substance, which alone is immutable and simple,
is varied by no conceptions of things or any other forms.
For although the custom of human speech presumes to
speak of the creator as of creatures, since of course it
calls him either provident or intelligent, still nothing
in him should be understood or can be diverse from
him, that is, neither his understanding nor any other
form. And consequently any question concerning the
understanding with respect to God is superfluous. And
to speak the truth more expressly, it is nothing other
for him to foresee the future than for him, who is true
reason in himself, not to be in darkness concerning the
future.

Now, however, that many things have been shown
concerning the nature of abstraction, let us return to
the *conception of universals* which must always be
formed by abstraction. For when I hear *man* or *whiteness* or *white* I do not recall from the meaning of the

noun all the natures or properties which are in the subject things, but from *man* I have only the conception
although confused, not discrete, of animal and rational
mortal, but not of the later accidents as well. For the
conceptions of individuals, too, are formed by abstraction, when namely, it is said: this substance, this body,
this animal, this man, this whiteness, this white. For
by *this man* I consider only the nature of man but related to a certain subject, whereas by *man* I consider
that same nature simply in itself not related to any one.
Wherefore the understanding of universals is rightly
spoken of as alone and naked and pure, that is, alone
from the senses, because it does not perceive the thing
as sensual, and naked in regard to the abstraction of all
and of any forms, and pure with respect to discreteness
because no thing whether it be matter or form, is
designated in it; in this latter respect we called a conception of this sort confused above.[25]

Consequently, *having examined these things, let us
proceed to the resolution of the questions concerning
genera and species proposed by Porphyry,* which we
can do easily now that the nature of all universals has
been shown.

The first question, then, was to this effect, whether
genera and species subsist, that is, signify something
truly existent, or are placed in the understanding alone
etc., that is, are located in empty opinion without the
thing, like the following words, chimera and goat-stag
which do not give rise to a rational understanding.

To this it must be replied that in truth they signify
by nomination things truly existent, to wit, the same
things as singular nouns, and in no wise are they located
in empty opinion; nevertheless, they consist in a certain sense in the understanding alone and naked and

[25] See above, p. 240.

pure, as has been determined.[26] There is nothing, how-ever, to prevent one who states the question from taking some words in one way in inquiry and one who solves it from taking them in another way in solution, as if he who solves the question were to say: you ask whether they are placed in the understanding alone, etc. This you can take in the manner (which is the true one) which we discussed above. And the words can be taken in absolutely the same sense on both sides, by the re-solver and by the inquirer, and then it is made a single question not by opposition of the prior members of two dialectical questions, to wit, these: whether they are or are not, and again whether they are placed in the sole and naked and pure understanding or not.

The same can be said in the second question which is as follows: whether subsisting they are corporeal or incorporeal, that is, when they are conceded to signify subsistences whether they signify subsistences which are corporeal or subsistences which are incorporeal. Cer-tainly everything that is, as Boethius says,[27] is either corporeal, or incorporeal, that is, we take these words corporeal and incorporeal for substantial body and non-body, or for that which can be perceived by the cor-poreal sense, such as man, wood, whiteness, or that which can not, such as soul, justice. Corporeal like-wise can be taken for discrete, as if the following were inquired: since universals signify subsistences, whether they signify them discrete or not discrete. For he who investigates the truth of the thing well, considers not only what can be said truly, but everything that can be stated in opinion. Whence even though it be certain to some that nothing subsists except the discrete, never-theless because there can be the opinion that there might be other subsistences, it is inquired not without reason

[26] See above, p. 250.   [27] See above, p. 92.

concerning them too. And this last meaning of corporeal
seems to fall in better with the question; namely, that
the question be raised concerning discrete and non-discrete. But perhaps when Boethius says that everything
that is is either corporeal or incorporeal, the incorporeal seems superfluous since no existing thing is incorporeal, that is, non-discrete. Nor does that which
comes to mind in relation to the order of the questions
seem to afford any help, unless perhaps in this respect,
that as corporeal and incorporeal divide subsistences in
another sense, so too it seems they divide them in this
sense, as if the inquirer were to say: I see that of
existing things some are called corporeal and others incorporeal, which of these shall we say are the things
signified by universals? To which the reply is made:
in a certain sense corporeal things, that is, things discrete in their essence and incorporeal with respect to
the designation of the universal noun because obviously
universals do not name discretely and determinately,
but confusedly, as we have set forth sufficiently above.[28]
Whence the universal names themselves are called both
corporeal with respect to the nature of things and incorporeal with respect to the manner of signification,
because although they name things which are discrete,
nevertheless they do not name them discretely and determinately.

The third question, of course, whether they are
placed in sensibles, etc., follows from granting that they
are incorporeal, because obviously the incorporeal taken
in a certain manner is divided by being and by not
being in the sensible, as we have also noted above.[29]
And universals are said to subsist in sensibles that is to
signify an intrinsic substance existing in a thing which
is sensible by its exterior forms, and although they

[28] See above, p. 240.   [29] See above, p. 219.

signify this substance which subsists actually in the sensible thing, yet they demonstrate the same substance naturally separated from the sensible thing, as we determined above in relation to Plato.[30] Wherefore Boethius says that genera and species are understood, but are not, outside sensible things, in that obviously the things of genera and species are considered with respect to their nature rationally in themselves beyond all sensuality, because they can truly subsist in themselves even when the exterior forms by which they come to the senses have been removed. For we grant that all genera or species are in sensual things. But because the understanding of them was said to be always apart from sense, they seemed in no wise to be in sensible things. Wherefore it was inquired rightly whether they could ever be in sensibles, and it is replied with respect to some of them that they are, but in such fashion that, as has been said, they continue to be naturally beyond sensuality.

We can however take corporeal and incorporeal in the second question as sensible and insensible, in order that the order of questions may be more appropriate; and since the understanding of universals was said to be only from sense, as has been said, it was asked properly, whether universals were sensible or insensible; and since it is answered that some of them are sensible with respect to the nature of things, and that the same are insensible with respect to the mode of signifying, because obviously they do not designate the sensible things which they name in the same manner as they are perceived, that is as discrete, and sense does not discover them by demonstration of them, it remained a question whether universals named sensible things only or whether they also signified something else; to which

[30] See above, p. 244.

it is replied that they signify both sensible things and at the same time that common conception which Priscian ascribes particularly to the divine mind.

And in accord with them. With respect to that which we understand here as the fourth question, as we noted above,[31] the following is the solution, that we in no wise hold that universal nouns are, when, their things having been destroyed, they are not predicable of many things inasmuch as they are not common to any things, as for example the name of the rose when there are no longer roses, but it would still, nevertheless, be significative by the understanding, although it would lack nomination; otherwise there would not be the proposition: there is no rose.

Questions, moreover, were raised properly concerning universal words, but none concerning singular words, because there was no such doubt concerning the meaning of singular words. For their mode of signifying accorded well with the status of things. As things are discrete in themselves, so they are signified by words discretely, and the understanding of them refers to a definite thing, which reference universals do not have. Besides although universals did not signify things as discrete, they did not seem on the other hand to signify things as agreeing, since, as we have also shown above,[32] there is no thing in which they agree. Consequently, since there was so much doubt concerning universals, Porphyry chose to treat of universals alone, excluding singulars from his intention as clear enough in themselves, although for all that, he sometimes treats of them in passing because of other things.

It must be noted, however, that although the definition of the universal or of the genus or the species includes only words, nevertheless these nouns are often

[31] See above, p. 219.   [32] See above, pp. 237-238.

transferred to their things, as when it is said that
species is made up of genus and difference, that is, the
thing of the species from the thing of the genus. For
when the nature of words is examined with respect to
signification, it is question sometimes of words and
sometimes of things, and frequently the names of the
latter and the former are transferred reciprocally. For
this reason most of all, the ambiguous treatment of logic
as well as grammar leads many, who do not distinguish
clearly the property of the imposition of nouns or the
abuse of transference, into error by the transference of
nouns.

Boethius, moreover, makes this confusion by transfer-
ences in the *Commentaries* most of all and particularly
in connection with the inquiry into these questions, so
that it may even seem right to pass by the inquiry into
what it is that he calls genera and species. Let us run
over his questions briefly and let us apply ourselves,
as is necessary, to the aforesaid opinion. In the investigation of the questions here that he may resolve the
problem better, he first throws it into confusion by some
sophistical questions and reasons, that he may teach us
later to free ourselves from them. And he sets forth
such difficulty that all concern with and investigation
of genera and species must be put off,[33] as if to say, that
clearly the words genera and species can not be said to
be that which they seem, either with respect to the
signification of things or with respect to the understanding. He shows this with respect to the signification of
things in that no universal thing, whether single or
multiplex, is ever found, that is, no thing predicable of
many, as he himself shows carefully and as we have
proved above.[34] Moreover, he first establishes that there
is no one universal thing and therefore no genus nor

[33] See above, p. 95.   [34] See above, p. 222 and pages ff.

species, saying:[35] everything that is one is one in number, that is, discrete in its own essence; but genera and species which must be common to many things can not be one in number and therefore can not be one. But since some one may say against this assumption that genera and species are one in number in the sense of one that is common, he offers such an one the following refutation, saying:[36] each thing one in number in the sense that it is common either is common through its parts or whole through the succession of times or whole in the same time, but in such wise that it does not constitute the substances of those things to which it is common. He removes at once all such modes of community from genus as well as from species, saying that they on the other hand are common in such a way that they are in the same time whole in each and constitute the substance of each of their particulars. For universal names are not participated in by the different things, which they name, by parts, but they are the names, whole and entire, of singulars at the same time. They can likewise be said to constitute the substances of the things to which they are common either in that they signify by transference things which constitute other things, as for example animal names something in horse or in man which is the matter of them or even of men subordinated to it, or else in that they are said to make up the substance, because they come in a certain manner into the knowledge of the things because of which they are said to be substantial to them, seeing that *man* denotes all that which is animal and rational and mortal.

Moreover, after Boethius shows with respect to a simple thing that it is not universal, he proves the same

[35] See above, p. 93.   [36] See above, p. 94.

with respect to a multiple thing showing that clearly the
species or genus is not a multitude of discrete things,
and he destroys the opinion by which some one may say
that all substances collected together are the genus *substance* and all men the species which is *man,* as if the
following were stated: If we assert that each genus is
a multitude of things agreeing substantially, still every
such multitude will have naturally another above it, and
that again will have another and so *ad infinitum,* which
is inconsistent. Consequently, it has been shown that
universal names do not seem to be universal with respect
to the signification of things, whether of a simple or of
a multiple thing, since obviously they signify no universal thing, that is, no thing predicable of many.

Therefore he argued also that they should not be
said to be universals with respect to the signification of
understanding, because he shows sophistically that it is
a vain understanding, because clearly, since it is by
abstraction, it is constituted otherwise than the thing
subsists. He resolves sufficiently and we have resolved
carefully above [37] the knot of this sophism. He did not
think the other part of the argumentation, by which he
shows that no thing is universal, needed limitation, since
it was not sophistical. For he takes a thing as thing,
not as word, because clearly the common word, since it
is in itself as it were a single thing in essence, is common by nomination in the appellation of many; according to this appellation clearly and not according to its
essence it is predicable of many. Nevertheless, the
multitude of things themselves is the cause of the universality of the noun, because as we have stated above [38]
only that which contains many is universal; yet the universality which the thing confers upon the word, the

[37] See above, p. 246.   [38] See above, p. 254.

thing does not have in itself, inasmuch as the word does not have meaning because of the thing and inasmuch as a noun is called appellative with respect to the multitude of things, even though we do not say that things signify or that they are appellative.

ROBERT GROSSETESTE (circa 1175-1253)

To judge from the criticisms and enthusiasms of Roger Bacon our present day reconstructions of medieval philosophy are unbalanced, and our judgments of the relative importance of the thinkers of the thirteenth century are misguided. Alexander of Hales, Albert the Great, Thomas Aquinas were, according to Bacon, overrated and their writings did not reflect the important problems or the significant tendencies of the century; indeed, their erudition was not sufficient to permit them to penetrate far in philosophy, for they were not versed in linguistics, mathematics, perspective or experimental science. Grosseteste, on the other hand, was most learned among men of science, as Boethius had been most learned in languages. *The ordinary run of those who philosophize is imperfect, and few of the wisest have attained to the perfection of philosophy, as Solomon and later Aristotle, in their time, and . . . in our days Robert, late bishop of Lincoln.* His distinction was to have turned from Aristotle, not because of ignorance but because of knowledge of other authors and because of his own experience; with his pupil, Adam Marsh, he worked for the application of mathematics to experience, for both conceived mathematics to be most necessary not only to all science but to theology. Roger Bacon's estimation of his master indicates surely enough, if his polemical attitude be reckoned in his praise, at least an important philosopher and a philosophical tradition distinct from the metaphysical aristotelianism of Paris.

259

The indicated importance of Robert Grosseteste extends over too many fields to be exhausted in the analysis of any one of his activities. As bishop of Lincoln, the most important diocese in thirteenth century England, his opinions have left a notable impress on ecclesiastical administration in many of the questions with which he dealt. His attitude was definite and became traditional with respect to episcopal visits in monasteries, the support of a resident vicar in each parish by monasteries with large benefices, the conferring of benefices in the english church on foreigners; his methods against the monks were so forceful that Matthew of Paris called him a persecutor of monks; his stand against the pope was so determined that he was in repeated controversy (in which he protested that he disobeyed only by a higher obedience) and at the time of his death he had suffered excommunication at the hands of Innocent IV. He organized philosophical studies at Oxford and on the foundation of the Franciscan Order there, in 1224, instituted courses in its house. He was one of the great translators from the greek, translating among other works, the writings of the pseudo-Dionysius, *the De fide orthodoxa* of St. John Damascene, extracts from the *Lexicon* of Suidas, the whole of the *Nichomachean Ethics* with commentaries of various greek writers, the *Posterior Analytics,* the *Sophistical Refutations,* and the *Physics* of Aristotle. His contribution to philosophy is contained chiefly in the number of diversified opuscules he left on various subjects. The following three were selected from these, but though they are concerned with metaphysical problems, the greater bulk of Robert's philosophical work was directed, as Bacon intimated, to the investigation of physical, optical, cosmological, astronomical problems, to questions concerning perspective, color, the rainbow, tides, heat, sound, the formation of the universe, the movement of planets and comets, the reform of the calendar. But the problems are, none the less, guided according to a philosophical plan, and the diversified inquiries are united in their philosophical bases.

Fundamentally the philosophy is augustinian, and the aristotelian physics, logic and ethics are made to fit the platonist frame with no serious metaphysical derangement. The science of perspective indeed makes the capital contribution to metaphysics: light plays a principal part in the production and the constitution of the universe. In one of his works, *On Light, or the Commencement of Forms,* Robert states his fundamental doctrine of form and matter. All corporeal things are form and matter, and the form of corporeity is light. The characteristic of light is to engender itself perpetually and diffuse itself spherically about a point in an instantaneous manner. Originally the luminous form and matter were equally unextended, but the first form created by God in the first matter multiplies itself infinitely, and spreads equally in all directions, distending thus the matter to which it is united and constituting thus the mass of the universe. The diffusion continues to the extreme limit of rarefaction of light (*lux*); this extreme limit of the sphere constitutes the firmament; and from it illumination (*lumen*) is reflected toward the center, engendering in its passage the nine celestial spheres.

The conformity of this doctrine of light to the augustinian metaphysics need scarcely be insisted on. For God is the light of all things by which their light is lighted. To be true, to be good, or simply to be is to be supported in the eternal Word. Grosseteste defined truth in the traditional phrase: it is the adequation of thing and understanding. But there are two truths for each thing as there are two understandings with which it may be adequated, divine and human. There is the truth by which the being of the thing is conformed to its reason in the eternal word, and there is the truth by which that which is is signified to be. It is consequent to this analysis that Truth follows even from the denial of truth, for if there is no truth, the proposition which asserts that, is and is true. It follows further that there is a single Truth which is one in itself but multiple and diversified by appropriation in particulars. Truth is so at the bottom of all things that a necessity may be observed even in contingent statements; the contingent follows on the necessary, and even the impossible follows only on the destruction of the contingent. God is knowledge; he is seen involved necessarily and without contradiction in all things, even contingent things, and in all knowledge. Any truth, any being, any good suggest the source by which alone it is intelligible that propositions be true, that things be, that ends be desired. And whereas philosophers in the earlier augustinian tradition found philosophy almost entire in the discovery of God at the center of all things, Grosseteste seeking to develop the consequences of that philosophy hit upon mathematics as the perfect dialectical instrument for its development; the effect of the application of mathematics was so to turn the search for God in things to the elucidation of things, that the inquiry for God was to inspire the first systematic experimental investigation of things.

ROBERT GROSSETESTE

On Truth [1]

I am the way, the truth and the life.[2] Here the very Truth says that he is the truth. Therefore it can be doubted, not without cause, whether there is any other truth or whether there is no other truth than the supreme truth itself. For if there is no other truth, then truth is unique and singular, nor does it admit of distribution or plurality that one may say *all truth* or *many truths.*—But on the other hand, one reads in the Gospel: *He will teach you all truth.*[3]

Again: if there is no other truth, whenever something is predicated to be true, God is predicated of it, although contiguously and denominatively and nominally. Is it, then, the same to be true and to be divine? It seems so by syllogisms on these grounds. If there is no other truth than God, to be true is to be divine, and that is a true tree because it is a divine tree, and that a true proposition because it is a divine proposition, and so of others.

Again: in future and contingent things there seems to be a corruptible truth. The truth, however, which is God, is in no way corruptible. There is, therefore, another truth than that supreme truth.

[1] *Die Philosophischen Werke des Robert Grosseteste, Bischofs von Lincoln, besorgt von Dr. Ludwig Baur,* in *Beiträge zur Geschichte der Philosophie des Mittelalters,* Münster, 1912, Vol. IX, pp. 130-147.
[2] *Joh.* 14:6.   [3] *Joh.* 16:13.

Again: the truth of proposition is an adequation of speech and thing. God, however, is not this adequation, because this adequation was not before speech and thing were, and God and the supreme truth preceded the word and created things signified by speech. There is, therefore, some truth which is not the supreme truth.

Again: Augustine says in the book of *Soliloquies* [4] that truth is that which is. Therefore, the entity of each thing is the truth of it. But the entity of no creature is the supreme truth, which is God. Therefore, there is another truth than the supreme truth.

Again: Augustine reconsiders this opinion which he expressed in the book of *Soliloquies:* [5] *Thou God who wished only the pure to know the truth,* saying this,[6] *it can be replied that many who are not pure know many truths.* Many, therefore, who are not pure see the truth by which the true, which they know, is true. But only the pure in heart see the supreme truth: for *Blessed are the pure in heart, for they shall see God.* [7] And according to Plato, as Augustine points out in the book *on the True Religion,* by the pure mind truth is seen, and clinging to it the soul is made blessed.[8] Again Augustine asserts the same in the book *on the Christian Combat:* [9] *Whosoever errs thinks he knows the truth while yet he lives evilly.*—There is, therefore, another truth than that supreme truth, and that other truth those who are not pure in heart see.

Again: it is written in the *Gospel: But he that doeth the truth cometh to the light.* [10] Man, therefore,

[4] Augustinus, *Soliloq.* II, 5, n. 8.
[5] Augustinus, *Soliloq.* I, 1, n. 2.
[6] *Retractationes,* I, 4, n. 2.   [7] *Matth.* 5:8.
[8] Augustinus, *De vera relig.,* cap. 3, n. 3.
[9] Augustinus, *De agone christiano,* cap. 13, n. 14.
[10] *Joh.* III, 21.

does some truth; but no one does the supreme truth. There is, therefore, another truth from it.

Again: from the words of Augustine in the book *on Falsehood*,[11] it can be gathered that truth is double: namely, one in contemplation and the other in proposition. And the former, which is in contemplation, Augustine sets above the mind, saying this: *as the mind must be set above the body, so too truth must be set above the mind, since the soul desires it, not only more than the body, but even more than itself.*[12]—But since nothing is to be set above the mind except God, it is evident that the truth concerning which Augustine is thinking here, is God.—After that, he does not dare to prefer the truth which is in proposition above the mind, but he intimates that it is to be preferred above all temporal things, saying this: [13]

> If any one should propose to himself so to love truth, not only truth which is in contemplation but likewise that which is in true proposition because it is true too in its genus of things, and if he should propose to bring forth opinion not otherwise by the motion of the body than it is conceived and observed in the mind, to the end that he might set the true beauty of faith above not only gold and silver and gems and pleasant estates, but above even the whole temporal life and every good of the body, I know not whether he could be said wisely to err in anything.

In this Augustine distinguishes evidently enough two truths, the second of which he does not dare to equate

[11] AUGUSTINUS, *De mendacio,* cap. 3, n. 3; cap. 16, n. 31; cap. 20, n. 41.

[12] AUGUSTINUS, *De mendacio,* cap. 7, n. 10.

[13] AUGUSTINUS, *De mendacio,* cap. 20, n. 41.

to the mind, much less prefer it. But, if he did not believe, or at least if he doubted, that the truth of proposition is other than the supreme truth, he would not doubt that it is to be preferred to the soul.

It seems, however, that there is not another truth than the supreme truth according to Anselm, who in his book *on Truth* [14] concludes finally that there is a single truth of all truths and that that is the supreme truth, even as there is one time of all things which are together in one time.

Again: it is probable that if the truth of any one statement by which the statement is true of creatures, be the supreme truth, and if the truth of all statements and all that can be stated be the same truth, nothing then lacks beginning and end except the supreme truth. But the truth of this: *seven and three are ten,* lacks beginning and end. Therefore, this truth is the supreme truth.—To this Augustine agrees in the book *on the Free Will*,[15] saying this: *seven and three are ten, and not only now, but always; nor have seven and three in any way at any time not been ten, nor will seven and three at any time not be ten. I have said, therefore, that this incorruptible truth of number is common to me and to any one at all who reasons.* The truth of such things is, therefore, eternal and, by that, is the supreme truth.

In the same way, it was true without beginning that *something will have been;* but it was not true except by its own truth. Therefore, its truth is eternal and supreme; similarly, the truth of all conditional propositions as: *if he is man, he is animal.* By hypothesis, therefore, all statable truth is the supreme truth. More-

[14] ANSELMUS, *De Veritate,* cap. 13: see above, pp. 183-184.
[15] AUGUSTINUS, *De libero arbitrio,* II, cap. 8, n. 21; see above, p. 36.

over, Augustine says in the book *on the True Religion*,[16] that truth is that which shows that which is. Its truth, therefore, reveals the being of each thing. For since this is the definition of truth, it is proper for all truth to show that which is. But any truth will show the being of nothing other than the being of that of which it is the truth. Therefore, if nothing else shows the being of any thing to the inspection of the mind than the light of the supreme truth, there is no other truth than the supreme truth.

It seems, however, from the carefully examined statements [*auctoritates*] of Augustine, that the light of the supreme truth and no other shows to the eye of the mind that which is. For he says, in his book of *Retractations*,[17] reconsidering something he had said concerning the opinion of Plato on reminiscence and correcting it with these words: *For this reason, even they who are unlearned in certain disciplines give true answers concerning them, because that is present to them, when they can grasp it in the light of eternal reason, in which they see these immutable truths.*

The same Augustine says in the book *on the Free Will:* [18]

> The supreme truth reveals all goods which are true . . . but just as they who choose in the light of the sun that which they look on willingly and are rejoiced by that sight; whereas if perchance there were any among them endowed with very vigorous and healthy and very strong eyes, they would look upon nothing more willingly than the sun itself, which lights up likewise all the things by which weaker eyes

[16] AUGUSTINUS, *De vera religione,* cap. 36, n. 66.

[17] AUGUSTINUS, *Retractationes* I, cap. 4, n. 4.

[18] AUGUSTINUS, *De libero arbitrio* II, cap. 13, n. 36; see above, p. 53.

are pleased: so the keen and vigorous perception of the mind when it has gazed with sure reason on many and immutable things, directs itself to that truth itself by which all things are shown forth, and inhering in it, as it were, forgets other things and at once in it enjoys them all.

Again in the book of *Confessions:* [19] And if we both see that what you say is true, and if we both see that what I say is true, where, I ask, do we see it? not I in you nor you in me, but both in that immutable truth which is above our minds?

The same Augustine in the book *on the Trinity:* [20] When we seize by simple intelligence the ineffably beautiful art of corporeal figures above the keen vision of the mind, we see by the sight of the mind in that eternity, from which temporal things are made, the form, by which we are and according to which, whether in ourselves or in bodies, we occupy ourselves by true and right reason with anything.

The same Augustine *on John* in homily 14: [21] *No man can say that which belongs to truth unless he is illuminated by him who can not lie.*

These statements affirm evidently that everything which is known to be true is observed to be true in the light of the supreme truth.

But if some one should say: since one and the same truth is shown at the same time both in the light of this truth and of that other truth, does that light of the supreme truth, then, not suffice to show what it illumines, or if it suffices, how is the other not superfluous?

[19] Augustinus, *Confession,* XII, cap. 25, n. 35.
[20] Augustinus, *De Trinitate* XII, cap. 14, n. 23.
[21] Augustinus, *Tract. in Joh.* XIV, 8.

Besides, if the light of the sun wipes out the other luminaries so that when it is present they reveal nothing to the sight of the body, how is it that that light, incomparably more lucid than any other spiritual light, will not all the more overcome every other, so that when it is present every other light will accomplish nothing? These shadowy clouds of contrary opinions would, perhaps, scatter and be dissipated, if the light of truth should for a short time grow clear for us. Therefore our attention must be turned for a time to understanding *what truth is*.

We are accustomed to speak commonly of the truth of *propositional discourse*. And this truth, as the Philosopher says, is no other than being in the thing signified, as the speech specifies. And this is what some say truth is, *the adequation of speech and thing* and the *adequation of the thing to the understanding*.— But since the speech is truer which is silent within than the one which sounds without, namely, the concept of the understanding through vocal speech, truth will be rather an adequation of interior speech and the thing, than of exterior speech; but if interior speech itself were an adequation of itself to the thing, it would be, not only true speech, but truth itself.—Wisdom, however, and the word, or *the Speech of the Father* is in the highest degree adequated by this manner of adequation to the thing which it speaks of and states. For thus each thing is most fully as this speech says, nor is it otherwise in anything than is stated in this speech; nor is it only adequated but it is itself the adequation of itself to the things it states. Therefore, the very Speech of the Father is, according to this definition of truth, in the highest degree truth.—Nor can this Speech not be spoken nor not be adequated to that which it says. Wherefore, truth cannot not be.

There is, however, in the things which are said by this eternal Speech, a conformity to the speech itself by which they are said. Moreover, the very conformity of things to this eternal speaking is the rightness of them and the obligation to be what they are. For a thing is right and is as it should be, in so far as it is in conformity to this Word. But in so far as a thing is as it should be, to that extent it is true. Therefore, the truth of things is for them to be as they should be and is their rightness and conformity to the Word by which they are said eternally. And since this rightness is perceptible to the mind alone and in this respect is distinguished from visible corporeal rightness, it is evident that truth is defined appropriately by Anselm when he says [22] that it is rightness perceptible to the mind alone. And this definition embraces also the supreme truth, which is rightness rectifying as well as the truths of things which are rightnesses rectified. Rightness, however, is in none a departing from one's self or a deviating from one's self.

Again: each thing in so far as it falls short of that which it tends to be, to that extent that which tends or contrives to be is false. For that is false, as Augustine says in the book of *Soliloquies*,[23] *which contrives to be what it is not or in any way tends to be and is not.*—Again, the same author says in the same work [24] *That is false which is accommodated to the likeness of anything and nevertheless is not that to which it seems like. Wherefore, everything is true which is free from, defect.*—Wherefore truth is the privation of defect or the plenitude of being; for a tree is a true tree when it has the plenitude of being tree and lacks the deficiency

[22] ANSELMUS, *De veritate*, cap. 11, see above, p. 172.
[23] AUGUSTINUS, *Soliloq.* II, 9, n. 16.
[24] AUGUSTINUS, *Soliloq.* II, 15, n. 29.

of being tree, and what is this plenitude of being except conformity to the reason of tree in the eternal Word?

The being of things, however, is double: a first and a second: a thing can have full first being and lack the plenitude of second being. And because of this the same thing can be true and false, as a true man is an animal, which is composed of body and rational soul. Augustine also makes the same distinctions: *if he is mendacious and vicious, he is a false man.*—Similarly, the proposition is true that man is an ass, because it has full first being of discourse, but it is false because it lacks the plenitude of second being. For the second perfection of discourse is this, to signify that that which is, is, and that that which is not, is not. And when one thing is said at the same time to be true and false in this way, it is not a contrary assertion concerning the same thing, because a plenitude and deficiency of the same being is not asserted. But when falsity is spoken of, it is true falsity, and the false is truly false. Is the contrary present in its contrary and does the rule of logicians fail in these terms, as it does, according to Augustine, in the case of good and evil?[25] And if it fails in true and false as it does in good and evil, are there no more contrarieties besides these two in which it fails?—And what is the difference between the contrarieties in which the rule of logicians fails, and the contrarieties in which it does not fail? Does the rule of logicians fail only in those contrarieties of which one of the contraries follows being? For every thing which is, is good; and everything which is, is true. Wherefore, they are not in the least false and evil, or they are not false and evil except in the true and the good.

Further, the true is anything whatever whose being

[25] Augustinus, *Enchiridion*, cap. 14.

is conformed to its reason in the eternal Word; and the false that which contrives to be and is not conformed to its reason in the eternal Word. Since, however, everything that is, is only that and is wholly that which it is said to be in the eternal Word, everything that is, so far as it is and so much as it is, is true.—But, on the other hand, is all that which is without God, something false? For since that is false which is accommodated to the likeness of something and, nevertheless, is not that to which it is like, yet every creature has a likeness to something which it nevertheless is not, it seems that every creature is something false. But if this is true, is man, who is the likeness and image of God and still is not God, a false God, as the statue of a man is a false man? To say that seems absurd. And since at present no authority occurs which determines that, let us put off the solution of it for the time.

God, however, is in no way something false, because all likeness is of equal to equal or of inferior to superior, but God has neither equal nor superior to whose likeness he may be accommodated. The Son, moreover, who is most fully like the Father, is that which the Father is. Whence, there is no falsity in him from any part, but full truth and light, *and there is no darkness in it.*[26]

Since, however, as was said above, the truth of each thing is the conformity of it to its reason in the eternal Word, it is evident that every created truth is seen only in the light of the supreme truth.—But how can the conformity of something to something else be observed, except by having observed also that to which it conforms? Or, how can the rightness of the thing be recognized, since it is rightness although it is not

[26] *I Joh.* I, 5.

rightness according to itself, except in the rule of that which is right according to itself and according to which the thing is rectified? This rule is nothing other than the eternal reason of the thing in the divine mind. Or, how may it be recognized that the thing is as it should be, unless the reason be seen according to which it should be so?

But if it be said that this is the right reason according to which the thing should be thus, it is asked again: where is this reason seen to be the right reason of this thing and such as it should be, except, in turn, in its reason? And so there will always be a regress until the thing is seen to be as it should be in its first reason which is right according to itself. And, therefore, the thing is as it should be because it conforms to that. All created truth, then, is evident in so far as the light of its eternal reason is present to the person observing, as Augustine testifies.[27] Nor can any thing be known to be true in its created truth only, as a body can not be seen to be colored in its color alone without an extrinsic light spread upon it.

Created truth too, therefore, shows that which is, but not in its own illumination [*lumen*], but in the light [*lux*] of the supreme truth, as color shows body, but only in the light spread upon it. Nor is this an insufficiency of light, that it reveals body through color, since color itself is not a shining light added to a superfused light; but the power of light is this, that light does not obscure color which lights up beyond itself, but, on the other hand, it does not illumine that which lights up beyond itself.—In the same fashion is the power of the light of the supreme truth, which so illumines the created truth that, illumined itself, it reveals the true object. Consequently, the light of the supreme truth

[27] Augustinus, *De Trinitate*, XII, cap. 9-14.

is not to other truths as the sun is to other luminaries
of the sky, which it obscures in its brightness, but rather
as the sun to colors which it illumines. The light alone,
therefore, of the supreme truth shows first and through
itself that which is, as light alone shows bodies. But by
this light the truth of the thing, too, shows that which
is, as color shows bodies by the light of the sun.—It is
true, therefore, as Augustine testifies,[28] that no truth
is perceived except in the light of supreme truth. But,
as the weak eyes of the body do not see colored bodies,
unless the light of the sun is spread upon them, but are
not able to look upon the very light of the sun in itself,
except only as it is spread upon colored bodies, so, too,
the weak eyes of the mind do not look upon true things
themselves except in the light of the supreme truth; but
they are not able to look on the supreme truth itself
in itself, but only in a kind of conjunction and super-
fusion in the true things themselves.

In this manner, I think that many impure men, too,
see the supreme truth and many of them do not perceive in any wise that they see it, as, if anyone should
see colored bodies for the first time in the light of the
sun and should never turn his gaze to the sun, nor
should have learned from any one that there is a sun
or any other light that illumined bodies which are seen,
he would ignore wholly that he sees bodies in the light
of the sun and he would ignore that he sees anything besides only colored body. The pure in heart, however,
and those perfectly purified, look upon the light of
truth in itself, which the impure are not able to do.—
There is no one, therefore, who knows any truth, who
does not also know in some manner, knowingly or igno-
rantly, the supreme truth itself. It is evident now,

[28] Augustinus, *Tract. in Joh.* 35, n. 3; *De lib. arb.* II, 13,
n. 36, see above, p. 53; *Soliloq.* I, 6, n. 12.

therefore, how the pure in heart alone see the supreme truth and how not even the impure are kept wholly from the vision of it.

We think too, as Augustine intimates in the book on *Falsehood*,[29] that the truth of things is multiplex. Otherwise the name of truth would not take on plurality and distribution. For the simple comparison of one to many does not make that one many, as the comparison of one time to many temporal things which are at the same time, does not make it many times. There are not, in fact, many times at once. In the same way, if there were no truth except the supreme truth which in itself is single because of the collation of its name to many, there could be many true things, as there are many temporal things at one time. But there would not therefore be many truths, as there are not many times at the same time. For the plural name or the distributed universal sign requires many subordinates. Wherefore, they could not be called *many truths* or *all truth* if there were not many subordinate truths.—The truths of things, therefore, which are the conformities to the reasons of things in the eternal truth, are subordinated in such expressions. But perhaps the name of truth is nowhere applied except to signify in some way, at least adjacently or obliquely, the supreme truth as form of the name. For as the truth of a thing can not be understood except in the light of the supreme truth, so perhaps it is not to be hypostasized through the name of truth except when it bears the signification of the supreme truth. Truth, therefore, signified and predicated everywhere by this name truth, is single, as Anselm insists, to wit, the supreme truth. But that one truth is called many truths in the many truths of things. Since, however, truth is consequent to all things, even

[29] Augustinus, *De mend.*, cap. 20, n. 41.

to its contrary, because the false is necessarily the true false, likewise, contrary to the rule of the logicians, the affirmation of truth is consequent also to every negation, and moreover it is consequent even to the destruction of itself, because it follows: if there is no truth, it is evident that there is truth, because truth is that which is necessarily through itself. For whence, save because it is necessarily through itself, is it consequent to all things even to the destruction of itself?—Truth, therefore, is that which is necessarily through itself or at least that which is the consequent necessarily to a being necessary through itself. For otherwise it would not be consequent to every affirmation and negation.—But does the rule of the logicians truly fail here? Or does being fall outside the division of any negation, so that when being is affirmed the affirmation of truth follows from division? In whatsoever way it is, the light of truth is manifestly inextinguishable, which illumines even the extinction of itself and can not be corrupted in any way.

But it can be doubted whether any truth of things, which is the conformity of the things to their eternal reasons, be eternal and without beginning. For the truths of mathematical propositions seem to be eternal and the truths of all conditional propositions and of all negations concerning the existence of creatures seem to have had truth without beginning before the creation of things, inasmuch as *the world is not* was true, and true without beginning, before the creation of the world and was in conformity with its statement by which it was said in the eternal Word. Therefore, the conformity of the statable to its statement in the eternal Word is not God. Therefore, something other than God was without beginning.

In the same way truths of such sayings as *something*

will have been are without beginning, and they are different from each other. For the truth of the saying *something will have been* is not the same as that of sayings of this sort, *seven and three are ten*. For the one truth is the conformity of the former to its statement in the eternal Word, and the other the conformity of the latter. There are therefore many, indeed innumerable, truths without beginning, and they will be without end.

In the same way it can be inquired concerning *propositions* themselves. For it is eternal that *something will have been;* similarly *seven and three are ten;* and neither of them is the other and neither is God; therefore, they are other than God, and a great many of them are eternal.

To reply to these contentions, however, I suggest this example: let it be asserted that there was from eternity a praising of Caesar and, similarly, a praising of Socrates. According to this assertion it is true from eternity that *Caesar has been praised and Socrates has been praised,* because if there is a praising of Caesar, Caesar has been praised. Let there be, then, this word A of which the definition is *Caesar praised* and this word B of which the definition is *Socrates praised;* then, it is true that A is eternal and B is eternal, so that the predication is *per se* and not *accidentally,* as it is true *per se* that *white can not be black.* It does not, however, follow that Caesar and Socrates are eternal or that anything is eternal except the praising, because eternity is not assigned when A is said to be eternal except because of praise which is eternal in praising. Because of the eternity of this, its correlative, praise, takes on the predication of eternity. However, such correlations as praise or passion, do not require an eternal subject or being or anything or any existence outside the praising except the assertion. An example of the same sort is that God knows all things from eternity. Wherefore, if he knows A of which the definition is *Socrates known by God* and B of which the definition is *Plato known by God*, it will be true, speaking *per se*, that *A is eternally, B is eternally*, because clearly B itself is known eternally by God and A is not B nor conversely, and neither of them is God and, nevertheless, God alone is eternally; because, when it is said *A is not B and B is not A, and neither of them is God* the predication is made of corruptible subjects. But when it is said *A or B are eternally*, the predication is made *per se* thanks to the form by which these names are imposed, which obviously are called eternal because of the eternal knowledge of God. Nor does the truth of such a statement require the existence or coeternity of anything outside of God. Similarly, therefore, when it is said *this truth is eternal or this statable fact is eternal*, the predication is made by the form correlative to the statement in the eternal Word; for this relation, however, nothing is required to be except God.

Consequently, the objections listed above will be replied to thus, or else we shall be compelled to confess that statable facts are nothing else than the eternal reasons of things in the divine mind. It can, however, be inquired, since truth and being are the same, because truth is, as Augustine says [30] *that which is*, whether, as there does not seem to be any truth except in the light of the supreme truth, so there does not seem to be any being, except in the supreme being.

This is seen in an example such as the following: fluid water has in itself and of itself no determined figure, but is figured always by the figure of the container. Wherefore it can not be known and observed truly by the mind that this water is square except by

[30] AUGUSTINUS, *Soliloq.* II, 5, n. 8.

thinking and observing that the figure of its container is
square and except by observing its shape in connection
with the figure containing, figuring, and supporting in
its shape the water which is fluid and which slips of
itself, if it were left to itself, from that shape. In the
same way, every creature of itself, if it were left to itself, as it is from nothing, it would thus slip back into
nothing.—Since, therefore, it is not of itself, but considered in itself alone, it is found apt to slip into non-
being: where or how will that which is be seen, except
in connection with that which supports it lest it flow into
non-being and except in view of the fact that it is supported by that? For any creature to be, therefore, is,
as it seems, for it to be supported by the eternal Word.
Concerning which Word Paul says: [31] *Upholding all
things by the word of his power.* Nor is it known truly
that any thing is created, unless it seems in the mind
to be supported by the eternal Word. And so, in all
being, that which is to adhere to first being seems in
some manner first being, although in seeing, one may
even ignore that one sees first being, nor is posterior
being seen except in the comparison of it to the first
being which supports it.—However, we said above that
the healthy eye of the mind seeing the first and supreme
light in itself would see, too, all other things more
clearly in it than if it examined the same things in
themselves.—But, perhaps, it is not clear to some
that a thing can be seen more clearly in its exemplar
than in itself. But since the knowledge of a thing is
double, one in itself, the other in its exemplar or likeness, when the likeness or exemplar is of more lucid essence than the thing itself of which it is the likeness,
the knowledge of the thing in its likeness or exemplar
is more noble and more clear and more open. But

[31] *Hebr.* 1: 3.

when, on the contrary, the thing is of more lucid essence than its likeness or exemplar, the knowledge itself of the thing in itself is more clear and more open to the healthy eye of the mind than the knowledge in its likeness or exemplar. And according to this, since the divine essence is the most lucid light, all knowledge of it by likenesses is more obscure than knowledge through itself, but all knowledge of a creature is more certain and more pure and more manifest in the most lucid eternal reasons of creatures in the divine mind (which are the most lucid exemplars of creatures) than in the creature itself.—The example of this thing, however, namely that a certain thing is seen more clearly in its likeness, is found obviously in corporeal sight: for when a direct ray from the eye, by which ray, clearly, the body is seen in itself, goes into a dim light, and when a ray reflected from a mirror to the same body, by which ray, obviously, that body is seen in its likeness, goes into a bright light, it will be seen obscurely in itself and perspicuously in its likeness, as happens when in the evening hours or at night trees are seen more clearly in the water than they can be seen in themselves because of the ray reflected from the water to the tree which passes to the lucid sky, while the ray direct to the tree itself passes into the obscure light of some shadowy thing opposite. On the other hand, when the ray reflected from the mirror passes into obscure light and the ray direct to the body passes into lucid light, the thing will be seen obscurely in its likeness and perspicuously in itself.

The definitions of truth given above are common to all truths. But if one descend to single things, a diversified principle [ratio] will be found for each truth. For the truths of particular things are the definitions of their first or second being, inasmuch as the truth of proposition, by which a proposition is true, is nothing other than the statement of something concerning something or the statement of something from something; and that is the definition of its first being. —The truth, however, of proposition, by which a proposition is true, is nothing other than the signification of being of that which is or of non-being of that which is not. And this is the definition of its second being. Wherefore, the intention of truth, as the intention of being, is ambiguous: from one part it is one in all truth and, nevertheless, by appropriation it is diversified in particulars.

ON THE TRUTH OF PROPOSITION

It is not necessary that the thing, which partly is or was and partly will be, be or have been totally before its completion. But when something has been completed, it is necessary then and for the rest that it be or have been absolutely. Between the beginning and the completion it is necessary that it be or have been in some respect [*secundum quid*].—And so, in the case of contingent things which are made in time, it is possible that they will not be completed. For example, let the total motion from A to B be called C. Between the beginning and the end of C motion, C with respect to that which it has been, is necessary, and C in the respect that its future part will not be, is possible. But, between the beginning and the end, C motion is always spoken of truly, since C is. This being, however, is not complete being and determinate and definite, but it is incomplete and indeterminate and indefinite. Wherefore, although in the middle of the motion C, it is said truly that C itself is, nevertheless, it can not consequently be said: it is necessary that C has been, because, since it is present, part of it has passed and part is future; it is said truly that C is partly past, because it is. But, when something is past, it is perfect. C, however, before its end is neither past nor perfect. Nor is it truly said that C has been, because that would be to say that that which is still future has been.

It is manifest, therefore, that it is said truly of something that it is, and yet it does not follow thereafter, that it has been; on the contrary it can not not have been, with respect to something of it, and it can not be, with respect to something of it which is still future: so, it is true now that this year is, but still, it will not be true immediately hereafter, that this year has been. And, if time were to have its end before the end of this year, it would then be true that this year is now, and it would never be true that this year has been.— But it is said of anything that it is completed and finished or that it has been completed and finished, immediately after it can not not have been, or rather, immediately after it is necessary that it have been.

I believe the truth of proposition and of opinion of a future contingent thing is such as that of a thing whose being is unterminated. For the truth of speech or of opinion is the adequation of word or opinion and thing. However, this adequation is nothing other than for it to be in the thing as the speech or opinion states, and in future things it is for the thing to be in the future as the speech or opinion asserts that it will be. The truth, therefore, of speech or opinion concerning a future thing is the present assertion of the existence of the thing in the future together with the existence of the thing in the future. But the present assertion of speech or opinion is, and it will not be able not to have been. The existence, however, of the future thing is not yet, but will be able not to be; and so, the truth of a future thing in respect to something of it is now and has necessity; it is not yet in respect to something of it and has contingency.

Although, therefore, the truth of this proposition *the antichrist is* may be spoken of truly, nevertheless, it does not follow that it will be necessary forthwith that he have been, because the truth of it is incomplete and indeterminate being. For to impose necessity on this truth is the same as to impose necessity on the assertion of a future thing that it will be and to impose necessity on the existence of the future thing. Any truth, therefore, of such propositions as *the antichrist will be, the antichrist is future,* is not necessary but contingent, because it is possible that any such proposition be false. —But the truth of them is partly the present assertion concerning the future antichrist, that he will be, and it is partly the future existence of the antichrist.

But from part of the assertion, this truth is immutable. For any such proposition asserts the same thing always and in the same manner as it now asserts it. But it is impossible that a change be made from existence which is not yet to non-existence. For all change is from that which is, not from that which is not yet changed, and is future. Therefore, none of these propositions or statements is changeable from its truth which partly is and partly will be, because that part of truth which is at present will always remain in one manner. Of the part which is not yet, no change can be made before it takes place. Whence, if it never takes place, change will never be made from it. Whence, whether the antichrist will be or whether he will not be, it will not be changed from truth into falsity, unless that contingent which it has, changeable from truth into falsity, is necessary. For it is said to be changeable from truth into falsity in two ways: either because it is not susceptible of falsity, or because with respect to this order after truth it is not susceptible of falsity. In the first manner it is necessary, but in the second manner it is not necessary.

ON THE KNOWLEDGE OF GOD

If God knows that the antichrist is or was or will be, the antichrist is or was or will be. But the antecedent is necessary. Therefore, the consequent too is necessary. If, however, the antecedent is contingent, it turns out that change and deception can befall in God. And, likewise if the consequent were contingent, since it is convertible with the antecedent, other inconsistencies seem to turn up: for if the antichrist will be, God knows it or else something is concealed from him, which is inconsistent. On the other hand, if he knows it and it is contingent, because it is contingent that it can come to pass that it never be, then, when it does happen, since God does not know the false, God will not know that the antichrist is or was or will be, and thus it is possible that God should not know what he knows; and a change befalls him or, if he remains in the prior opinion, a deception befalls him, which can not be supposed. To posit the impossible, that I now see as present the future running of Socrates tomorrow, it would be forthwith true and necessary in me that I have seen the future running of Socrates. And, nevertheless, the running of Socrates would still be contingent. In the same way, since all things have been present to God from eternity, is it not necessary that he know things which in themselves are future and contingent, and that his knowledge concerning changes be unchangeable? And since he can not be deceived in his knowledge, the being of things follows from his knowledge and contrariwise. Who is there

285

who doubts that the contingent follows from the necessary and that on the contrary the impossible follows from the contingent on the destruction of the contingent?—It must be conceded, therefore, that the contingent follows from the necessary and the impossible from the contingent. But necessity is double: one which forces a thing to being and is the *antecedent necessity;* the other which follows the being of a thing and does not force it to being and is the *consequent necessity.*— For the necessity of the solar and the lunar motion forces the eclipse to being. But the necessity of the following sort, that I have seen Socrates run yesterday, does not force Socrates to run, but it followed from the running of Socrates.

Further, that which is necessary, is incessantly. But to be incessantly is either to be in all time or to be in the simplicity of eternity. Consequently, that necessary which forces the thing to being, will be incessantly in all time and can not precede the contingent. That necessary, however, which follows the being of the thing and whose being incessantly is in the simplicity of eternity, necessarily precedes the contingent, as it is necessary that God know that the antichrist will be. From which it follows that the antichrist will be, which is contingent. And again, from this: *the antichrist will not be,* which is contingent, it follows that God does not know that the antichrist will be, which is impossible.

That, however, which is said in logic to the effect that the contingent does not follow from the necessary and the impossible does not follow from the contingent, must be understood of the contingent and necessary and impossible of which there is one measure, as for example the measure of the necessary is time according to its universality, as it is of the contingent according to its part.

When, however, we imagine for the measuring of infinite eternity a measure from the totality of time, we are deceived in that imagination, and we can not be free from that deception until the eye of the mind, purged of the composition of time, ascends to the contemplation of simple eternity.

And note that it is in different senses that the sun is said to be moved in all time and that God is said to be in all time. For God is said to be in time, because he is absent from no time or because he is in the simplicity of eternity, from which all time flows, according to the following: *Thou who commands time to go from eternity.*

THE SUMMA PHILOSOPHIAE

Up to the time of the publication of the *Philosophical Works of Robert Grosseteste* by Dr. Baur in 1912, scholars had from time to time lamented the loss of a reputed *Summa of Philosophy* from the hand of the bishop of Lincoln. Not infrequently they hazarded guesses concerning its contents; the tendency was to make it a compendium of the sciences similar to that of Roger Bacon. The *Summa* has now been published in Dr. Baur's edition, but the effect of the publication of the long sought work of Grosseteste is to make clear that Grosseteste is not its author; it may even be doubted, notwithstanding the similarity of its doctrines to those of Grosseteste, that the author is, as Dr. Baur insists he is, of the school of Grosseteste. The *Summa* is, however, for all the doubts concerning its authorship, an outstanding statement of humanistic scientific augustinism as it flourished at Oxford in the thirteenth century and at Chartres in the twelfth century. Since Alexander of Hales and Albertus Magnus are quoted by name in it, and since there are several mentions of doctrines attributable to Thomas Aquinas, though Thomas is not mentioned by name, it may be supposed that that treatise was written during the averroistic debates between 1260 and 1277.

The work covers in the course of nineteen treatises and two hundred eighty-four chapters, the sum of human knowledge. It opens with a history of philosophy, and progresses through the problem of knowledge, metaphysical questions, theology, cosmology, psychology, optics, perspective, astronomy, natural philosophy, meteorology, mineralogy. The selection which follows is the second and third treatises of the nineteen, which are concerned with the problem of knowledge and the implications of truth. Fundamentally the analysis is augustinian and might very plausibly have been the work of a follower of Grosseteste. Three truths are distinguished, an incomplex, a complex and a medium truth: the incomplex truth is the very entity of a given thing; the complex truth is the adequation of thing and understanding; the medium truth is of symbols. The existence of contingent things, once more, can be made the warrant for concluding the existence of a necessary being, uncreated and uncaused, but in the manner of latterday augustinism the illumination of God is not only pursued back to its source that God may be known, but the things lighted up by God are examined that he may be known more fully.

THE SUMMA OF PHILOSOPHY

(attributed to Robert Grosseteste)

TREATISE II.[1]

CHAPTER I.

That truth is necessarily eternal.

That truth is follows absolutely from the fact that something is true, because every being of a concrete thing brings with it necessarily the being of its abstract. But every necessary thing is true. That truth is, therefore, follows necessarily from the fact that anything necessary is.

That truth is, moreover, follows necessarily, for like reason, from the fact that something true or necessary has been. But it is necessary and necessarily true that either something or nothing is or has been from eternity. That truth has been from eternity follows necessarily, therefore, from the fact that something or nothing has been necessarily from eternity. Moreover, it is highly inconsistent and very much contrary to natural reason to deny the proposition: *something or nothing has been from eternity,* or the statement that *something or nothing has been from eternity.* But it follows absolutely from the statement that *truth eter-*

[1] DIE PHILOSOPHISCHEN WERKE DES ROBERT GROSSETESTE, pp. 290-302.

nally is not or has not been that this statement is or has been eternally true, and therefore, whether it is supposed that truth has not been from eternity or whether that is posited, it follows necessarily that truth is and has been from eternity, and also that it is necessary or that the necessity has been absolutely from eternity. Therefore, it is wholly necessary that the being of truth be, and truth as well as its being is an absolutely eternal necessity.

Chapter II.

That the eternal truth can not be created nor even caused.

If the eternal truth has been created however it follows necessarily that it has been caused. For every created thing is necessarily also caused. If, therefore, every caused thing has its effective cause, and every effective cause is prior in nature or origin or causality or eternity to the thing caused, it follows definitely that it is true that another truth necessarily precedes this truth which we showed above as eternal and it by consequence is more truly eternal. If that were posited in turn to have been created or caused, it would go back *in infinitum,* which is vain, or it would be necessary to set up a circle of eternal truths causing each other and caused by each other; and so, prior to themselves, they would be posterior, and they would be caused by themselves, and they would be at once eternal and not eternal, all of which are entirely absurd. It remains, consequently, that the eternal truth is wholly uncreated and uncaused.

Chapter III.

That from the fact that the eternal and uncreated truth is, it follows absolutely that some being is truly eternal.

But the eternal truth, whose being has now been declared to be most necessarily, is either some being in itself by the mode of substance—and it is this that we intend—or else it is the disposition or accident of some eternal being. But every disposition or accident is other than and posterior to that of which it is. But if the truth is absolutely eternal, and that of which it is the truth is also eternal, and moreover the one is truth, the other that of which it is the truth, and the truth itself of the latter is the disposition or the accident of the prior, there will necessarily be many eternal things diverse from each other in nature, and there will be real priority and posteriority in eternity; and there will be these two impossibilities: that two things diverse in nature be coeternal, but still not be coeval, and again that they be coeternal but still by nature not be together, and both be true and both be eternal, but still the truth of the subject not be prior to the truth of the disposition or of the accident, which are wholly contrary to reason. But since truth is the disposition or accident of the other, it will have its being from that of which it is the disposition or accident, and so it will have been caused necessarily and will have been separable mentally from its subject or its causing, which is the common characteristic of every accident. There will therefore be a subject and a causing of it truly intelligible apart from the positing of its coeternal truth, and thus something can be understood to be truly without that which would be the true being itself.

These however are grave inconsistencies and contrary to reason.

The eternal truth therefore is not other, and can not be other, than that of which it is the truth, which is a being of the genus or manner [*maneries*] of substance. But even though it were feigned that non-being, for example a chimera, be eternal, and even though it is true by an eternal truth that the chimera is not, it would follow necessarily that this negative truth is rooted in some positive or as it were affirmative truth. For it is positively true that this truth *the chimera is not* is necessary. And if this negative truth is eternally true, this positive truth is necessarily so, that is, it is true that *this negative is eternally true.*

CHAPTER IV.

That it is impossible that there be many eternal truths or many eternal substances different in species.

It follows necessarily from the fact that there are many truths different in species or nature which are equally eternal that no one of them is prior by any causality or eternity, because nothing is prior to an eternal thing either by causality or by eternity, and so none of them is prior to the other. However all other things which are different differ in that they are divided by the specific difference of some genus, and they agree in something common which is prior by nature to the things which are different and even to the differences themselves. There will therefore be many things— that is differences and what is common to them—prior by nature to the eternal things, the positings and truths of which precede necessarily their being, just as they themselves by nature precede these eternal truths. And so it will be possible- to understand that it is true that before the absolutely eternal truth there are other truths; which are most grave inconsistencies. But if perchance the eternal truths are imagined not different in the proper sense of the word, but only diverse, just as the ten first categories of things are only diverse from each other and not properly different, whether truth be applied to them univocally, or analogically, or even equivocally, or finally with many meanings, they will nevertheless necessarily agree in something common, as in some being of these four mentioned modes, and still it would be impossible for them to be the first genera of things, whether they are posited in some genus of being or not, but they are necessarily diverse from each other not only in their essential properties, but altogether, so that they differ from each other as things that differ by species; which has just been declared to be impossible.

Truth will therefore be an eternal uncreated substance, wholly unique, and whose being of necessity must be, and can not but be.

Chapter V.

That truth is multiplex, and what each truth is in fact or in definition.

There is however one truth simple and incomplex, another complex, another medium.—But the incomplex truth is the very entity of any thing, that is the indivision of the thing that is and its being. And since there is one being substantial and another being accidental, and since that of accident is mentally separable from its subject without injury to the substance or entity of the subject, the truth of each thing will be of its substantial being undivided from it rather than of its accidental being. Wherefore the more incorruptible anything is in itself, to that extent this indivision of the thing that is from its being is stronger and therefore truer; the more corruptible, the more remote it is from the truth of being. The accident, however, the being of which consists only in inhering in something else, has in itself extremely little of the principle of being; but its truth depends on the truth of its subject.

The complex truth, in the next place, is the adequation of the thing and of the understanding joining the intention of the predicate with the intention of the subject or disjoining the latter from the former. Wherefore it is divided only into affirmative and negative. This truth however is the adequation of two things, that is, the thing and the understanding either in actuality or in condition and potentiality alone—and in the latter case it would be called the adequability; for the understanding is either in potentiality alone of understanding, as the possible or material intellect, or in potentiality at the same time as in condition, as in those who sleep or those who have turned away from sense or are not paying attention; or it is in potentiality and in condition and at the same time in actuality, as the acquired intellect—but none the less it is a condition; or it is in potentiality and actuality with a certain medium disposition between the existence of understanding apart from the condition and actuality of understanding, as the intellect of those learning.—And it is manifest that the actual or even conditional adequation is the consideration of the understanding related in all to the object knowable or intelligible to the understanding. For knowledge is of the class of relatives.—But the adequation of the understanding and the thing is in potentiality alone, or it can be considered from the part of the understanding only, or from the part of the thing only, or from the part of both. For it is true that A is a letter or that A is not B, even though no understanding should understand that and consequently even though it were understood by no one.—The medium truth finally is in signs, which the understanding uses to express complex truth, and in things themselves. For truth is in these as if in its material principle without the adequation necessary for the understanding.

CHAPTER VI.

That we do not believe the complex truth is properly in the first and uncreated intellect.

But since there is one uncreated intellect, which is the first intellect, and another created, and the created intellect is either the separated intelligences or the souls —nor indeed are there more beings than these with understanding in the nature of things—it must be observed that in the first intellect there can be found no combination whatsoever of predicate and subject. For all acceptance of predicate and subject is naturally prior to the connection and combination of them with each other, but it is impossible to find such acceptance in the first understanding, as we shall demonstrate elsewhere. This moreover seemed to be true of the intellect of the created intelligence too, since it is an intelligence in effect lacking complexity and potentiality connected with the operation of many things which have to do with the part and not the whole. And more concerning

this at another time.   The soul however first chooses
predicable and subjectable intentions, and consequently
compounds or divides and has its actuality above itself, discerns itself by turning about upon itself and
pronounces that the true or false is, as soon as an accidental adequation of that which judges and that which
is judged turns up, that is, an adequation of understanding or intellect and that which is understood by
itself; and that latter which is understood by itself is
just as things themselves are constituted or are not constituted, and it perceives nothing more or less in understanding.   But since in our case we are reduced in like
manner to conjecturing even in the understanding of
first simples, we err in fashioning the complex truth of
the eternal statables, and it can not be true that there
is in the understanding of the intelligence an absolutely
consimilar composition of perpetual statables.   But more
of this at another time.

CHAPTER VII.

*That truth is expressed in many ways and accordingly
it is also defined or accepted variously by different
people.*

The complex truth is sometimes conceived only by
the mind or the understanding, and is sometimes expressed in signs.

And of these the first, according to Anselm,[2] is *rightness perceptible to the mind alone,* while the second
must be declarative of the complex, according to
Hilary, and the latter is brought forth outwardly by
word or writing or nod or gesture or, universally, by

[2] *On Truth,* ch. 11; see above, p. 172

some act or permission, and so it is an adequation of active signification on the part of a sign, that is, of the word or writing or of any of the others named above and of passive signification of the thing signified by any of these signs.

But the truth of active signification, that is, on the part of the sign signifying outwardly the motion of the soul, is the adequation of the soul and of its exterior sign signifying according to the common acception of that which signifies the thing signified without. Wherefore if this word *man* signified *ass* in another nation and conversely the word *ass, man,* it would be true for an interpreter of that nation that man is ass and conversely. In the same way in the other signs mentioned above, it is possible that apparent equivocation or amphibolies be made.

Chapter VIII.

On the truth which is in things as if by a material mode.

But the truth which is in things themselves from the relation alone of things to each other (or because A is a letter and is not B, apart from any action of the understanding) is the adequation of understanding and things only in potentiality, just as we should say, even though every understanding were circumscribed, that there are infinite truths in things which result from the relation of the subject to the predicate by the mode in which the one can be present in the other, that is, the predicate in the subject, or perhaps not be present, as has been said above. And the truth of this can be either eternal, since true relations and many modes of being or understanding and even of understanding as if in a passive mode are in divine things, or else non-eternal. But the non-eternal is either continuous and stable, as that *man is animal,* and that *A* is not *B* and infinite similar truths, or else transitory and temporal or mutable, which is contingent truth.

Consequently all truth which can be conceived from the relation of two things, related to each other by the mode of inherence or agreement, is either eternal or non-eternal.—Further the non-eternal is either perpetual or non-perpetual. But the perpetual is either necessary through itself, as that *man is animal,* or necessary by accident, as that *this man is animal.*—One variety of the non-perpetual is of the contingent; on the other hand, the other is necessary by accident but conditionally, as that *A is moved when it is moved.*

CHAPTER IX.

That it follows from the fact that there is mutable truth that there is an immutable created thing, and it follows as consequence to that that there is something immutable uncreated.

It follows necessarily from the fact that there is a mutable truth that there is something continuous, and the mutable is not immutable, and the contingent is not necessary, or conversely.—And in the same way it follows from the truth necessary by accident that there is something necessary through itself, because at least *this thing necessary by accident is not necessary through itself* or conversely.

But it follows necessarily too from the non-eternal truth, whether perpetual or mutable, that there is something immobile and eternal, because this mutable truth will be mutable, or the mutable will not be immutable. For both statements were true from eternity. And we understand here truth as it is in things themselves apart from the action of the understanding compounding or dividing.

If therefore the uncreated truth which is the uncreated being or not other than it by the mode by which it is being, is cause of all caused being, it will likewise, by the mode by which it is incomplex truth, be cause of all incomplex caused truth, and it will be posited absolutely, by the mode by which complex truth can be made to be, the cause and root in a certain manner of all complex truth. For just as all being is because of first being, so too all truth is because of first truth. Complex truth, however, is actual in the understanding as in its efficient cause, in things themselves as in matter, and in uncreated truth as in form and end.

Chapter X.

That the contradictory opposition derives from uncreated truth the truth of one extreme and the impossibility of the other.

It is necessary that the uncreated truth, as well the complex as the incomplex estimation of our consideration, admit of complex negative opposition. For whether truth is regarded as the indivision of being and the thing that is, which is the principle [*ratio*] of incomplex truth, or whether it is regarded as rightness perceptible to the understanding alone, which is the principle of complex or apparently complex truth, there will be assigned a negative opposition to it such as non-indivision, non-rectitude, infinitely removed from it. For not even an understanding of infinite comprehension can comprehend a greater distance than the contradictorily opposite. The distance therefore between them is absolutely infinite. Eternal truth is therefore known in only one or the other part of the contradiction. If therefore first being is absolutely, which can be understood either of uncreated or created being, it will be plain that an eternal contradiction in being and non-being is established.—It will therefore be eternally true by incomplex truth that its being is extremely far removed from non-being, and by complex truth that two contradictory opposites absolutely can not be true at the same time.

In like manner it will be true of any truth, that is, the incomplex and the complex caused truth, and of the truth of signs and the potential truth, which we said above is found in the things themselves from the relation of things to each other, that truth is present in only one or the other part of the contradiction, and it is impossible that two contradictory opposites be true at the same time.—The truth of this philosophic principle, as has been declared, is absolutely eternal and of every opposition the affirmation or the negation is true, which according to what has been said above is the truth of sign. And these two are the first principles of knowing and philosophizing. Moreover because it is impossible for the understanding to judge between contradictory opposites by distinguishing that which is completely unknown, it will be necessary that the understanding know both principles, but one through itself and the remaining one through the other, and that both be in the understanding at the same time, but in different manners. And concerning these things more at another time.

CHAPTER I.

On the unity [3] *of knowledge and on its eternity as well as its perpetuity.*

It is true that something or nothing is known, and that is true by a complex or an apparently complex truth. Let A therefore be the name of that which is some thing and B the name of that which is nothing: then either A is known or it is not known. However for A to be known is for the knowledge of it or about it to be—and this is what we intend. But for A not to be known is either true by a complex truth or an apparently complex truth or else it is not true. But if the first of these is supposed, since complex truth is an adequation of the understanding and the thing, it follows necessarily from the fact that A is not known that something is known, and so from the fact that A is not known, it is known.—But if the second be supposed, that is, that *A is not known* is not true by a complex truth, it will be most true by real truth, that is, by the potential truth, which we said is in the things themselves, that A is not known, because there is nothing to be known; this *nothing to be known* can be from a double cause: either because it would be true that

---

[3] The word *anitas* in the text has been interpreted throughout as an error for *unitas,* and has been translated *unity.* It should be noted however that not only the printed edition, but the three manuscripts at Cambridge and Oxford, have *anitas* and not *unitas.* It is not impossible that the word is a contraction of *antiquitas;* the translation should then read the *antiquity of knowledge,* and the sense would be much that in which Eriugena says that *understandings are more ancient than things understood.* See above, p. 114.

nothing is, or having supposed that something is, it is nevertheless not known; but whether it is true that nothing is or that something is and is not known, it will be absolutely necessary that truth be not only incomplex in the first and uncreated understanding but also apparently complex. For we have already shown that the complex truth or the apparently complex truth is a thing of the understanding forming something affirmatively or negatively. Therefore since the unity of the first intellect is proved later and its necessity, and since it is assumed for the time being as well as the eternal actuality of the first intellect, it will be manifest that its knowledge is absolutely eternal and for like reason that the knowledge of the caused intelligence and the active intellect, the perpetuity and actuality of each having been proved in its proper place, are absolutely perpetual.

But also in the intellect acquired in us it is absolutely necessary that knowledge be formed truly from the adequation of thing and understanding. For either it is known truly by the understanding that *two and two are four* and likewise an infinite number of similar things manifest to the understanding—and it is this for knowledge to be true for the understanding—or it is not known truly; but this can occur from a double cause: namely, either because it is held only by opinion and therefore is not known truly, or because it is in no manner true; the first of these is inconceivable and inconsistent, since both parts of the contradiction in opinion are judged possible in the understanding of those holding contrary opinions; and so, by that reason by which it is reckoned that *two and two are four,* it can be reckoned that *two and two are not four;* which is inconsistent. The second moreover is manifestly false. It remains therefore that something is known truly and that knowledge is truly.

CHAPTER II.

What is knowledge with respect to the thing in the un-created understanding and also in the created under-standing, whether the intelligence or the rational soul?

Knowledge is a passion or perfection resulting from the union of an intelligible and an intellective power. And this is its ground reason in the mode by which it is generated or is made in the understanding. But in the mode by which it is as it is in fact, it is a condition [*habitus*] by which the true is discerned from the false and by which one of them may be judged to be true.

The intellectual, to be sure, is present first, and the intellectual is the thing outside, for example, the wood or the stone, and all things divided by species and essence by the understanding but according to that which the species or intellectual idea of the thing is, taken in the way mentioned above. For it was de-termined elsewhere that only the essence of the thing is known truly and the thing itself is known by its essence, which in the understanding is called its species or idea and sometimes too its form and occasionally its universal and common predicable.—Concerning each of these we shall treat more fully later. Knowledge however in the first and uncreated intellect or even in the intelligence is not univocal in any of its modes with our intelligence, concerning which we are treating here, nor similar except by a remote similitude, which is with the greatest dissimilitude. For although, according to Aristotle,[4] the forms or species of intelligible things in the soul are not other than the very essence of the thing which alone is known truly, nevertheless they

[4] *Metaphysics* VII, 1, 1042 a. Cf. too *De Anima* II, 12.

differ in reason from the essence. And indeed the essence of wood or of stone and of other things is not truly in the soul, but still that which is understood truly of the thing is not other than the essence. Otherwise if the essence of the thing were understood by another species, while the essence of the thing is truly the quiddity and form of it, there would be an ulterior form of the form which is known truly and is not the essence itself of the thing; which is incongruous. And these things will be stated more precisely elsewhere.

Consequently the forms united to the understanding or to be united to it or the species or ideas or universals are, some of natural things, and some of things which are produced by free will or chance.—Natural things, however, are some, of the genus of substance, and some, of the genus of accidents. Therefore the species or forms or ideas are united to the understanding with nothing mediating, as the natural form is united to matter, since the understanding is a spiritual mirror bringing into actuality by an innate light the idol or the phantasm in the human imagination where it is in potentiality, just as light brings color into actuality. The phantasm itself however once it has been brought into actuality perfects the understanding by its own property and makes of the possible intellect the acquired intellect or the intellect in condition, just as the species of color moves and perfects the sense by its own property. These things are treated more fully elsewhere.

If however the intelligible species were united to the understanding with some medium intervening, the incongruities mentioned above would return, and the intelligible species would not themselves move the apprehensive power, but their idols would, and the idols would be understood more truly than the species themselves. We however see manifestly that the excellent sensible corrupts the sense because it can not be made by the mode by which every idol is, but only by the mode by which the natural thing is. And this at another time.

CHAPTER III.

On the knowable and its nature and variety.

The subject of knowledge, generally speaking, is double: for the understanding is the subject through itself as that in which the knowable is immediately or as that of which it is. The knowable, moreover, like truth, is either incomplex in actuality and potentiality, or complex in potentiality alone. For it can not be said properly that the knowable is conditionally or actually united to the understanding, but rather that the known is. And the incomplex is properly the thing itself or its essence. For everything which is known, as was said above, is known through its own essence.

Being however is one thing by itself, another by accident. But being by itself is either by itself and first, which is properly first substance and this something and individual, or else it is by itself but secondarily, and this has to do either with the genus of the substance of things, as genus and difference and species in the genus of substance, as rational animal, man, or else of the genus of the substantial accident of things.—Another is being by accident as when the musician builds and similar beings.

Consequently there is, through itself and first, incomplex knowledge of being, but still it is not properly knowable in so far as it is individual and particular, but rather sensible, except in its universal, since truth in nature is preserved in particulars. For these are the principles of universals; but they are known in their universal. For the particular is properly the first knowable or intelligible, and the second knowable or intelligible is the species itself and idea of the thing, which is called universal.

The knowable therefore is the individual itself or the individual form. But united more immediately to the understanding is the universal form itself which contains the individual. And this is rather known than knowable. It is clear too that the knowable, complex in potentiality, alone is statable potentially or really true or false, and this too is particular; for in the same way the statable has been said to be particular.

CHAPTER IV.

On the division of knowledge in genus and in relation to the understanding knowing or considering.

Knowledge is either the name of the condition by which the understanding speculates easily what is true, and what false, and understands actually—and thus it · is properly called *knowledge*—for condition is midway between potentiality and actuality, by which potentiality passes easily into actuality; or else it is that act of speculating or understanding—and thus it is properly called *consideration;* or it is the disposition to the act of knowing or the condition in learning, whether the learner begins to know by proper exercise, and that is called *investigation,* or instructed by some one else, which is properly called in the person teaching, *doctrine,* in the person learning, *discipline.* But knowledge in the first manner is a thing in no way univocal either of the uncreated intellect or of our knowledge or even of the caused intelligence.

Understanding of the caused truth is this: a condition from the actual thing or reason—or it is distinguished in both ways. This condition however is either concreated with the caused intellect or is acquired by discovery or is acquired by doctrine or is infused upon one.

But sensitive knowledge is not properly knowledge, but is a way to it. For human knowledge is most of all generated from the relation of it to the understanding.

Chapter V.

On the division of knowledge in genus in relation to that of which it is.

Knowledge however, as has been said above, is either simple and incomplex or complex or apparently complex. Simple knowledge is either of the unity of the thing or of the quiddity in one manner. The quiddity moreover is either incomplex, which is the true essence of the thing, of which the property is to be known or understood in the manner stated above, or else the complex quiddity, namely, when it is known what the thing is by definition. For definition is the speech indicating the being of the thing.—And knowledge of the quiddity of the thing in the first manner supposes that the thing is absolutely in nature, but knowledge of it in the posterior manner, not at all. For if we know what a phoenix is or an eclipse or a frenzy and many similar things, it will not therefore be necessary that they be.

Knowledge is complex which is concluded from subject and predicate or is designated by some single statable, as that *man is an animal* or *man is not an ass.*

But apparently complex knowledge we rather construct in the uncreated understanding, since that is absolutely the most simple, as will be pointed out at another time. And in the understanding of the intelligence and of the active intellect, certain of the statables are likewise known first or in themselves as that *every whole is greater than its part* and similar things. Others are not first. And it happens in two ways that there is knowledge of these: one namely by the cause and the other by the effect or not by the cause. And of these the first is knowledge because of something. In this class of knowing it is impossible that first principles be known absolutely, but only understood. The second knowledge which is spoken of is particular knowledge, which has its origin from the sense; it is also universal knowledge, which is collected from many parts; and it is knowledge caused by the joining of the particular to the universal, according to which knowledge and action is. For very often knowing the universal we do not know particulars, because we do not relate the particular to that universal, as, whereas *every square is an equilateral* or *every mule is sterile,* we nevertheless consider this a tetragon or that this has offspring in womb.

Moreover faith and opinion differ from knowledge since the former two are of the phantasy or the imagination, where error is found more frequently, whereas knowledge is of the understanding alone. Sometimes however faith as well as opinion approaches science, since in both there are grade and breadth, but in knowledge there is none at all.

CHAPTER VI.

On the division of sciences in particular according to the subject or matter concerning which it is.

It has already been declared that knowledge is divided according to subject matter. For knowledge is referred to the knowable as it is—whether it is taken by us essentially or relatively—but not conversely. Moreover the knowable is commonly called the thing. Knowledge therefore follows the variety and characteristic of the knowable.—Some things however are divine and uncreated, which are at the extreme of nobility of being, so that they exceed very much the knowledge of creatures and most of all of mortals; others on the other hand are created, but perpetual and spiritual; others are perpetual but corporeal, and the most important difference of these needs not be taken up by us at present; others too are of the genus of accident, and of these some are related more to the speculative part of the soul, and others to the affective and motive part.

Universally however knowledge of the better and the most wonderful, as Aristotle affirms elegantly,[5] is the nobler. And therefore theosophy is incomparably more eminent than all mundane philosophy, and the knowledge of spirits is more eminent than that which is concerning bodies, and the practical is more eminent than the speculative simply. There are indeed three kinds of speculative knowledge according to Aristotle;[6] this must be understood of the speculative alone. For every practical science is in a sense speculative, but the statement is not convertible.—Aristotle moreover did not want the speculative sciences which treat of things either wholly abstracted from motion and matter, or only from motion but not from all kinds of matter (and the mathematical sciences are of this sort), or having their being in motion and matter (and the natural sciences are of this sort) to be understood to be the same as those which

[5] *Metaph.* 1, 2; III, 2 and X, 7, 1064 a.
[6] *Top.* 1, 14, 105 b sq.; *Metaph.* V, 1, 1026 a.

deal with the intentions of things (and dialectic and demonstrative science are of this sort) or of speech (of which sort is grammar which treats of the congruity of speech, or rhetoric which treats of the ornamentation of speech).

The practical sciences, however, of which the principal end is not that we may know but that we may be made good, regard principally the morals arising from free will and, as end, the felicity of living well. And since some morals are gratuitous, that is, divinely infused, some natural, and some acquired, it is plain that that science which evolves the gratuitous morals and which is the other part of theosophy, is incomparably more useful than all the other sciences. For theosophy too like philosophy is divided into the speculative simply and the practical.—That science however which deals with acquired morals by which natural morals are improved rather from the point of view of nature, concerns the passions of virtue rather from the point of acting according to virtue. And of these Aristotle describes the first in the *Ethics;* the other Plato first but incompletely describes in the book of *Laws.* For civil knowledge is the more notable part of moral philosophy. Knowledge of canon likewise, which ecclesiasts use, falls under and serves practical theosophy.

Plato divides knowledge more generally into natural and moral and rational,[7] and Alfarabi [8] and Algazeli [9] much more particularly. For they say that one science is of language, another of logic, and one doctrinal, another natural, another divine, and one civil, and another

---

[7] Attributed to Plato by Cicero *Acad. Post,* 1, 5, 19. See Sextus Empiricus *Adv. Math.* VII, 16.

[8] *De Ortus scientiarum* and *De Scientiis.*

[9] *Philosophiæ tractatus,* I, 1.

of judging and speaking.—Moreover they divide the doctrinal science into arithmetic, geometry, the science of appearances and the science of the stars and also into music and the science of weights and the science of natural qualities, the particulars of which moreover Alfarabi works out, and Algazeli followed him.

CHAPTER VII.

On the difference between science and art.

Moreover there seems to be this difference between science and art, that science contemplates and examines principally certain causes of its truth, but art considers rather the manner of operating according to the truth transmitted and proposed. Consequently the philosopher and the artist have a common matter but different precepts or principles and end. The sciences of the trivium [*triviales scientiæ*] therefore since they are referred to the operation of proper pronunciation, or persuasion, or argumentation, are, to be sure, called arts, since they rather inform the cognition of the true. And it happens that a certain theoretic and speculative part and a practical or operative part are assigned in almost all matter of science. First Philosophy is the only one which is concerned only with speculating on the principles of being and of knowledge.

Universally therefore those treating of any science and those eminent in it can be called philosophers. But in any art those outstanding and honorable are to be designated by the name of masters. By appropriation then and excellence those who were most eminent in first philosophy are called philosophers, and those learned in theosophy were called wise or theologians.

CHAPTER VIII.

On the origin of philosophizing and its occasion or cause and its impediments.

The origin of philosophizing was first from a double want, namely, of knowing and desiring. For just as all men by nature desire to know, so too every man is desirous of honor according to Aristotle [10] and the love of instructing and the ambition for gain mix themselves with these later.

For knowledge, since it is a certain perfection of the understanding, is of the class of the supremely lovable. But the soul, affected by passions from its union to the body, is thence according to Plato rendered mad. And therefore according to the testimony of Aristotle (?) he compares a boy to a drunken or a weak person whose soul barely knows itself, but because of its vehement intention toward sensible things, according to Saint Augustine, it does not notice this. Wherefore when the motions of the passions have been quieted for a little while, the understanding is conditioned to look upon the truth, and by diligence and learning knowledge is generated in its next potentiality. In the first place therefore under the sway of the affective power the task is one of retraction from the activity of dangerous phantasms so far as man may follow the species of the intelligibles. And thus the affect is for a double reason the beginning of philosophizing, namely, of knowing and further of avoiding the impediments to it. And therefore boys and wantons are unable to philosophize, and they are not able to judge in like manner as venerable elders according to

[10] *Ethica Nicomach,* I, 2, 1095 a.

Aristotle, and it matters very little whether a person be puerile from age or from character.

There is however a multiplex impediment to philosophizing, one natural, as dullness and bad comprehension and proneness to the contrary to knowledge, another casual or voluntary, as slight training in the art of argumentation, habit with regard to the fabulous, presumption and private love for one's own or another's opinion and similar things.

Nevertheless comprehension of the truth even of difficult things is not wholly impossible, notwithstanding the testimony of Averroes. The desire for it would otherwise be vain; this however is not the case; for nothing in nature is in vain. It is, none the less, difficult, the sign of which is that no one has been able to arrive at the comprehension of truth as he should.

ALBERT THE GREAT (1193/1206-1280)

The work of determining the significance of the writings of Aristotle, newly translated into latin, and the work of assimilating them to current thought and philosophy, would have been an imposing task for the thirteenth century to accomplish, even if the task had remained only one of erudition and science. Unfortunately it came to involve questions of religious orthodoxy no less than questions of philosophical relevance and precision. Much of the intellectual movement and much of the philosophic debates of the thirteenth century center around the circumstance that christian philosophers were convinced that the tenets of Aristotle ran contrary to christianity, and equally christian philosophers recognized on the other hand that the sum of antique science and learning, the only existing body of positivistic data and the only comprehensive theory of knowledge and being, were in the works of Aristotle and his followers and commentators. The repeated prohibitions of Aristotle's scientific works at the University of Paris and other universities during the thirteenth century, the commission appointed by Gregory IX to expurgate Aristotle of doctrines dangerous to christianity, the growth none the less of the study of Aristotle at the universities, accompanied by the spread of averroism, the condemnations of averroism in 1270 and 1277 which endangered even thomistic aristotelianism, are only some important points of the outline history of the aristotelianizing of christianity. Properly the work of Albert falls in the line of the history of that process, after the translators, among the adaptors of Aristotle, who made available to the western world the doctrines which were already in part interwoven with christian philosophy and which were in detail to form the basis of the discussions of the thirteenth and succeeding centuries.

Albert's statement of his purpose is explanation of the body of his work: it was his intention to make intelligible to the latins the major parts and instruments of philosophy: real philosophy (metaphysics, physics and mathematics), practical or moral philosophy, and rational philosophy or logic, and to that end he purposed to write a book for every book Aristotle had written, had planned to write or should, for the clarification of his scheme, have written. The importance of the venture may be judged by the condition of Aristotle in the new translations which were infiltrating during Albert's time: much that had been translated was unintelligible to a degree that philosophers of the power of Grosseteste (himself an important translator) and Bacon were said to have foresworn the use of Aristotle's works; manuscripts were scattered, and Albert had an opportunity in his travels as provincial general, bishop, preacher of a crusade, such as few scholars could rival, to come upon all the unsuspected bits of the aristotelian corpus hidden in out of the way libraries; finally, the attempts at organization of ancient lore which were in progress at the time, such as the *Specula* of Vincent of Beauvais, were seldom on the background of a systematic, organic view of the doctrines expounded. Only when Albert's enterprise was terminated, was there a well-conceived and detailed statement of a christian aristotelianism, not thoroughly self-consistent in its parts, to be sure, nor of undisputed accuracy in its interpretations, but an intelligible statement of an aristotelianism such as might be defensible from attacks of unorthodoxy and free therefore to develop its philosophical consequences.

The reputation of Albert is some indication of the extent of the influence his statement of philosophy wielded. Roger Bacon protests that even in his own lifetime he was quoted by name as an authority, contrary to the custom of the thirteenth century when contemporaries were seldom named explicitly in a doctrinal work; wise and judicious people, according to Bacon, esteemed that they had the complete body of philosophy in Albert, and they were accustomed to cite him as they would Aristotle, Avicenna and Averroes. Bacon even admits that Albert was a man of infinite energy and study, who had collected a vast number of things from the ocean of facts; yet Bacon esteemed that on the whole his influence was bad, since he like Thomas Aquinas, for all his assiduity and metaphysics, was ignorant of mathematics and science and perspective, and had begun to teach before he had learned. The disciples of Albert mix rather less criticism in their praise. Ulric of Strasbourg sums contemporary admiration in the statement that Albert was a man so divine in his knowledge that he may properly be called the stupor and miracle of his time. His erudition merits him the praise even today: he was widely learned in greek, hebrew and arabic thought no less than in the doctrines of his latin predecessors; of the greeks, he was particularly well versed in Aristotle, the pseudo-Dionysius, and John Damascenus; of the jews he seems to have known Isaac Israeli, Avicebron (ibn Gabirol) and Maimondes; of the arabs he refers confidently to Algazeli, Abubacher (ibn Tofail), Avicenna (ibn Sina), Averroes (ibn Roschd). These at least among the vast number of writers from whom he draws doctrines for confirmation or refutation, he quotes or interprets constantly. But none the less, despite the breadth of his reading, his erudition is not accurate, and his work has furnished, from the time of Bacon to the present, inexhaustible materials for the fascinating game of discovering erroneous attributions, questionable interpretations and downright errors in history of philosophy.

In a project of the magnitude and nature of that which Albert executed, it would not be surprising if inconsistencies were discovered. Modern scholarship, indeed, so far as it has been turned on the work of Albert, has been devoted, when it is not concerned with tracing esoteric doctrines and legends to their sources, to pointing out that his attempted reconciliations of philosophic doctrines were unsuccessful and inaccurate. His reputation has been made to suffer needlessly by a double comparison. His philosophy is not an organized system of thought comparable to the expression which his pupil Thomas Aquinas gave to much the same material, and in many of the questions to which Thomas gives an excellent resolution, Albert's position is either vague or at apparent variance from Thomas; on the other hand, Albert was convinced that a man might come to philosophy only by way of both Plato and Aristotle, and therefore neither his platonism nor aristotelianism conforms to later interpretations of Plato or Aristotle. By either comparison his use of terms and his perception of problems either is or seems to be vague. Add to this that much of his work is actually or virtually commentary on aristotelian or neoplatonic works, and quotations from the one group set besides quotations from the other may work violence to historical sensibilities. And finally, in the interests of completeness, he not infrequently expounds doctrines which he will not acknowledge as his own. He gives warning that all his statements should not be taken as his own opinions, and sometimes as in the case of the *de Animalibus* he closes his exposition with the explicit statement that he has expounded the position of the peripatetics as best he could, that no one might be able to criticize what he himself held in questions of natural philosophy.

If it is remembered, however, that by this time in the east as well as in the west, Aristotle had been platonized, that a hierarchy of being had been discovered in Aristotle which could be fit to the neoplatonic scheme so well that the *Liber de Causis* and the *Theologica Aristotelis,* two neoplatonic works, could pass as genuine works of Aristotle, it becomes possible to read Albert, not as an erroneous platonism or aristotelianism, but as a philosophy nicely adapted to the statement of philosophic problems. The selection from the *Parva Naturalia* which follows illustrates the philosophic dilemma of one who would distinguish Plato and Aristotle in Albert: it might be read as platonic in its upper metaphysical realm and as aristotelian in its lower empirical reaches; or it might be read as a derivative of both, identical with neither. The problem of knowledge is posed by Albert much as it appeared in the philosophy of Augustine; the question, how the intellect knows, carries the investigator from the intellect to the realm of the eternal and the changeless which is reflected in knowledge. But the aristotelian logic had added other emphases to the problem and the averroistic interpretation of Aristotle had pointed out heretical dangers in the augustinian doctrine of divine illumination. If the mind in knowing attains to eternal ideas which are either in the mind of God or dependent on the divine ideas, does it follow that the human mind is merely passive in knowledge, receiving from God or the world soul or the active intellect ideas, which in the words of Augustine are impressed on it as the image of a seal on wax? If it is, the human intellect is only a possible or passive intellect and has no active phase. Heretical consequences follow thick: for since the active intellect alone is immortal, there is then no personal immortality, but rather one immortality for the eternal generic reason of all the human species; if man is passive in receiving ideas, he has no freedom, he has no moral responsibility. The averroistic doctrine of the active intellect was sufficiently like the traditional augustinian doctrine of divine illumination to seem to implicate philosophy in heretical consequence concerning freedom, immortality and the creation of things; averroism had come to be so generally considered the interpretation of Aristotle that the whole aristotelian position was endangered in the condemnation of these errors. The accomplishment of Albert and Thomas was to disentangle aristotelianism from unchristian consequences in the interest of orthodoxy that they might be free thereafter to elaborate subtly a metaphysics which is justified sufficiently as philosophy.

The intellect, then, for Albertus, is derived from God and dependent on him; one may even speak of knowledge as divine illumination; but it is the human intellect which is active and forms judgments by joining or separating concepts abstracted from sense perceptions. The intellect is dependent wholly and solely on its first cause, the first cognitive nature. There is no intermediate between the two save only privation; there is a descent from the being of God into regions of dissimilitude in which the cognitive essence is more and more deprived of its simplicity and power, for the first cognitive nature communicates proportionally to its

effects. This is to say, if we were pure intellects, like
the angels or Adam before the fall, we should see in
individual things the principles which constitute them.
We, however, are far removed in perfection, that is, we
are far removed by privation from the first cognitive
nature, and we see principles evinced only through abstractions and inductions from experience. Our soul is
the mode of operation of the cognitive nature suited to
a being of our grade of perfection; it is a single essence
with a multiple power, intellective, sensitive, vegetative,
motive. Now, as the cognitive nature recedes further
from the first being it becomes mixed and corporeal
and mortal; in us, though there is no intelligence like
that of the angels, there is none the less an active intellect which is separated; the active intellect can operate
in virtue of its connection with the possible intellect; the latter is concerned with continuous and temporal things. Both aspects of knowledge are accounted
for: its universal aspect, in which the active intellect
is illuminative, like light, and its definitive reference,
in which the possible intellect is determined by the
active intellect working upon the phantasms of sensation. The intellect reflects in its nature God, the place
of man, and the things it is designed to know; it may be
said to be in man in three ways: as the nature which
gives being to him, as the power on which the operation of the understanding depends, as the form acquired
from many intelligibles.

The intellect is caused by a cognitive nature; it depends on God and its highest power is that of attaining
to God by contemplation. Yet all knowledge arises
from experience; indeed, in the biological sciences
Albert insists repeatedly that there is a range of questions which can be certified only by experience. Despite that, of course, scientific knowledge is not of

experience or of particulars. The universal alone is intelligible. None the less, particulars alone exist, and therefore the double problem arises of the relation of universals to things and to the intellect. To solve the problem the universal must be considered in two ways; in one it is the essence distinct from the nature of that of which it is the essence, in another it is individuated through matter to the thing in which it is. In both ways again it can be considered doubly: as essence it may be considered either as essence absolute in itself or else as communicable with many things; in that latter sense it is universal. As participated in by the individual in which it is, it may be considered either as the end of the generation or composition of the substance, and then it is its actuality, or it may be considered the whole being of the thing, and then it is its quiddity. By such distinctions the principles of metaphysics and of logic are disentangled, and one is justified in the conviction that the principles of understanding, the principles of being of the thing and the actual knowing of the thing are no different, save only that the causes of knowledge and the causes of the actually existent thing are taken differently: taken universally, they are the causes of knowledge, taken specifically and appropriated to a particular thing they are the principles of things in nature.

The problem may be stated in another way. All things are determined in their existence, and all things are potentially intelligible; yet in their particularity, until understood, they are not, at least for us, actually intelligible. The intellect is a cognitive nature, but it is in the beginning a *tabula rasa*, without content. Only in the light of the intellect are things given intelligibility actually, and only by experience of particular things is the intellect determined and given content.

As light confers color on things, so the intellect confers intelligible being or *intention* on things. The process of abstraction accomplishes the transition from the particular to the universal. There are four stages in the process according to Albert: first, the sense organ separates form from matter but not from its power or its appendages; second, imagination, one of the faculties of the sensitive soul by which the forms of sensible things are preserved when the things are not present, distinguishes matter from the presence of matter but not from the condition or the appendages of matter; third, inclinations or qualities which are not impressed on our senses, but which could not be noted without our senses, are distinguished; fourth, the quiddities of things denuded of all appendages of matter, without the inclinations of sense, but simple and separate, are apprehended. The analogy of light permits the explication of the powers of the intellect. For some things can not be known because the very intensity of their own intelligible translucence overpowers the intellect; the most manifest things in nature are to the eyes of our mind like the light of the sun to the eyes of a bat or an owl. Some things are unintelligible because they are too much intermixed with privation, like motion or time or first matter. But others are made manifest because they are illumined in precisely the right degree by our intellects themselves, and such things we know from the true first principles. From this distinction can be seen why the divine truths of theology exceed our knowledge, why the truths of motion and matter of physics fall below the powers of our intellect, while the truths of mathematics are nicely proportioned to it. Only the universal is intelligible; the universal may be abstracted from particulars; but knowledge of particulars as particulars can only be probable knowledge, never certain. By reminiscence, sense, and imagination, the intellect proceeds from potentiality to actuality. When it acquires knowledge (*scientia*) it is the acquired intellect (*intellectus adeptus*). Only by means of sense perceptions in the light of the active intellect can the possible intellect become actual, but when it has received all that which it understands, it has the light of the active intellect adhering to it in form; and when it becomes its own light, the active intellect clings to the possible in form; this is the acquired and divine intellect, the most perfect state by which man becomes in a measure like God.

Many legends have grown about the name of Albertus Magnus. For centuries his repute as a scientist made him the form and type of magician and sorcerer, and about that reputation accumulated stories of brazen statues that talked, of philtres and curing chalices, of spells, enchantments and divinely inspired architectural projects. The modern legend of Albert differs somewhat from the medieval but its basis is as accidental. The importance which he as an aristotelian gave to experience as the origin of knowledge, has not infrequently led to his selection, together with his contemporary Roger Bacon, for the honor of being the heralds of the experimental method. Suffice it that experiment had its place in his version of the aristotelian method, and that he made, particularly in botany and zoology, observations of extreme importance. He was moreover the authority of a century on the sum of the sciences, and his influence was extensive, and his knowledge has been praised, in the sciences of geography, physics, astronomy, botany, zoology, mineralogy, alchemy, medicine, physiology. His great task none the less was the philosophic labor of preparing Aristotle for the west, for although nearly all the works of Aris-

totle were known to philosophers before the writings of
Albert were ready, to Alexander of Hales for example
or Robert Grosseteste, it is only after Albert that the
force and power of Aristotle is felt through every division of the philosophic encyclopedia. Philosophy becomes truly everything that is knowable, *quidquid est
scibile,* and a modified aristotelianism is extended wherever thought penetrates. Albert's achievement is overshadowed in retrospect by the less extensive but more
perfectly articulated statement of Thomas Aquinas;
perhaps he was unfortunate in the discovery of such a
pupil to carry on his work in a system beside which his
own philosophy has been found confused and un-
ordered; or possibly his reputation is safe in legend,
and his only misfortune is to have conceived a project
too vast to tempt readers frequently to the examination
of so monumental an achievement.

ALBERT THE GREAT

THE SHORT NATURAL TREATISES ON THE INTELLECT AND THE INTELLIGIBLE.[1]

TREATISE I.

ON THE NATURE OF THE INTELLECT

CHAPTER I.

What is the intention of the work and what is the order of exposition?

As we said at the beginning of this work, the science of the soul is not complete enough in that which, in the book *on the Soul,* has been determined concerning the soul in respect to itself alone. For in addition to that it is necessary to know about the objects which occasion the passions proper to the parts of the soul. Of these objects of which the soul has passive qualities for parts or powers, some occasion passions peculiar to the soul, and some arouse passions common to soul and body. For passions are common which are such that the soul uses a corporeal instrument in operating with them, such as the passions which have to do with the vegetative and the sensitive soul. Because of that circumstance, more-

[1] B. ALBERTI MAGNI, *Parva Naturalia, De Intellectu et Intelligibili,* in *Opera Omnia,* ed. A. Borgnet. Paris: *Vivès,* 1890, Vol. IX, pp. 477-502.

over, the ancient peripatetics said that the sciences of such common passions were sciences of the soul and the body. We have already treated in part, in our small measure, of these passions in the books *on Nutriment and the Nutrible* and *on Sense and the Sensed*. There remain still however the books *on Sleep and Waking, on Youth and Old Age, on Inspiration and Expiration,* and *on the Motions* which are called *Animal, on Life and Death,* which are all concerning the common operations of soul and body.

But since the interpretation and nature of sleep can not be determined definitely, unless one have knowledge first of the intellect and the intelligible, it is necessary that we interpose here the science of the intellect and the intelligible, even though understanding [*intelligere*] is proper to the human soul apart from the body. For we consider, as we have often insisted, principally the facility of doctrine: because of this we follow in the translation of the books of natural sciences the order by which the auditor is more easily taught, rather than the order of natural things. And for this reason we did not hold, in the sequence of these books, to the order which we set forth in our introduction where we stated the division of the books of natural sciences.

In treating of the intellect and the intelligible, moreover, we shall take for granted any principles which have been determined appropriately in the third book of our work *on the Soul*. But whatsoever it seems necessary to inquire into here, we shall treat, so far as we shall be able to investigate, by demonstration and reason, following in the footsteps of our prince, for although we have not seen his book on this science, we have examined a great many books and letters of many of his disciples which treat of this matter very well.

Moreover we shall bear in mind the position of Plato too in these doctrines in which he did not in the least contradict the doctrines of the peripatetics.

Since, moreover, according to a great many of the sounder philosophers, the intellect makes the intelligible in the form of intelligibility, it is necessary that we speak first of the nature of the intellect with respect to what the intellect is, and then of the intelligible with respect to what it is in relation to the intellect, and then of the unity and diversity of the intellect with respect to intelligibles: for when these points are known, one has a sufficiently perfect knowledge of the intellect and the intelligible. The value of the investigation moreover is this, that when the above things are known, man knows properly what he himself properly is, since he is intellect alone, as Aristotle says in Book X of the *Ethics,* and he knows moreover the principle of those actions which make for contemplative felicity in him. Therefore in beginning the investigation of the nature of the intellect, we shall state first the things which are prior in nature.

CHAPTER II.

It is demonstrated in this chapter that everything cognitive in animals is caused by some other cognitive.

Let us say then that every nature which has the power of knowing any thing either has the power of knowledge from itself or from some other nature which is anterior to it. But it is known that it does not have it from itself, for then it would itself be the principle of cognition in all other things, and its own cognitive power would not be imperfect, but perfect,

not passive but active; all of these conclusions are not
in accordance with the souls of animals, as is clear from
what was stated in the book *on the Soul*.

If, however, any one should say that the soul of animals has its cognitive power from itself, in that its
cognitive power is in its own nature, just as the triangle
must from its own nature have three angles, etc., and
because of this there is no principle causing any thing
in other things, we shall say that a thing may be said
to have a property from itself in two ways. In one way
according to the efficient cause, and in another way according to the formal cause. We however are inquiring here concerning that which is cognitive through itself according to both causes, just as in physics the
first mover is moved by itself as well because it does
not have an efficient cause of its motion anterior to itself as because it is by its nature and its essence a
mover: because of it, furthermore, all that it moves has
motive power from it, and its motive power influences
like a fountain all motive powers in all other moving
things. For in inquiring thus whether the soul of animals is cognitive by itself, the things which have been
determined before follow. For since everything which
is created by that which is nobler falls away necessarily
from the first cause, the defect of cognition which is in
the cognitive power of the soul of animals shows not
only that it has its cognitive power from something
other than itself, but also that it is far removed from
that which is the first cause and fountain of cognition.
What it has from some certain thing other than itself,
which is first and perfectly cognitive of all things, must
therefore be stated. For if the soul should be said to
have it from something else which is not first and perfectly, there would be the same question concerning

that, and the process would go on *in infinitum,* or else the soul will be in the first and perfect cognitive.

Moreover, every cognitive element of mortal animals, is the same in genus with every cognitive element of mortals; or if one were said to be prior or posterior, it is with respect to some one thing. But everything which has such an agreement and unity of genus or nature, proceeds from some one thing which is the cause of the agreement of that genus in all its members. It is necessary therefore that that which is cognitive of animals be caused by some one first cognitive with respect to efficient cause as well as formal cause.

If, however, some one should say that this conclusion holds only for things caused univocally, as man generates man, but cognitive things do not have a univocal but an equivocal cause in genus, we shall convince our adversary of the truth by the fact that every equivocal is reduced to some thing univocal, which is anterior to it. Here the generating therefore will be equivocal, which, as he says, has something univocal before it, which is its first cause; and thus the conclusion will be the same as that arrived at above.

Moreover, we see that it is thus in all things, because whenever some powers and forms are found in many things, and are imperfect in certain of them but perfect in others, the imperfect are caused by the perfect, and the imperfection comes from the diversity and imperfection of the matter. Thus therefore it is necessary that this be the case too in cognitive natures. The nature therefore by which other animal natures are cognitive, will be from some cognitive and perfect first nature.

This entire discussion however is derived from a certain letter of Aristotle which he wrote *on the beginning of the universe,* which Avicenna mentions in his *Metaphysics.* Eustratius says in his commentary on the sixth book of the *Ethics* of Aristotle that all cognition of animals flows from a first cognitive cause.

CHAPTER III.

How does the imperfect vegetative and intelligible flow from the first and perfect intellective?

Let us inquire then what that first nature is. For since the first in the order of nature flows into the second, and not conversely; and since living is prior in the order of nature to perceiving, and perceiving to understanding, it seems to some perhaps that the first fountain of all knowledge would be only living, and not sentient and intelligent; especially since the first in the order of nature is by the mode of one, and the second by the mode of two, one of which is added to another, the third by the mode of three following each other in the order of the nature of added units, if perceiving is added to living, and understanding to perceiving, because as we said in the book *on the Soul,* the constitution [*ratio*] of soul is the same as the constitution of figure. For just as in figures the triangle is in the tetragon, so the vegetative is in the sensible and the sensible in the intellective. This opinion is proved to be erroneous by the fact that according to nature the imperfect is never the univocal cause of the perfect: but living separated in being from sensible and intelligible is the most imperfect in the genus of living things, nor does it have any nobility of life by which it could be a principle.

Still it is true in all things caused univocally with respect to nature, that whatsoever is present essentially in the thing caused, that is present more powerfully and more nobly and more clearly and prior and more perfectly in the cause of that which is caused. In all things cognoscitive there is present essentially a cognoscitive principle; that therefore is present more powerfully, more nobly, prior and more perfectly in the cause of those things which are cognitive. Therefore the nature by which they are sometimes cognitive does not flow from some one living thing, the living of which is separate from the cognitive.

Moreover, among things which are caused the more noble is nearer to the first principle which is the cause because it approaches with more nobilities and goodnesses; but the intellective approaches with more nobilities and goodnesses to the first and perfectly cognitive: and it is intellective rather than living only or only perceiving and living; it is necessary therefore that the fountain and origin of the knowledge of life be some intellectual nature.

Moreover, we see that all things which are perfective of sight are caused by that which is visible through itself and perfectly. For every diversity of colors is caused by light, and the diversity of colors comes from the multiform permixture of an opaque and determined body with a diaphanous body, of which the actuality in itself is illumination. Similarly therefore all cognition flows from that which is most perfectly cognitive, and the diversity of cognitions comes from the multiform overshadowing of the cognitive light radiating over those things which are cognitive in the diversity of creatures with souls [animalium].

From all these considerations, moreover, very excel-

lently grounded reasons have determined that every intelligible and sensible cognition of animals flows from
an intellectual nature perfectly and intellectually cognitive. For since it may be said that the first cause influences more than the second, the peripatetics held that
this is true of the true cause. The living, however,
separated from the cognitive, is not the cause of the
cognitive, and therefore has no influence. But although
the first cause pours all its goodnesses on that which
is caused, and goodnesses have no distinction and order
in it, because the first cause itself has all simply before
that which is caused, still in the effects those things
which are poured, are poured from the first cause under
an order and distinction: and thus that influences first
which according to the order of understanding is more
general and prior, because if the causality of the first
is removed, none of the second has influence, but on
the other hand if the causality of the second is removed, the first still influences. In the same way in
the cause which is the fountain of life and knowledge,
the living does not add something above the others, for
its living is its understanding, but in the effects in which
living has its distinctness, the living is in some other
thing as if the foundation of it. With respect however
to attributed nobilities, nothing is as multiplex as the
first cause, but that multiplicity of nobilities removes
no simplicity in the first cause, because it has all these
nobilities simply and in unity anterior to that which is
caused, and therefore the Philosopher says very well
that the first cause is pre-named for all its effects and
that it is rich in itself in respects in which it is given
to none and dispensed to none of its effects, and it is
rich in other things which it communicates proportionally to its effects.

CHAPTER IV.

That the cognitive nature is caused by the intelligence, as Plato says.

Now that these things have been stated, it is necessary to investigate further what that nature is which like a fountain pours forth every cognition and life. And it seems that Plato holds that intellectuality in man and sensibility in brutes, as well as the principle of life in vegetables and brutes, flow from the movers of the orbs and the stars, for he argues in the *Timæus* from the greatest of the gods to the movers of the heavenly bodies, remarking and saying, *I shall make a sowing of these, and I shall bestow them on you: and it is proper that you follow after.* Moreover platonists seem to agree in the same thing, however many souls of animals they derive, drawn from and caused by the intelligences.

They confirm their statements very cogently with three reasons, of which one is that every last effect in the order of things caused does not derive from the first cause except by way of the causes which are intermediate. The last effects, however, are forms of generable and corruptible things. The intermediate causes are the movers of the celestial orbs, which the Philosophers called the celestial intelligences. The nearest of these, pouring forth souls, is the intelligence moving the last orb. The second reason is that the intelligence impresses on the soul, as the soul on the nature of the animate body. Therefore as we say that the soul is the cause of the animate body and of the movements and passions of it according to which it is animated, so we must say that the lowest intelligence is the cause of the cognitive soul according to which it is cognitive, because the cognition of the soul is a certain result of the light of the intelligence. The third reason is that, just as the body is animated under a celestial body, and is caused, and ruled by it, so the soul of the body is under an intelligence and ruled by it.

The contrary of this, however, appears. For if the cognitive element of mortals should flow from and be ruled by the intelligence of the lowest orb or of some one of the other orbs or of all, then it would itself necessarily be subordinated in its own movements and operations of knowledge and emotion to the motions of the stars, because all that flows from any thing is contained and restrained by it in powers of operations. However, that the soul is especially restrained under the motions of the stars is contrary to all the peripatetics and contrary to Ptolemy. For it itself apprehends the higher movements in the spheres, and turns freely from those things toward which the motion of the stars inclines, and directs itself toward other things by wisdom in understanding, as Ptolemy says.

Moreover, the order in nature is of the first to the intermediate and of the intermediate to the last, because something which is not perfected by the first cause may be caused in the last by the intermediate. I speak of these effects, which carry some nobility in their name, for otherwise there would be no recourse from the last to the intermediate to the first; and this can not be, since everything which is, desires some goodness of the first cause, and because of that it does whatever it does. Therefore whether or not we say that the intermediate contributes something in the production of the last, the goodnesses of the last are always principally and efficaciously from the first cause, and those which are intermediate operate as instruments if they do anything with reference to the last.

Once again, we see in the light which is the universal cause of colors that although it constitutes the last colors by a commixture of the prior, still every constitution of color is by the nature of the perspicuous preservation of light as the first hypostasis of colors; and whatever any color has of the nature of color, it has from light, and if there is anything else in it, it is rather from the privation of the nature of color than from that which deserves to be called the essence of color.

In quite the same way, therefore, when the first cause pours its goodnesses upon the intermediate and last, if something should flow from the intermediate into the last, the constitution of the last will still be only from the participation of the goodnesses of the first, and if something else is in the last, it is something of privation; and this was the opinion of the best wise men of Greece, of Theophrastus and Dionysius and other philosophers. Moreover they used the simile of the light of the sun which pours itself out in the limpid air and in different earthly clouds: and although it is in the cloud by way of the air, and it is in the earth by way of the cloud, still because the intermediates give only what they have received from the sun, that which is in the last is entirely from the sun; and if the light in the intermediate and the last terms is far from the limpidity of the sun, that is rather because of the privation of matter than the result of any efficient cause.

Since we hold these opinions, therefore we say that when Plato says that the property of celestial bodies is to follow after the goodnesses of the first cause, the sowings of cognitive substances follow in the manner that instruments lead to the things which are in the art of the artist who moves those instruments, and it is clear that these instruments of the mover do not make the things from any influx proper to themselves. For there is in all intelligences an order of practical forms, which descends through the forms themselves into the matter of generable things, and the forms are the same in all, but in inferior things they are more and more determined, just as the form of light [lux] is the same in the sun and in the air and in the cloud and in a determined body, although the illumination [lumen] in the degree that it descends further from the sun is more and more constricted and determined to the nature of color. It is moreover the same in the case of the form of the art in the mind of the artist, which the hand follows through and which falls under the instrument, and which the iron assumes, which is proportionally the same in all, and yet it is more determined to matter in the hand than in the mind of the artist, and more in the hammer than in the hand, but it is determined most in the iron, because the iron assumes it materially. And in the case of the many intelligences this simile would apply both to the first cause and the matter of the generables, if the hand and the hammer had an intellect by which they might make explicit and follow through the form conceived by the mind of the artist. Wherefore, just as notwithstanding the existence of such an hypothesis, in art, all things will be from the mind of the artist, so all things are in potentiality from the first cause, although the intelligences make explicit certain goodnesses, and they are introduced by the celestial motion into matter. The first Philosopher however treats of these questions more fully. What has been inferred indeed is sufficient for the question; but however many of the later philosophers have treated of the souls caused by and poured forth by the intelligences, they have understood this manner of flux which has been spoken of: and for this reason they have asserted that the soul is first from the intelligence and that it is the offshoot of the intelligence and subject to the illuminations of the intelligence, in this undoubtedly speaking the truth, as the divinations of dreams show and many other phenomena concerning which we shall treat in other books. Because of this the soul is said likewise, in the book *on the Motion of the Heart,* to be perceptive by a second revelation of illuminations which are from the first cause.

Likewise, from what has been said, it is sufficiently clear how the movers of the lower spheres pour forth and how they do not: for the first and complete fusion of the soul and all nature is from the first cause. But the lower orbs operate organically by determining and inclining natures to matter. Because of this Plato says that in every orb the soul takes on something, memory in the orb of Saturn, and other functions in other orbs, as we have stated in the first book *on the Soul.* And in this manner the essence of the soul is wholly and solely from the first cause, but the application and determination to the body is by other things instrumentally subject to the first cause; and in this respect it is subjected to the intelligences of the other orbs to be ruled in illuminations and to be moved in temporal motions: and since the whole harmony of the heaven is referred thus to the first cause, therefore the philosophers who have understood this thing best have said that the whole has a single mover, and they have said that the lower movers to the spheres are powers and members of the first heaven and of its mover. We made mention of these things however in the second book *on Heaven and Earth.* There will moreover be a thorough examination of them in the *First Philosophy.*

CHAPTER V.

Whence arises the diversity of the genera of the soul, namely, the vegetative, the sensitive and the intellective?

The consequence of these doctrines moreover is that we determine a manner of descent of souls. For since the first cause, illumining souls in its light, is a single simple intellectual nature, it will seem strange how many genera of souls there are, namely, vegetative, sensitive and intellectual. For this can not come about from intermediate motors, for all these are said by the philosophers to be intellectual. Nor is what Pythagoras said true, that all souls are intellectual, and all bodies are animate; and he says that the motion of sense or intellect cannot follow the soul into certain bodies because of the gravity of matter. For the stone, as he says, is animate; but the soul in it is oppressed because of terrestrialness, so that it does not display the motion of vegetation, or understanding, or sense. In plants, however, because of a slighter terrestrialness, the soul displays and performs vegetation, but not sense. In less terrestrial brutes, further, it operates one or two or all senses, but not understanding. Finally, in the human body which is least terrestrial of all and which recedes most in incomplexity from the excellence of contraries, the soul has all operations completely.

This indeed can not be, since nature is never lacking in that which is necessary. For if the sensitive and intellective soul were perfect in the stone or the plant, nature would certainly have given to the stone and the plant the organs by which sensible things could make explicit the operations of the sensitive and intellectual soul.

Yet, all diversity of matter is because of diversity of form, as has often been stated before in the books which have been completed. How therefore can it be said that the genus of the soul is the same in all bodies, which are obviously different in figures and in quantity and in nature?

Nor is the reason of Plato cogent when he says that the forms are infused according to the worth of the matter, because according to this the material diversity would be the cause of the diversity of forms, although this is not true, for the diversity of matters is not the cause but the sign of the diversity of forms. For if it were said to be the cause, then it would be necessary that the matter be before the form according to nature and understanding, and it would be the cause of the form; but whosoever is well instructed with respect to those things which have been proved in the books on *Physics* does not doubt that all this is absurd.

There remains therefore the question, whence arises the diversity of genera of the soul, vegetative, sensitive and intelligible? For that which is derived from one in the same manner can not be other than one according to what all philosophers have commonly held.

But this question is solved more readily, if one consider subtly by what manner of bestowing of natures souls proceed from the first cause. For all forms are bestowed by the first cause on the nature of the whole universe; but the further they are removed from it, the more they are deprived of its nobilities and goodnesses; and the less they recede from it, the more they are noble and the more forces and powers of goodnesses they have; and as we said in the *Physics,* those things which are undistinguished in it, when they proceed from it, are distinguished with respect to being and essences and diverse species, just as the rays, coming from the sun into air and clear glass and colored glass, take on a different being and different species. And in this manner diversity arises, for it flows single from a single source through things diverse organically making it explicit and in diverse things informed by it, as was determined in part in the eighth book of the *Physics* too. And there are grades of dissimilitude in this descent, since the descending principle of life, which is the soul, possessed of a noble operation, divine and intellectual and animal, remains even down to the organic body composed of contraries, the combination of which is proportioned by celestial equality, for it is formative; otherwise it would be generative of the things which are reformed in these things; for nothing generates something else, except by something divine which is in it; moreover, the soul is intellectual because it operates without using the body and animal because it uses the organic body; but nevertheless its intellectual aspect is overshadowed in that it is inquisitive, not certain like the intellectual aspect of the celestial intellects which are not overshadowed by the disturbances of bodies. Receding further however in the region of dissimilitude it is more overshadowed, so that it loses the intellectual entirely, retaining only knowledge of sensible things. Still further removed moreover it retains only the lowest power of the soul, which is to vegetate, and functions of this sort. There is an example of this in the light receding from the sun into the limpid air and the subtle cloud and the body colored with a white color or a black or a red; for this light little by little is closed in and loses the strength of its power more and more, until it comes to privation; in all things in which it proceeds it has a different being and species. Nor is it one except by procession from one first fountain of light, and since the procession of forms from the first cause is similar in all respects to this, Plato says that the first form is unique, and from it alone all things are made. But Democritus and Leucippus also said that all things are one, and the same is made diversity by order and composition.

Both sects however were in error, for that which is one by procession from one simple being and many with respect to being and figure, is still one with respect to its relation to the first unique efficient cause; and if the natures of souls and of forms were considered with respect to that diverse being, then they are the proper natures of souls and forms, and the diversity of matter is because of them and not conversely, and they give being to matters; and this consideration is properly of them, and they are defined and known according to that which Isaac says in his book of *Definitions*, namely, that the rational soul is produced in the shadow of the intelligence, and the sensible soul in the shadow of the rational, and the vegetative soul in the shadow of the sensible, and the nature of the heavens in the shadow of the vegetative, since essence which gives being proceeds from the first cause, and so, since it is far removed and is taken by similitude, it will be the most simple in being and the most powerful and the most noble and the most universal nature with respect to abstraction; but according to what we say, that the more universal nature causes and influences more, for that reason, this essence is vegetative, intellectual, causative, motive, and possessed of many other powers of goodnesses; and with respect to all these, it is given in the first effect, which is the intellectual being causative of the motion of the orb. This essence, however, descending is deprived of simplicity and power more and more, as we say, even to the final being which receives a minimum difference of being and power; and this privation is called its overshadowing by philosophers. From this the true understanding of the matter is clear, because all things are from the idea itself of one; and it is clear also how the idea is unique in the first cause, possessed of no plurality except by procession and by the vicinity of things caused. For it is not true that life in the first cause is separated from being, but it is a simple emanation of essence from the simple first being. And as the cognitive and motive faculties of the first being are one, so too is the essence emanating in the same powers, so long as it is not overshadowed by the distance of dissimilitude.

From this, three corollaries follow. One, that where there is intellective and sensitive and vegetative and motive being, there is a single essence there and simple substance, but it is multiple in power, and both these characteristics it has from the propinquity of its procession to the first being from which it proceeds. The second is that if any substantial form is motive of its subject with respect to place, it has that power from agreement with the first being which, existing immobile, moves with respect to place, and it does not have it from the fact that it is composite, as certain of the latins asserted. Third, that when it does not recede necessarily far from the first being by privation of nobilities, as intellectual it remains separate and perpetual; but when it recedes far, it is mixed and it is made mortal and corporeal.

From these statements it is known how animals [i.e., creatures with souls] move themselves, and not other beings, and how the intellectual soul is not the actuality of the body, and is not corrupted when the body is corrupted, as Alexander mistakenly said.

CHAPTER VI.

Whether the intellectuality of the soul is matter or derived as an influx from the first cause.

It is, moreover, easy for us to come to a decision concerning the nature of the intellectual soul, since it has its nature from the fact that it is a procession from the first cause, but not emanating to the point of intermixture with matter; and therefore it is even called by some wise men of our dispensation the *image of God.* For it has from its assimilation to the first cause, a universally active intellect, which is like a separated light, as has been shown properly in the third book *on the Soul.* Nevertheless, from the fact that this nature is appropriated to the organic physical body, its intellectual nature is immersed a little, and therefore it has a possible intellect which derives its material from imagination and sense: and since this nature is separated and not immersed in matter with respect to itself, it is necessary that it be universal; and therefore the soul is universally cognitive of all things intellectually, and not only of certain things, for certain things are not made determinate except by matter; but we said that the intellect is separate. Sensible cognition, however, which is the act of a material organ, is sensitive only to certain things, as was decided sufficiently in the book *on the Soul.*

From this it is clear that the author of the book the *Fountain of Life,*[2] which is said to be about matter and form, is mistaken, for he seems to hold that from the nature of matter the intellect has the power of understanding all things. For he says that first matter is

[2] Avicebron.

that which is all things in potentiality, and the more
that it is determined by forms, the more its potentiality
is enclosed and determined, since if this form which is
intellectuality is added to first matter, then it is no
longer in potentiality to intellectuality, but to all other
things. And if the next form which is corporeity is
added to it, then again it is of a more determined potentiality, and therefore it will not then be in potentiality
to the intellectual. But if contrariety is added to corporeity, then it will be in potentiality only to those
things which are in the power of contraries, and they
are the forms of generable and corruptible things.

This statement, of course, is erroneous and opposed
by all peripatetics, for the intellect is by no means all
things in potentiality as first matter is all things in
potentiality, because the forms which are individual
with respect to material being are not separate from
those which are in potentiality in matter. The forms,
however, which are in potentiality in the intellect, are
universals, separate from individuating elements, and
especially from matter, existing not here and now, but
everywhere and always.

For all this, however, matter does not make forms
to be in themselves by means of something which is of
the same nature and genus as matter. But the intellect
has something of its own, namely, the active intellect,
which makes forms to be in the intellectual soul.

Yet the intellect, which is in potentiality all intelligible things, is related to them as a *tabula rasa,* and
matter is not related in this manner to universal forms
which are in potentiality in it. Even more, matter understands nothing of these things which are in potentiality or in actuality in it, but the intellect understands
all things. All these points are touched on briefly here,

for in the book *on the Soul* they are worked out and proved in detail.

Wherefore, although we assert that there is in the nature of the soul something potential and something which is the actuality of it, still we can not say that the potential which is in the soul is first matter, because it does not have the properties of first matter; but it is said much more properly that, since the intellectual soul retains its noble separated being, the possible intellect is effected by that part by which it attains to the continuous and time; and by that part by which it remains in every manner separated it is active and perfective of that same possibility. Avicenna gives a fitting example of this in the flame which adheres to the combustible parts of dry wood. For the flame is in some degree smoky in the part which adheres to the wood, but in the part in which it mounts upward into the pure air far from the wood, it illumines the air with full light, and it illumines even the smoky part of the same flame. So it is with the intellectual soul, for it is in some manner the perfection of the body, and yet separated; and therefore it is, as it were smoky, and it is made intelligence in potentiality but not in actuality by the part by which it is inclined to the corporeal powers of organs, which are imagination (taking the continuous) and sense (taking the temporal and transmutable), but it is in the actuality of perfect light by the separated part.

These things, however, may be passed by now, for, as we have said, they have been treated of in the book *on the Soul*. But the following is what is understood by that which has been said, that the essence emanating from the first cause has the full power of life and cognition and motion by the fact that it emanates from that which is the fountain of life and of cognition and of motion; and it retains this essentially if it is not overshadowed by the distance of dissimilitude from the first cause, since the first essence which gives being to rational and intellectual things would not be furthest removed in dissimilitude; therefore it will be the principle of life and cognition and motion in all things; and it is this especially which we intend to distinguish and investigate here.

CHAPTER VII.

Whether the intellectual nature is universal or particular with respect to actuality, for there is no doubt that it is universal with respect to aptitude, since it is form.

However, some would perhaps ask whether this divine essence which is called the intellectual nature is universal, or determinate and particular (or individual). For although this question has been decided in the book *on the Soul,* it should nevertheless be interposed here also, because otherwise we can not know the nature of intellectual beings to the full. There were of course some peripatetics who said that this nature is universal and perpetual, and the most cogent of their reasons are three, one of which is that anything which assumes something, assumes it according to the power of its own proper nature; the intellect however receives into itself the universal, but the universal is not, in respect of anything of this sort, except in the intellect; it is necessary therefore that the nature of the intellect be universal, because if it were individual, it would individuate all that which is in it, for every form is individuated by the individuality of its subject in which it is. The second reason is that the intellectual nature is a substance separated from matter; but all individuality is

through matter, and therefore they said that the intel
lect is universal. Finally, the third reason is that if it
were individual, it would be individual only with respect
to its own proper matter, and then, just as sight which
is conjoined to a certain matter of its own receives only
that which is proportioned to that matter and no other,
so that intellect would receive only certain things proportioned to its matter and would not receive all things.
This however is false. Therefore the intellect is not
itself individual. Nor can that solution stand which
holds that there are two matters, one spiritual and the
other corporeal, and that the intellect is individuated
to spiritual matter, because that spiritual matter is made
proper to the intellect only through something which
makes it appropriate, and then the argument returns to
the same conclusion as the previous one, namely, that
the intellect does not know that which is not proportioned to its constitution. Nor can it be said that all
things are proportioned to such a composition, for nothing is proper except through that which is not in agreement with others. There will therefore be many other
things which are not proportioned to its proper composition, and these the intellect would not know. These
are the most cogent of the reasons why Abubacher and
Averroes and many others affirm that the intellect is
universal and can be appropriated to us only by imagination and sense, as we said in the book *on the Soul*.

If, however, the intellect is said to be universal and
essentially the same in all creatures with souls, many
absurd consequences follow, of which we made mention
in the book *on the Soul*; and therefore it seems to us
that the intellectual nature is in its genus like the sun
in the genus of bodies. For we know that the sun is a
single individual in number, and that the light which
is in it is to be considered in two ways. For if it should

be considered as it is in the sun, it is the form of the
sun, one in number.   But if it is taken as emanating
from the sun, it is thus illuminative universally of all
transparent things, as well the translucent things which
it makes to be luminous, as the impervious things which
it makes to be colored, as we have stated in the first
book *on Sense and the Sensed;* and considered in this
manner it performs and does many things.

Since, therefore, the Philosopher says that the intellect is like light, the intellect seems, as it is something
of the nature of the soul, to be individual, and still, as
it lets forth the actions of understanding, to be universal in power; and universals are in it in this manner, that it is abstractive and denudative of forms as
corporeal light of colors; although it is said to be individual in the respect that it is the form of man, still with
respect to its power and so far as it is the potency of
spiritual light, it is universal.   These universals moreover are not in the intellect as form is in matter or
accident in the subject, for in the soul, being is rather the
intention of the thing than the thing; and therefore just
as color is not individuated by the being which it has
in the corporeal light nor is even specificated because
in light being accords with every color in respect to that
which color is in actuality, so the intention of the thing
is not specificated or individuated by that which is in
the incorporeal intellectual light, but it remains universal; and in this there is knowledge according to the
congruence and faculty of the intellect, just as sight
with respect to actuality is according to the congruence
and faculty of the corporeal light.   What he says concerning the fact that the intellectual nature is separated,
is expounded in detail in the book *on the Soul,* and must
therefore be passed over here.

The third objection which is raised moreover is not

conclusive unless we were to affirm that universal knowledge was in the intellect according to that which the individual itself is. This however must not be conceded, because it would follow without doubt then that the intellect would know only those things which were in accordance with the congruence of its composition. For we said in the aforementioned book that the intellect is joined to man in three ways. In one way as a nature which gives being, and in this way it is individual. In another way as the power by which there is the operation of understanding, and in this way it is a universal power. In a third way as the form acquired from many intelligibles, as has been stated more clearly with reference to the active intellect which is not joined to contemplatives as agent only, but as it is their beatitude when they arrive at that which is in them as form. And the said intellect is not present in the second and third manners, as prudence and wisdom, equally in all men, but in some more and in others less, and in some perhaps there is present nothing of intellect.

CHAPTER VIII.

In which in a summary fashion the nature of the intellectual soul is deduced.

To state briefly, point by point, the things which have been noted, we have said with Dionysius the Areopagite that *every nature proceeding from the first cause is simpler and nobler and more multiplex in power the more intimate it was with the first cause by proximity of similarity, and in contrary wise, the more distant it was by dissimilitude the more material and the more ignoble and of fewer powers.* The wisest peripatetics moreover demonstrated this by the eighth heaven, the multiplicity of the stars of which showed how great its multiplicity was. And since that multiplicity is in the fact that it is moved, it is necessary that it respond by a congruence to the multiplicity of powers which are in the motor. Because of this it happens also that the intellectual soul is more multiplex than the form of stones or of minerals, and thus with other forms; however the more such natures are separated, the more they are called forms, as the ancients said. For this reason too the platonists asserted that forms were absolutely separated, and the more they were conjoined with matter, the less they were called forms, but it pleased them rather to call them images immersed in matter, as Boethius says in the book *on the Trinity*.

It is clear for this reason that the intellectual nature is more truly form than all other consequent forms, because it is most of all separated, and to this extent the separated incorporeal lights flow from it, according to which it is made capable of knowing all things which are abstracted and resolved from the obscurity of matter and privation and from the shadows of material conditions. Since however it is in proximity to the first cause, with many similarities to it, it has a great many powers which are its natural properties and potencies, as we said above; these nevertheless are not the same as it, nor is one of its powers the same as another, because in this it is far removed from the first cause which is the same as each of its powers and each of its powers is the same as the other; and since its powers are so many, it is itself with respect to itself, and not by common accident, operative of many; and in this it differs from the form which is simply the nature and form of the body and the actuality of corporeal matter only, with respect to which the natural body performs only one operation. Nevertheless among these parts one of the powers is more excellent than another in the degree that it may have been more separate, and therefore the intellect is more potent than the common sense, and the common sense more potent than the proper sense, and sensual nature more potent than vegetative nature, and it is found to be the same in all others.

Treatise II.

ON THAT WHICH IS INTELLIGIBLE
THROUGH ITSELF

Chapter I.

That nothing is understood except the universal.

After this it seems that the *intelligible* should be discussed. But it is the opinion of almost all that the universal alone is intelligible, for Aristotle as well as Boethius and Averroes attests that it is universal when it is understood, but singular when it is perceived. They give as the most cogent reason for this the following, which has commonly been promulgated, that the intellect receives that which is denuded and despoiled of matter and of the appendages of matter. Since therefore matter with its appendages is that which individuates forms, it will be thus denuded of that which individuates, and thus it follows that the universal is the object of the intellect, and so it is held generally that the universal is the object of the intellect.

Furthermore the universal either is in things, or it is in the sense, or it is in the intellect, or it is absolutely nothing. It is obvious however that it is not in the sense. But since nothing is in things except as it is singular and proper to a single thing, it is clear that the universal is not in things. It is necessary therefore that it be in the intellect.

Again, it is stated by Aristotle that the universal is

everywhere and always, and that it is one in many and of many. But no thing is everywhere and always. I speak however of those things which are in natural or artificial things without the mind. It is necessary therefore that that which is everywhere and always exist in the soul and not in things.

Moreover, the proper operation of the active intellect is abstracting, not only from matter, but universally from this particular of which the intention is in the sensible soul. This abstracting however is nothing other than taking the universal from the particular. For this reason Aristotle asserts that when many experiences have been accepted, a single universal acceptance is made, which is the principle of art and science. It remains therefore that the proper object of the intellect is the universal.

But some do not wish to concede this, asserting that in certain things so great a simplicity and immateriality is found that they can by no means be abstracted from matter and from the appendages of matter which they do not have, as the intellect itself understands itself and other intellectual natures which nevertheless are not universal. In these therefore they say that the intellect is acceptive of particulars.

Again, since only natural and mathematical things in respect to themselves are in matter and motion, but divine things are absolutely without motion and matter, nevertheless the former are not all universals, but in them there are the universal and the particular. Since therefore, these say, divine things are taken alone in the intellect, it is necessary that certain particulars be taken in the intellect. They draw to this conclusion likewise the fact that we understand and know any thing whatever truly, as has been said in the book of *Physical Hearing*, when we know the causes and the principles and elements of it. The causes and principles and elements of things, however, are things particularly constituent and certain particulars. It is seen therefore that the intellect is more truly of particulars than of universals. Those who deny that the universal alone is intelligible say certain other things similar to these.

It seems to us that the first opinion must be granted, namely, that the only intelligible is the universal and absolutely no particular, for the entire sect of peripatetics are in accord in treating it thus. Whether however the universal is in the intellect alone and not in things outside the intellect will have to be inquired later and in this very book; but for the present we say that nothing is understood in the pure intellect except the universal; and as the peripatetics hold, the reason is that the intellect, since it is simple and pure, with nothing in common with any thing and separated from all things, must have an object proportioned to itself, for to know and to understand is proper to it only in accordance with its power and congruence, just as passion is formed in any passive thing; for the object does not introduce the passion except in the proper passives; therefore if the particular introduces any passion in the intellect, it is necessary that it have a congruence in genus to that particular, and then it would be passive only to things of the genus of that particular. But this could not be, as we have often said, and therefore that which is denuded of matter and the appendages of matter is the object which introduces the proper passion in the possible intellect.

Nor is that which the adversary says true, that as much simplicity is found in particular things as he says, for in every thing there is the universal from the part of the communicable form, and the particular from the part of the substance of that form which is incommunicable and accords with one only; and because the principle of communicability is found in all perfect things in nature and beyond nature in the first cause, Boethius therefore says that *every thing has something which is and something which is this, and every thing is the one and the other*. We have often said moreover that abstraction, which is in the intellect, is from the particular, and not always from matter as matter is taken strictly as the subject of transmutation and motion, as line is abstracted from this line, and intellect from this intellect. When however I say *heavens,* I speak of the form as it is universal, and when I say *these heavens,* I speak of the form particularized and constricted in this matter. Furthermore this abstraction is in all things, and the intellect understands itself as it understands other intelligibles, as has been determined in the third book *on the Soul.*

From these considerations it is likewise manifest that not only material and mathematical things are separable, but also all divine things: or else some of them are separable as the intellect separates the universal from the particular. It seems however that that which they say to the effect that we understand and know each thing when we know the causes and principles, which nevertheless seem to be particulars, must be considered in the following respect, that according to the truth of the thing, the principles of the being of the thing and the principles of understanding and knowing the thing are the same, but the cause of knowledge and the cause of the thing existing in nature are not taken in the same manner, for taken universally they cause knowledge, and appropriated and particularized to some thing they are the principles of things in nature. How this is done however will be shown in what follows.

CHAPTER II.

Whether the universal is in the intellect alone or also in the thing without?

The question whether the universal is in the single, naked and pure intellects or also in things, Porphyry says is very lofty business and one requiring much investigation, and although this is a question pertaining to metaphysics, still mention must be made of it here because of the easier mode of teaching. Since everything which is in things, is only single and proper, it will seem that the universal, which is in many and of many, is not in anything, especially since Aristotle holds in the *First Philosophy* that it is the same to be universal and particular, and the principles of all things which are the principles of being are particulars and not universals, as Plato says.

Moreover, the universal is simple and pure of matter and separated from the appendages of matter, but because this is true of it, it does not receive matter. Since therefore it is necessary that it be in some being, for it is a simple form, it must in accordance with this being be in the soul, and thus the universal in so far as it is universal is only in the soul.

Again, if the universal were in the thing, it would be necessary that it be the same as the thing in which it is, because otherwise the predication of it would be false when it was said, Socrates is a man, or Socrates is an animal; man therefore or animal predicated of Socrates is the same as Socrates. For the same reason when predicated of Plato, man is the same as Plato. But whatever things are one and the same as the same thing are themselves the same; it would follow from this that Socrates and Plato would be the same, or else it is necessary to say that man and animal would be two different universals predicated of Socrates and Plato, which is false, since Porphyry says that by the participation of species many men are one man, and Aristotle says that isosceles and equilateral are several triangles and one figure. From all the incompatibilities of this sort, however, it is concluded that the universal is not in the thing but in reason. For this reason, too, John Damascenus says that *in such universals that which is common in reason but not in the thing is considered.*

Furthermore, form is individuated by matter. But individuated form gives being to the individual. Thus therefore both the form and the matter are made proper. Nothing then of the form and the matter which is in one individual is in several taken at the same time. Therefore the universal is nothing in the thing, whether it be taken with respect to form or with respect to matter, since the universal is in possible things taken at the same time. In this, likewise, almost all the peripatetics agree, namely, Avicenna, and Algazeli, and Averroes, and Abubacher and a great many others.

But some men of no little authority among the latins whom this opinion does not please, assert that the universal is in some respect in things. For if it were not in the thing, it would not be predicated truly of the thing, especially since this is the nature of the universal, that it is entire in each of its particulars.

Nevertheless, no thing is understood except through that which is truly the form of the thing. Since therefore the universal is that which is understood, it is necessary that it be truly the form of the thing, and thus it is something in things.

Again, nothing is more truly in things than that which is entire and one in many and of many, for it does not

lose the reason of being in things by the fact that it is
in many. By the fact however that it is of many, it has
that which in them is their true essence, substantial or
accidental existing. It is necessary therefore that the
universal be truly in things, since it is one in many
and of many.

We, however, following the middle way in this difficulty, say that the essence of each thing is to be considered in two ways. In one way, namely, as it is a
nature diverse from the nature of matter or from the
nature of that in which it is whatsoever it is. And in
another way as it is in matter, or in that in which it is
individuated through that which is in it. And in the
first manner it may again be considered in two ways.
In one way as it is a certain essence absolute in itself,
and it is called *essence,* and it is a single something
existing in itself, nor does it have being except the
being of such essence, and thus it is only one. In another manner, as communicability with respect to aptitude accords with it, and this happens to it from the
fact that it is an essence apt to give being to many,
even though it may never give being, and thus it is
called properly *universal,* for every essence communicable with many is universal, even though it never actually gives being except to one, as the sun and the moon
and Jupiter and others of this sort; for the substantial
forms of such things are communicable, and that they
are not communicated actually arises from the fact that
all the matter to which that form is communicable is
already contained under the form, as has been determined in *on the Heavens and Earth.* Therefore
through this universal aptitude the universal is in the
thing outside, but with respect to the actuality of existing in many it is only in the intellect, and therefore
the peripatetics said that the universal is only in the

intellect, referring that to the universal which is in many and of many according to actuality of existing and not according to aptitude only.

There still remains, however, a double consideration of the universal as it is participated in by that in which it is. One, as it is the end of the generation or the composition of the desired substance from matter or from that, in which that is, to which it gives being and perfection, and thus it is called *actuality,* and it is particular and determined. In the second manner, as it is the whole being of the thing, and thus it is called *quiddity,* and thus again it is determined, particularized and proper.

Nor must it be considered inappropriate that the form be called the whole being of the thing, because matter is nothing with respect to the being of the thing, nor is it intended by nature, for if the form could be in operation without it, it would never be introduced into matter, but because this can not be, matter is required, not for being, but for the determination of its being. Considered in this last way, therefore, form is predicated of the thing of which it is the form, and separated thus by the intellect it is universal in the intellect, and therefore the aptitude of its communicability is reduced to actuality in the intellect separating it from that which individuates.

CHAPTER III.

Concerning the solution of the doubts which arise from the foregoing considerations.

But perhaps some would question these things which have been determined, taking as occasion the fact that such a consideration of form in itself and in matter does not seem to be of the thing, but of reason; and therefore although the aptitude of communication seems to fit it in this manner, it seems to fit it only in respect to reason and the intellect. And thus it comes up again that the universal is in the intellect alone both in aptitude and actuality, and in no manner in the thing itself.

But to this objection it must be said that without doubt, as is determined in the *Metaphysics,* actuality is prior to potentiality, and not in respect to reason only or in the manner of understanding, but in substance itself and in definition, just as the cause is prior to the caused, and it has the being of cause and of essence, as we have said, although it does not have being except in the particular nature; and in this manner it is one essence, not by a unity of number, as we say that a number is one, but by a unity of being and of essence in itself and of form, which unity of multitude according to aptitude is not repugnant to communicability. And in this manner it is called one in many and of many.

If however any one should object that according to what has been said the universal is prior to the thing and not posterior to it, although Aristotle says that the universal is either nothing or posterior to its singulars, we say that that which is universal is without doubt prior to the thing; but the actuality of its universality which the active intellect makes, is from the fact that the quiddity of the existing thing, which is predicated truly of the thing itself, is in the thing, and in this respect the consequence is the thing abstracted from the thing itself; and thus it appears the understanding of predetermined things, and that both sects speak something of the truth.

It is clear likewise from these considerations that since matter is nothing with respect to the true being of the thing, no thing is in any manner intelligible through its matter but through its form; and then since the universal is the proper object of the understanding, because universal being is of the form and not of the matter, for all communicable form is incommunicable matter, and matter is not in the many with respect to aptitude or actuality through the same part of itself, but by diverse parts, so that with respect to one part it is in one thing, and with respect to another part it is in another, and because the thing is named according to what is understood, it is named properly from the form and the matter. Nor is it understood or named except by analogy to the form, as we said also at the end of the first book of the *Physics*. Since therefore the individual is individual through matter, it will not have its proper name, properly speaking, except perhaps as it is substance through the form which properly and principally and most of all it underlies [*substat*]. All these points however have been determined adequately in the first book of the *Logic*.

From what has been said, moreover, it follows that, since the universal is in the essence of the thing according to the aptitude which it has for existing entire in many, and since that aptitude is equally with respect of past and present and future things, the universal which is the substance of the thing or established in the substance itself, is univocal with respect of all past, present or future things.

Yet, since it has to do with the aptitude of the essence, which is before matter and the composite thing, it is clear that concerning no existent particular man is it true that man is animal, and other expressions of this sort.

From these considerations, moreover, it is understood that if all first substances were destroyed, even though it be impossible that anything of any other substances remain, yet science is of perpetual things, and the perpetual is also the incorruptible, because it is established only on the aptitude of the communicability of form and essence and those things which are its passions and differences. But this is perpetual and incorruptible whether there are particulars or not. But it has already been determined in the statements which have been made *on the Soul,* how one science is in all, and how it is not.

CHAPTER IV.

On the falsity of the opinion which holds that every form is everywhere and always.

Although this way is the more rational, still some are not satisfied to hold it but say instead that every form, whether it is substantial or accidental, is of itself common; and because it is in matter only by accident, as we have said before, since matter is not intended to being, but form is the entire being of the thing, they say that every form is of itself everywhere and always, for it is restricted in space to be something only by the contrariety of matter, and it is restricted to the present time only by matter itself determined by contrariety, for those things which are beyond contrariety and motion are above time and differences of time.

They say likewise that since the formal essence is of itself everywhere and always, and is by accident in matter, it is more truly everywhere and always than here and now; and it is more truly where it is according to its more formal being than where it is according to its more material being which diminishes its being and restricts the power of its communication. And it follows from this that it is more truly in the intellect than in matter.

And these philosophers say that if some forms are separated, like the intellect, they are wherever they operate, and they can be in many things at the same time.

And they conclude from the first that one universal is, which is understood in all souls and exists in all its particulars, and thus they concede that there is a science one in number in all souls, but they say that there are different continuations of that science to men because of a diversity of imagination from which the intellect receives concepts, as has been determined in the third book *on the Soul*.

From the second they conclude the cause of prophecy which necromancers and augurers indulge in, namely, because one of them hypnotizes another and impedes the animal operations in him. They have moreover the reasons of their first supposition, one which we have said is most cogent as well as others which we have stated in the book *on the Soul*.

And since it is long to consider all such arguments, it seems to us that it must be said without prejudice of the better opinion, that this opinion is exposed to falsity, for true being and being certain in nature is that which gives form to particular matter, but formal being is only according to the aptitude in the essence of the form and only according to the separating intellect with respect to actuality, as we have said: and therefore to speak most truly, the essence of the form is everywhere and always, only according to aptitude and not in actuality. And with reference to the statement that a thing is more truly where it is according to itself than where it is according to accident, it must be said that this would be true if being accorded with it everywhere and always according to actuality; this however is not true, and therefore that which is concluded does not follow, because to be according to aptitude is to be in some one respect and to be potentially, but to be in matter is to be truly and perfectly and according to actuality. And when it is said that this is accidental to the form, it must be said that this accident does not accidentally make the being itself to be which is the actuality of the matter and of the composite of it with form, for this is substantial and true; but it is said to be accidental at the same time because it is by means of something else, and not because of an accord of its own; because this is true, such being in matter does not accord with form and essence by means of itself and because of itself.

CHAPTER V.

On the confutation of the error of Plato concerning determined things.

It is necessary, however, to make mention of the philosophy of Plato, which distinguishes in the resolution of each faculty of this sort a threefold universal. That is, one before the thing, which is the formal cause, possessing in power beforehand the whole separated being and existing perpetually before the thing, for since it is the cause, it is necessary that it be before the thing, and since transmutation and generation and corruption are only in the subject matter, it will be before all things of that sort; and therefore it is ingenerable and perpetual, and in addition it gives all being to matter and is the being of individual things, just as the seal gives figure to wax. The figure, moreover, will possess beforehand the whole being and power of the thing. This universal therefore Plato said is separated and mathematical, existing according to itself, and it is the principle of knowledge and the formal cause of generation in all things generated, and it remains outside generation, as the wooden last on which shoes are made remains outside the leather, although nevertheless every shoe is formed to it. And because this universal is perpetual he said it is the principle of knowledge, and because it is immaterial, he said it is always and everywhere the same in all creatures with souls. The second universal, however, he said is only in the thing, and this is the form impressed in things from the first universal, and from the first universal the forms of things proceeded as from a certain *etymagium,* that is, seal. This second universal he said underlies motion and change because of the matter in which it is. The third he said is after the thing, because it is by way of a consideration taken from things; and by it, he said, not only is the thing known, but it is known in its proper nature and by the application of the form to that which particularizes and individuates it.

Aristotle however disputed this, showing that it was contradicted by many reasons, as for instance that it is true too that the proximate principles of particular things are particular, and the proximate principles of corruptible things are corruptible, concerning which it is not proper to the present consideration to speculate. But that which is relevant to the problem is that if the being and the perpetual and incorruptible essences of things are such, as he said, then they have absolutely nothing to do with the being of naturally existent things, nor are things known except by principles which have to do with their being; therefore, by universals which preexist and have beforehand the being of things, no thing is known; and thus they are useless to the knowledge of things.

Moreover, according to this, the universal, existing as one, was predicated falsely of many, because the second universal, which is appropriated, does not agree with many; and the first universal has nothing to do with the being of things, and therefore it can not be predicated of any thing. Because of this circumstance the philosophy of Plato is without doubt most unsuited in this part.

Moreover, natural things differ from mathematical things in that they are conceived by the definitive reason together with mobile and sensible matter: how then can it be supposed that such things exist separated?

Moreover, if they were separated, what would make them touch matter and cause a natural being in it? For the *etymagium,* which he speaks of, does not touch wax for the purpose of sealing except when some one moves it. But what there is to move separated forms of this sort is impossible to say, although some wish to suppose some thing.

These then are the considerations concerning the intelligible nature and essence.

ON THE COMPARISON OF INTELLECT TO INTELLIGIBLE

Chapter I.

How is the intelligible in the intellect?

The next consideration must be concerning the comparison of the intelligible to the intellect with respect to the unity and diversity of the one to the other. For since every conception is formed by a certain assimilation of the intellect to the intelligible, it is necessary that the intellect and the intelligible be made one. This one, however, is not wholly as of subject and accident. It is not absolutely one because it is made one from matter and form, as has been shown appropriately in the third book *on the Soul;* and therefore it is necessary to inquire more clearly here how it is one.

To know this, however, we must see those things which are united in light by colors which are abstracted from light. For among all bodily things there is nothing in which so much similitude to incorporeal things appears as in light. Because of this indeed the active intellect is said to be like light in the book *on the Soul.* Let us say therefore that in light there are three things; these are light, shining, and illumination [*lux, lucere, et lumen*], which if they are considered in themselves seem to have absolutely no real difference or only a slight difference. If however they are considered related to certain other things, then they have a great difference between themselves, because light is the form of illumination in the body which gives forth light, and to shine is to emanate that form into something else, and illumination is that form already received from that which first shines. Color however, as it is abstracted from the body and as it is effected according to a spiritual being in the transparent or the translucent, is in illumination not wholly as an accident in a subject, since an accident does not have from its subject the form and essence of the accident, but only is. Color however has the form and essence of color from illumination, as has been determined in the first book *on Sense and the Sensed.*

Moreover, color is not in illumination as form in matter, because form is educed by an alteration of matter and the generation of the composite thing is caused. But color is not thus educed from the clear transparent, but, as has been said elsewhere, it is abstracted by formal abstraction from the colored thing, as is the case with the figure from the seal.

Moreover, the form has material being in the matter in which it is, but color does not have material but spiritual being in the transparent. For that reason indeed the change is undergone from the transparent to colors and to illumination. But all these things have been declared in other books. If however we should call only the intellect the light which is in it, then the intellect and the intelligible and its intelligibles taken from something else, would not differ; but by understanding that which received its intellectual light, it would understand its own understanding: and by understanding anything at all of the intelligibles, it would also understand itself and its own action.

We must imagine in one and the same manner the intellect and the intelligible as spoken of according to the actuality which is in them, for the intelligible is abstracted from things; and when it is in the light of the intellect, it is in that which gives it the form of intelligibility according to actuality, and not as an accident is in a subject, nor as form in matter; and this is not improper because such things according to the spiritual being which they have in that which abstracts them, are not accident, nor substance according to the truest acceptations of these, nor are they the differences of being or any species, unless being is taken in some one respect; but they are certain intentions of beings, taken according to the powers of their agents, for the power of light is such that it confers being on colors, and the power of the intellect is such that it confers being on intelligibles taken according to the act of understanding.

It is clear, however, from what has been said that the intellect understands its own understanding, not by any other operation or action than by understanding its intelligibles, and that it understands itself in understanding any one of the intelligibles. We have already stated the cause of this, that the intellect sounds the incorporeal light of the intellectual nature, which whether it is received in the intellectual nature itself, or flowing from it, or received, or determined above the intelligible, has no formal difference in itself. But if they are referred to another, then they differ according to the things to which they are referred.

CHAPTER II.

On the diversity of intelligibles in kind.

There is a diversity in intelligibles which is the diversity in colors as compared to sight. For because of the great victory and intermixture of the clear transparent in determined bodies we see certain colors on the advent of illumination made to scintillate and scatter brightness to the illumination of other things; and sometimes when the colored body is truly completely transparent, if light supervene, those colors color other bodies opposite them, as we see in the case of colored glass; the illumination coming through it draws with it the color of the glass and sets it on the body on which the illumination falls through the glass. There are certain things moreover so overpowering in translucent purity that they are made so radiant that they overcome the harmony of the eye, and they can not be seen without great difficulty. There are others too which give forth so much illumination and translucence that they can hardly be discerned by sight because of the slightness of their composition from the transparent, the proper actuality of which is illumination.

It is the same in intelligibles, since the forms of intelligibles, by the fact that they are simples and universals, and have no intermixture because of the privation of matter, are aspects of the intellect as colors are of light; and according to this they are rather prior according to nature and more universal and simpler, just as they are more intelligible and confer the light of intelligibility on others as excellences. Some, however, by their light are overpowering to our intellect which is continuous and in time, such as the things most manifest in nature which to our intellect are like the light of the sun or of a powerfully sparkling color to the eyes of an owl or a bat. Some are manifested only in the light of something else, such as those things which take credence from first and true principles. Some because of a too great intermixture with privation can not be comprehended with perfect understanding, such as motion, time, and first matter.

From these statements it is clear that theological things, which are most manifest, are little understood, and mathematical things are most of all understood, and physical things have rarely a certain and firm conception. For this occurs because divine things overpower and beat back our intellect with their light; mathematical truths are proportioned in themselves to our intellect and are intermixed with the intellect and the light of the intellect; physical things fall away from intellectuality because of privation and matter and motion: hence it is that divine things are said to be above the intellect, mathematical things in the intellect, and physical things below the intellect.

It is further to be observed from what has been said, how the condition of the principles is said to be *intellect* and the condition of the conclusion *knowledge,* and the process from the principles to the conclusion is called *reasoning,* since principles have understandings of light and of form most of all, because of which they are named from the form; but the conclusion has understanding least of all, and as if through another medium, from illumination, and because of this another word arises, and it is called knowledge which is always effected according to what knowledge is and never causes illumination in anything else unless it is taken as principle. Reasoning however names inference and as it were the direction by itself of that which throws light on something else; and therefore this descent of principles into conclusions is marked in that name.

Observe further from these considerations that there are some things in which the illumination of the intellect is as if eclipsed by the interposition of the obscurity of matter and of privation, and a shadowy and obscure light comes upon them, as in those things which are said to be only probable, but the illumination disappears entirely in those things which are only sensible, as has been determined. in the first book of that science. And from this observe why arguments are imperfect in probable things and why conclusions are accepted with misgivings, for probable things are neither the first and true things which are in the full light of the intelligence, nor do they take credence from true things, but they are what are commonly found extrinsically in things, in which there is as it were a certain reverberation of the intellectual light with many shadows caused by matter and privation, and therefore universals are not true in such things, or they are not of immobile truth, and since all perfection of argumentation and all certitude is from the universal and immobile truth, it is necessary that the argumentations in such things be imperfect and uncertain; wherefore neither do they conclude well, nor will the conclusion be accepted without great fear of contradiction. We speak of this opinion and doubt and ambiguity in other books; moreover, there will be place to say something concerning them in the *First Philosophy*.

CHAPTER III.

On the diversity of intellects, as well with respect to themselves as with respect to intelligibles, and also with respect to the faculty of understanding.

There is however, a diversity of intellect which many of the philosophers asserted with respect to the parts themselves of the soul, because there is the possible intellect and the active intellect concerning which there is mention in the book *on the Soul*. There is a third more-

over which is the formal intellect, namely, when the
form of that known or operating by the light of the
intellect is in the soul; and this is divided into practical
and speculative, of which there is likewise a treatment
in the third book *on the Soul*. For this formal intellect
is divided into the simple and the composite intellect.
And the simple is the understanding of the uncom-
pounded; but the understanding of the complex is com-
pounded, either by the mode of proposition or else by
the mode of syllogism or of some other species of argumentation.   And that which is called composite is
divided into the understanding which is called of principles, which is in a certain respect innate in us in that
we do not receive the principles from anything else but
from a knowledge of terms which arise at once in us;
and the intellect derived from other things, which is
called among the philosophers the acquired intellect,
in that it is acquired through discovery or learning and
study.   And the reason for the divisions of these appears
from their very names.

With respect to the faculty of the intellectual nature
which is in men, a certain division of the intellect is
caused, of which some philosophers make mention, especially Aristotle and Avicenna, and certain others who
follow them.   For there is a certain intellect more intermixed with the continuous and with time, that is, with
imagination and sense; and one more separated; and one
of a medium sort; finally one which does not have the
powers of imagining and of accepting anything through
the senses.   And the first is obscure, receiving nothing
save with difficulty; and if it is taught anything that
must be done through sensible examples; and such
examples are impossible for the understanding of things
manifest through themselves or of divine things which

are treated in the first philosophy, and are called existences of that evil mode of thinking by the crowd.

The second, however, are capable of understanding, as it were through themselves or from a little learning, all things, because they do not have an agent as a power of the soul, or as it were a making by abstraction of intelligibles in the soul, but they have the agent as if for a form, through which the whole intellectual soul operates, for in the book *on the Soul* we said that felicity is that at which every philosopher attempts to arrive, and this intellect is called the blessed intellect or the world intellect by Avicenna. But it is called the divine intellect by Aristotle, and this intellect derives illumination from a little study for prophecies and for the truest interpretation of dreams.

The medium intellect is the one which aids learning to understand easily as well prophetic as divine things. But the third intellect can not be aided by any reason, because neither is it separated nor does it have instruments by which it is aided by the operation of the sensible soul, and this is sometimes from the defect of constitution, as in the case of insane men, sometimes from long habit of not going beyond the acceptance of sensibles, as in the case of those who are called idiots. From these observations it appears how those who have studied for a long time in particulars, as for example concerning human actions, as they study who turn their attention to the laws and do not inquire into the causes and reasons in the laws themselves, are rendered unsuited for philosophy.

Let this much be said, then, of the nature of the intellect and of the nature of the intelligible and of the comparison of one to the other and of the distinction of each. And this is the end of the first book.